W9-DEC-891

For the Love of Tennis

For the Love of Tennis

edited by Ronald Atkin
on behalf of the Lawn Tennis Writers' Association

Stanley Paul
London Melbourne Sydney Auckland Johannesburg

Stanley Paul & Co. Ltd

An imprint of Century Hutchinson Ltd

17–21 Conway Street, London W1P 6JD

Hutchinson Group (Australia) Pty Ltd
16–22 Church Street, Hawthorn, Melbourne, Victoria 3122

Hutchinson Group (NZ) Ltd
32–34 View Road, PO Box 40-086, Glenfield, Auckland 10

Hutchinson Group (SA) Pty Ltd
PO Box 337, Bergvlei 2012, South Africa

First published 1985
© Ronald Atkin 1985

Set in Century Schoolbook by
The Castlefield Press

Printed and bound in Great Britain by
Anchor Brendon Ltd, Tiptree, Essex

ISBN 0 09 162340 5

Acknowledgements

Grateful thanks are extended to the publications and authors named on the contents pages for permission, always readily given, to reproduce the material in this book.

Thanks also to Tommy Hindley for permission to reproduce his photographs.

Contents

A Funny Thing Happened . . .

Introduction

This anthology of tennis writing was suggested by Geoff Miller, of Associated Press. Geoff was at that time the chairman of the Lawn Tennis Writers' Association and, in that irresistible, charming way of his, he 'suggested' that I might like to edit a book to help keep the LTWA solvent.

This book now becomes a tribute to Geoff Miller, following his sad and untimely death at the Sarajevo Winter Olympics of 1984.

When I agreed to undertake the editing job, Geoff advised me – again in his charming fashion – 'be ruthless in your selection'. That advice has not proved easy to follow. Certainly, I was spoiled for choice, as the editors of anthologies always are, but the fact that virtually every member of the LTWA bombarded me with clippings or original material made the task trickier still.

It was my decision to invite the best (again in my opinion) of the American writers on tennis to appear in this book. After all, *players* from the United States tend to dominate huge slabs of the game's history, so it was only right that this book should represent that American involvement.

There are, inevitably, omissions. Not everybody's favourite player, or treasured reminiscence, is to be found in these pages but there is a rich store of writing from the top (English language) journalists and tennis experts, as well as autobiographical extracts from such respected figures as Fred Perry, Arthur Ashe and Ted Tinling.

For The Love of Tennis is divided into five sections: Players, a look at some of the world's leading competitors, from Bill Tilden to Billie Jean King; Points, descriptions of some of the most memorable matches and most fascinating tournaments; Places, comments on the leading stages on which tennis is performed;

11

People, dealing with some of the most fascinating personalities, on and off court, in tennis; and finally, A Funny Thing Happened ... in which journalists tell of the weird and wonderful things that occurred in the frantic dash to make a deadline in some well-known, and not so well-known, parts of the world.

My thanks to all who gave of their time and their typewriters to ease my task in putting this book together.

Ronald Atkin
London, July 1985

Players

Nastase, the Tragic Twilight

Peter Bodo

'Is fantastic, no?' Ilie Nastase asked me, as he waved at the cluttered table that stood like a defiant gesture against the stark, contemporary furnishings of the hotel room high above suburban Memphis. Nastase's voice filled with wonder: 'I never see nothing like it – never. I don't even know how it works.' Nastase laughed and then added: 'But it's fantastic, I can't stop looking at it.'

Nastase was talking about a clock, one of the three he had purchased on an impulse a few days earlier in Chicago. The 'fantastic' one was encased in a horizontal chrome cylinder about eight inches in diameter The face of the clock lacked numerals. Instead, two lines – set at right angles like the cross-hairs of a rifle sight – quartered the clock's face. The hour and minute hands were mere black slivers, and the second hand wasn't even a hand; just a disc as big as a silver dollar freely wandering around the clock's face. The most fantastic part of all was the way the clock's face changed colours, from passionate red to orange to magenta to melancholy blue.

Still dressed in his wet tennis clothes, Nastase flopped into a white wire chair. Just an hour earlier, he had lost in the first round of the US National Indoor Championships, lost in straight sets to Jim Delaney, a qualifier who ranked 270th in the world. Nastase looked at the television, but he couldn't resist glancing over to the clock. 'You should see it in the night,' he said. 'If I wake up in the dark and see the clock, it is really something – strong, like the sun . . .'

Nastase popped out of his chair. The only two rackets he had brought to Memphis fell to the carpet. The rackets were different models. Neither of them had a cover. The room went dark as Nastase switched off the lights, leaving it illuminated only by the vivid, slightly disconcerting light of time passing in colours – time passing for the vibrant, unforgettable genius of a tennis player whose career, like his moods, has been a sequence of dramatic colours.

The clock slowly turned blue, deep blue as the days have been for Nastase for well over a year. In the darkness, I could hear the words Peter Fleming had spoken earlier in the day, in the locker room of the Racquet Club of Memphis: 'Look, I know that everybody thinks Nasty's a big joke now, I know they say he's gone off the deep end. But I wish he'd get his stuff together. Physically, he can still play. Maybe he is a basket case mentally. I don't know. But I know he's better than number 79 in the world. And there's no need to trash him, he's a good man.'

Suddenly the lights went on again. Nastase returned to his chair and began to strip off his shirt. His eyes settled on the television that is always on to ward off the loneliness of a hotel room. Besides, he was going to talk about his troubles. And if you are going to reveal some of your deeper feelings to a guy like me with a notebook, it is easier for both of you if there is something to look at besides each other.

'I lost a little speed, maybe a step or two, and I lost some confidence,' Nastase began without benefit of a question. 'When you lose your confidence, everything else goes. You eat bad, you sleep bad, you don't practise.' Nastase paused. He continued in a quicker, anxious tone: 'One day, I'll wake up and decide I won't play any more. I don't enjoy losing. But I would miss the tour too much. The tour is something inside me.'

It was the fierce confession of a man who has spent almost two full decades playing tennis, playing more demanding, mentally debilitating tennis than any man alive. Many people feel he played too much, left too much of his fluid, poetic game on overnight flights between continents, and in cow-towns all over the world.

Nastase is 35 now, and critics whisper that his nerves are shot, burned to cinders like the elements of an overused appliance. Harold Solomon says he hasn't seen 'competitive fire' in Nastase for about four years. But Nastase doesn't see the cost of his fame and wealth in those terms. To him, it is more painful, more desperate.

'Tennis is a very dangerous life,' he said sombrely. His tanned, youthful face grew old and sad. He let the wet shirt fall to the carpet. 'Tennis cost me my family because it isn't a normal life,' he went on. 'To spend nine years with a person (his wife Nikki) and to have a child . . . to lose them because of a game, is a big, big price to pay.

'But what can I do, kill myself? I am not the first person to go through this.' Nastase's voice went flat. 'So I am losing now, I have no confidence. I suffer when I lose, but I want to be where the show is . . . because tennis is my life. I know people say I should retire, but what do I do then? I don't care about opinion; it's my own life. To tell me to retire tomorrow is like saying I must die tomorrow. And I don't want to die.'

The spark of defiance in Nastase's eyes died. He began to undo the laces of his shoes.

Some of Nastase's friends worry about his health. His frame of mind has been constantly coloured by the divorce proceedings that have dragged on in the French courts for nearly a year. Despite the state of his game, the promoters of tournaments and exhibitions line up for Nastase's services because he is still a big name. And no matter how far his ranking drops, he can still get into tournaments as a wild-card entrant admitted at the discretion of the promoters. But the way he has been playing drives him deeper into himself. Earlier, Gene Mayer had said, 'If Nastase stopped playing for a while, he'd probably realize how unhappy he is. But the circuit, it's like a fantasy, like college – an escape from the real pressures of life.'

Struggling with a lace, Nastase addressed his shoetops: 'Tennis is the strangest game ever. It is all in your head. Little things can bother you, destroy your game. So think what a big thing can do.'

The big things, like losing the companion of your best years. It was a storybook romance between Ilie and Nikki, a courtship played out across the verdant lawns and sun-dappled verandas of tennis clubs around the world, culminating in marriage when Nastase was at the zenith of his career. For a few years, Nikki was a delightful apparition at tennis tournaments, as cool and distant as Nastase was hot and close. After bearing their daughter, Nathalie, who's now six, Nikki stopped going to tournaments. Her husband did not.

'Exactly how do the big things affect you on the court?' I asked.

Nastase threw a shoe over toward the middle of the room, where a suitcase lay with its contents exploded all over the floor. Nastase calmly replied, 'I know I can't be on top anymore, but I know I shouldn't feel confused on a tennis court, and I do. Sometimes when I'm playing, I feel like the court is not my place anymore. It makes me sad and I just think, "OK, this is bad, so just finish the match anyway".'

After a minute he continued: 'I don't feel the pressure before matches now. Now when I go into a match, I'm not so nervous like I used to be and I miss that very much. When I was playing my best, I was never aware of the people, the fans. All I want was to win, and I played well when I was down. I fight like hell, that's how I was. Now I am there just to be in the game. It is like a fashion for me. But I have to be there or else the people, they forget you.'

I almost asked Nastase why he didn't just go home, but I remembered about the divorce. According to Nastase the fickle French, who adopted him so eagerly years ago, have all but abandoned him. Yannick Noah, the top French player, had told me, 'It's true the French love you when you are winning, but when you begin to lose, they have no more respect. But still, everybody knows him. Every time I take a taxi, the driver asks me about Nastase.'

One of Nastase's lawyers, Peter Lawler of Donald Dell's firm, told me that his client was booked to play for 47 weeks this year. The figure is preposterous, the itinerary of a homeless man. But that's how Nastase wants it. He admits he's a 'yo-yo' and claims that if he stops for two weeks, he gets sick.

Nastase's income will be enormous and the job of Dell's firm, as Lawler put it, 'is to make sure he doesn't end up sitting on a bar stool when he's 70, without a penny to his name.' Nastase had made some financial errors in his past. There were many 'friends' who came along offering spectacular deals that only trimmed Nastase's bank account. For a while, Nastase was managed by his brother-in-law. But money never occupied Nastase's mind.

'Is it normal for me to go in the street and buy three clocks?' Nastase asked, laughing. 'The people who work for me, they are more nervous than me about the future. In France, I have to pay a $25,000 fine because I have a Mercedes-Benz with German plates, a Ferrari with Italian plates and a pick-up truck with American plates. So I am crazy, just like on court. But if my plane goes down tomorrow, I don't want to be the richest guy in the cemetery. I want to go down in a good mood.'

The atmosphere in the room momentarily lightened. In a drama on the TV screen, Evita Peron stood before a cheering throng. Nastase watched her, with the eyes of a man who knew the same intoxication. But like most professionals, the respect of his peers has a deeper meaning than the cheers of the crowd for Nastase. That's why he feels bitter toward John McEnroe, who often makes fun of Nastase, denying him the respect Nastase feels he deserves.

'The ones who understand me are the ones who saw me at the top, who knew how I could play,' Nastase said. 'Arthur (Ashe) understands me. So does Borg. Jimmy (Connors) too. You know, Jimmy invited me down to Florida to practise with him. It was nice from him. Jimmy is a good man, he cares. But I know how I am. Maybe I am a little too proud. I never went.'

Because of his pride, Nastase comes and goes at a tournament, shrouded in mystery. The other players whisper about the man who was once the best player on the planet. 'Nobody considers him much of a factor anymore,' Trey Waltke had told me. 'Nasty's pretty much in his own world. He comes in, does his little routine, and then everybody lets him go off to his corner.' Waltke's voice dropped, and when he continued, it was almost reverentially: 'It's sad, because he's the most respected talent any of us have ever seen. I hate to say it, it's kind of weird, but everybody talks about him in a tragic sense.'

The great moments, the titles, won't be forgotten, though. When I asked Nastase about them, his craggy, mobile features relaxed. The mention of his four Masters titles brought a sheepish grin to his face. 'I don't know what I was doing to win four Masters titles,' he said. "I can't say. For me the nicest memories are always the jokes. How happy people were when I was in the dressing room.

'Wimbledon,' Nastase paused. He was obviously haunted by his failures in his two appearances in finals there. 'I can't think about Wimbledon,' he continued, 'because I had too many other good tournaments.'

'What else are you proud of?' I quickly asked.

'That I am professional,' Nastase answered. 'In almost 20 years of tennis, I average about 35 tournaments a year. I played non-stop and I never defaulted from one tournament. I had one broken ankle and one kidney stone and that was all. I did my job pretty good, I think.'

Pensively, Nastase picked up one of his rackets and began to heft it. He looked trim and fit, wearing just his shorts and the smile brought on by memories of better times – times when his nerves were like the strings of a violin and his game served as a bow to bring forth some of the most melodious tennis any mortal has ever witnessed.

'Everybody thinks it was easier for me with my attitude,' he said. 'But I don't think so. All the extra things took the energy out of me. When I was younger, I didn't realise it. I just go out to play. But I see it now, how much it hurt me in some big matches.'

Nastase let the racket drop. He muttered, 'I know I can still win, but I'm not strong enough to say, "OK tomorrow I will win the tournament." Even when I was No. 1, I never thought I could win for sure. It was always maybe I can, maybe I cannot. I wasn't a killer, maybe I had too much fantasy. I had to feel how my game was going, then I could say, "OK, today I win." '

I forgot what I wanted to ask Nastase next because a little incident that occurred just after he lost to Delaney occupied my mind. We were upstairs in the club, watching a match through a big window. Nastase had decided to skip the locker room; he was just cooling off before going back to the hotel. A ball girl reached through the crowd around us, hoping Nastase would autograph a ball. She finally had to touch him to get his attention.

'You work my match?' Nastase said as he took the ball. 'Were you scared?'

The girl bravely shook her head, pretending that she hadn't been scared at all.

'Good,' Nastase said. 'Sometimes they get scared. You don't have to be scared of me, I'm an OK guy.'

A ball boy from the match stood nearby, munching a corndog, staring. Nastase grinned at him, saying, 'You were so slow tonight because you didn't eat, yes? Next time, you eat a big dinner before you ball boy. Then you'll be the best.' The boy shyly smiled.

Nastase's life is full of such vignettes. He has always craved communication, hungered for the touch of passionate feelings in his relationships with everyone, including umpires. Yet he has made very few close friends, as if such a relationship would inhibit his freedom, cramp his need to express his individuality on the stage that is both larger and smaller than life.

I remembered something that Solomon had said: 'Nastase always avoided real close relationships. That's probably been the chief thing missing in his life. Nastase's reaction was always to put others down. It was a way of keeping people at a distance.'

Then I remembered what I'd wanted to ask Nastase. It was, 'Do you think you'll every marry again?'

'No, I don't think so,' he replied. 'It would be nice to have a child who likes to play tennis, I would like that.' Crestfallen, he added, 'My daughter, she is not interested in tennis.'

'And the future, what do you want people to say about you in the future?'

Nastase pondered the question. The fantastic clock was silent, but the disc kept moving and the cross-hairs were pointing right at the almost naked man sitting in the wire chair. 'I was a crazy player, a fantasist,' he finally replied. 'I don't want them to say that I was the best, just how I really was – a complicated player. Now there is still the controversy, but I know that in some years all that will be gone. The titles, they will stay.'

It seemed like the right time to go. Nastase saw me to the door. When it softly closed behind me, I had to beat back an impulse to knock again, to go back inside and throw all those clocks out of the window, especially the 'fantastic' one that kept turning blue.

Junior Puts the Knife in
Ronald Atkin

It's the face that gets John McEnroe into trouble, according to his doubles partner Peter Fleming. It is a pugnacious face to start with, unsmiling, pale, freckled and spotted, an Irish-potato-type face, surmounted by a mass of Medusa curls barely restrained by a bright red headband when he's on a tennis court. But it's what he does with that face while he's playing that has made McEnroe the most unpopular tennis player to emerge since Ilie Nastase's antics became merely boring. He pouts. He scowls. He hardly ever smiles, certainly not on court.

'It rubs people up the wrong way,' explains Fleming, who is partnering McEnroe in the World Doubles Championships at London's Olympia this weekend. 'From the very start of a match, people get a bad impression. They think "Who is this sourpuss?" I'm telling you, this guy can't pick his nose without people booing him.'

Lack of popularity appears to concern McEnroe not at all. 'I don't care if I don't smile on court,' he says. 'OK, I make faces. The faces are me. People pay to watch me play and if they want to boo me, that's fine. Let's put it this way. I'd rather get some attention than no attention. If it's bad, that's life.'

If his behaviour is sometimes worse than Nastase's, his playing record is considerably better than most people's as a matter of fact. John Patrick McEnroe Jr, aged 19, is the son of a lawyer (and is known as 'Junior' on the tennis circuit). He has risen so fast since abandoning his law studies to turn professional seven months ago that he ought to be checked out for nitrogen bubbles in the bloodstream.

Two hundred and seventieth on the Association of Tennis Professionals' computer list 18 months ago when he burst virtually unheralded through the qualifying pack to reach Wimbledon's semi-final, McEnroe now stands among the world's top five.

Just where he stands in that five (Borg, Connors, Vilas and Gerulaitis are the ones McEnroe ranks himself with) is uncertain, since he has never played Vilas or Gerulaitis in official competition. Perhaps this week's Masters tournament in New York, with Connors defending the crown in an eight-man field which includes McEnroe, may help to clarify things a little.

'I think he is the most talented player in the game,' says Fleming, who knows his doubles partner so well that he has beaten him three times at singles, something no one else has managed to achieve in recent months. After McEnroe's astonishing autumn run from the US Open when he won four tournaments out of the nine in which he competed and was a semi-finalist in the other five, at the same time collecting six doubles titles, the 1975 Wimbledon champion Arthur Ashe called him 'the best player in the world right now'.

Though he was flattered, McEnroe said: 'I don't know how Arthur can say that. I've played Connors four times and never beaten him yet, so how can I be the best?' On each occasion, however, the margin has been closer and in Stockholm two months ago, Junior pulled off the finest victory of his short professional life by beating Bjorn Borg 6–3, 6–4. It was the first time Borg had ever lost to an opponent younger than himself. McEnroe dropped only seven points on his own serve in the whole match, and afterwards Borg said he had tried to attack McEnroe's weakness but couldn't find one.

Strength he has in abundance, however. He is incredibly fast around the court, his volleying touch is stunning, his left-handed serve is fast and laced with deadly spin. 'Snaky' is how Fleming describes it, adding 'on grass it is probably the best in the game'.

Ashe says: 'Against Connors and Borg you feel like you're being hit with a sledgehammer. But this guy is a stiletto. Junior has great balance and he just slices people up. He's got a ton of shots. It's slice here, nick there, cut over here. Pretty soon you've got blood all over you, even though the wounds aren't deep. Soon after that you've bled to death.'

'I am fairly happy with what I've done over the past six months,' is McEnroe's way of describing his explosive arrival on the professional scene. In that case, why doesn't he *look* happier sometimes? He has a ready wit and has shown it at press conferences, deflating pompous or pedantic interviewers.

Fleming, who shares tennis courts and hotel rooms with him, says it is because McEnroe is 'a great competitor who doesn't put up with any bullshit'. Fleming feels that despite what he might say to the contrary, McEnroe is working hard at improving his public image. 'But it's going to take a while. In one year he has improved his deportment so much. Now he's halfway towards where he wants to be.

'When we played each other last month in Jamaica we had a misunderstanding and I screamed at him. I won the match and we didn't talk to each other that night or the next day. Eventually we decided to have a couple of drinks by the pool and discuss it. We talked for about an hour. He was really upset that I had yelled at him.

'The problem is that on court he only thinks about winning the next point. Nothing else counts.' Not even popularity, obviously. McEnroe has been known to pull more than faces on a tennis court and the history of arguments with officials, undeleted expletives and rows with spectators dates back to the days when Junior *was* a junior.

He also spits a lot, in the way that footballers used to spit until they realised that Match of the Day's cameras were focused on them. 'I guess I always had too much Irish,' is McEnroe's explanation.

His childhood friend and former mixed doubles partner, Mary Carillo, says McEnroe has no subtlety. 'He doesn't go out of his way to impress people. He just doesn't care what people think. The game is so simple for him he just gets mad when anything goes wrong.'

Not much has gone wrong for a while now, but McEnroe emphasises, 'It's not luck. I worked for this, I deserve it. The amount of tennis I played over the past six months has been a strain, and after the Masters I'm going to take things a little easier. I have only had about two weeks off in 25, but this year I am not going to play more than two or three weeks in a row.

'What are my goals? I don't like to set goals. My goal is to do well. Of course, I'd like to win Wimbledon and the US Open. They will be my top priorities.'

Those particular priorities might be closer than even

McEnroe thinks. After Borg had captured Wimbledon for the third successive time last July I wrote that there was no reason why he should not go on to a fourth or even fifth title 'unless another superman floats to the top of the pack of ambitious youngsters thronging the courts of the world'.

John P. McEnroe has broken surface and a sharp triangular fin is aimed at Connors and Borg.

Guillermo Vilas

Curry Kirkpatrick

'Boom. Ba-boom.' The floor is made of ceramic tiles that are the colour of buttermilk. 'Bip-bip. Ba-boom.' The walls are marble halfway to the ceiling. 'Baba-da-boom. Baba-da-boom.' There is chipping plaster, and water pipes all around. 'Bip-bip. Boop-ba-boop. Boom.' And mirrors and stalls and a long wooden bench. 'Ba-boom. Bip . . bip . . babadaboom. Ba-boom . . ba . . boom.'

In the faded elegance of a dressing room underneath the stadium of the Buenos Aires lawn tennis club, Guillermo Vilas waits to go upstairs for another tennis match. Waits and sits. Stands and dances. Sings and taps a small stick.

'I should have been a Brazilian,' Vilas says. 'How fantastic they are with the music. Unbelievable. So natural with the music. You go into a bar and there they are drumming and tapping on everything. Ba-boom. Ba-ba-da-boom. Metals, wood, the floor, the chairs. They click glasses and spoons and fill the bottles at different levels so they get the different notes. Bip-boom. They become a band. People singing and laughing and dancing on the tables. Ba-boom.

'I fly away with the music,' Vilas continues, now working on the marble and the pipes. 'Boop-bip-ba-boom. Yes, sometimes I wish I was making music. I speak to Burt Bacharach in Caracas. He said he went crazy listening to the Brazilians. He said he will come here and I will go to California and meet the big guys. My songs will be love songs. But not for lovers, you know? Love songs for all people. I want that. Yes, I want to make music . . I will . . I know I will.'

The reason professional tennis has established itself as one of the big sports of the '70s is that it has grown far and wide and variegated enough to have at its highest level such disparate personalities as Jimmy Connors, Bjorn Borg and Guillermo Vilas. Though much has been made of their diversity, the notion persists that Connors and Borg are not so dissimilar after all. It is Vilas who is different. Vilas, the poet. Vilas, the romantic. Vilas, the mild bull of the Pampas. Though probably lacking the raw ability of his two rivals, Vilas may have the greatest appeal to the public.

Connors has earned a reputation for nastiness while wearing his heart, not to mention his middle finger, on his sleeve. Conversely, Borg is well mannered but exhibits no recognizable human emotion past a wink. And although they have performed prodigies on the tennis court, they are sadly deficient in the social graces and general knowledge. Indeed, it sometimes seems that they went directly from childhood to manhood, while cutting classes, as it were, in the lessons of youth. Perhaps that is why, in their press conferences and public utterances, Connors, 25, and Borg, 21, can express themselves only in jock rhetoric or downright baby talk. Conversation? Forget conversation. They don't know what conversation is. If all the nets of the world suddenly were ripped asunder by Darth Vader, Jimbo and Bjorny would have to take to the streets selling sausage.

This is not the case for 25-year-old Vilas. Besides being one of the three best tennis players in the world, Vilas is a published author of prose and poetry. He has written a screenplay and collaborated on songs to be recorded in Argentina. He is a philosopher, a musician, a reader, a thinker. Even if Vilas's book of poetry were nothing more than recipes for 'carbonada criolla' and his musical notes badly off-key; even if his Renaissance-man reputation is based on nothing more than 'phantom depth' as one touring pro charges, that is besides the point. On his own the man reads, writes and composes, and he does it for only one reason. The self. Himself.

Vilas is bright, handsome, articulate. He is honest, witty, sensitive. He makes tons and tons of pesos. You might not want your daughter to marry a tennis player, but Guillermo Vilas you'd approve of.

This is a simplification, of course. Vilas's passion for the aesthetic, his artistic nature, derives in large part from the circumstances of coming from a broken home and from the hurt inflicted by incessant reference to him in the Argentine press as a loser and 'the eternal second'. 'I am a very complicated person to get involved with,' Vilas says. 'I am not easy to know on a superficial basis.'

Significantly, the two men who say they know him best – does anyone know Guillermo Vilas *well*? – disagree on the subject of Vilas's state of mind.

'Willie is, you know, counterclockwise,' says Luis Alberto Spinetta, Argentina's leading jazz-rock musician. 'You tell him what's white, he'll tell you what's black. You act hard on him, he'll be sweet. It's all reversed. He's contradictory. But he is young, a champion, sensible. He has fun. His future is now. He has found the world already.'

Arturo Romero, who was Vilas's roommate during law school at Faculdad de Derecho y Ciencias Sociales and now serves as a kind of secretary for his friend, demurs. 'Travelling is a lonely time for Guillermo,' says Romero. 'He has no home left, but he needs the charm and closeness of the family. When you force Guillermo to think, he's pessimistic. Because he's not happy, he must discover a place to settle and find peace. The problem is Guillermo doesn't find his peace.'

There are other contradictions. Vilas has said that money means nothing, that he 'plays for fame'. But last year he entered an astonishing 34 tournaments (winning 21), played 153 matches (winning 139) and earned $434,065 in tournaments prize money, an all-time record. He plays and plays and plays and plays. He also won the $300,000 first prize in the Colgate Grand Prix bonus pool, as well as an additional $30,000 in the season-end Masters showdown in New York city, for a year's total of $764,065. That is quite a bit of fame.

And Vilas's interest in only the fame of the Masters title is suspect. He cabled Colgate before the tournament to ask if they could send his $300,000 down to Buenos Aires ahead of time 'for tax reasons'. (There were no tax reasons; tennis players are taxed where they earn their money.)

Moreover, Vilas resigned or, rather, Ion Tiriac, the brooding Romanian who is Vilas's friend, aide, mentor, agent, corner-man, coach and general manager, resigned both of them from the Association of Tennis Professionals last spring (over a petty gossip item in the ATP newspaper). Vilas was the only major player who refused to sign a pledge not to play exhibitions in conflict with ATP-sanctioned tournaments this season. As a result, this winter and spring Vilas (whom Tiriac has come to refer to as 'I', the way fight managers say, 'We fought so-and-so') has been lazing around, playing in only a few tournaments. He does appear in a whole lot of exhibitions. For fame? For money?

In defence, Tiriac argues that Connors, Borg, Ilie Nastase and other big names have been 'collecting guarantees on contracts' from Lamar Hunt's WCT tour, and that his man either deserves the same largess or else should be left alone to make up the cash in exhibitions.

'Guillermo is bored with deals I make,' says Tiriac. 'He doesn't want to hear about them. Anyway, money is not a factor with these guys anymore. It just depends on who wants to win. This guy won non-stop last year. God, we're tired.'

Be that as it may, Vilas, or Tiriac, or those spinners and weavers from Fila, the Italian clothes manufacturer that makes Vilas's two-tone outfits, or somebody, must be yawning all the way to the Buenos Aires Savings and Loan.

Arthur Ashe puts in a word for Vilas. 'What Guillermo did last year – to reach that many finals and win that many tournaments – was extraordinary,' says Ashe. 'It's trivial to complain that he hasn't played much this year. He must have accounted for an extra 50,000 spectators in the last six months of each season. He more than supported the tour.'

This season the tour has had to make do without Vilas. After injuring his ankle at the Masters in January, he rushed home to rest for nearly three months before gingerly venturing back into competition, in which he has been rudely beaten by a whole draw sheet of players. But this appears to be another typical Tiriac production; go slow, practice hard, work like a pack mule, then sneak up on everybody in the world's big clay championships – this week's Italian Open in Rome and next week's French Open in Paris.

Tiriac deservedly has taken credit for the technical and mental improvements in Vilas's game since he joined up with him permanently in 1976. Other players sense his influence on Vilas's personality as well. There was a time in South Africa, after Vilas had lost a long point, when he appealed to the chair that coughing spectators had disrupted his concentration. The umpire allowed a replay. Last spring during the Davis Cup match between Argentina and the US, American representatives accused Vilas of arousing the crowd to use drums, bugles and whistles.

'Tiriac is the guru and Tiriac's forte is gamemanship,' says Ashe. 'We know not to give Guillermo anything on the court because he'll nail you if he can. He has come to the superstar point. He plays on that image of the romantic poet, but he uses the grand gesture the way Newcombe used to in influencing an inexperienced linesman. Newk got away with it because he was Newk. This guy can do it because he is Vilas.'

The 'superstar' hasn't been conceived who would avoid exploiting such an advantage. Still, for Vilas to engage in such gamesmanship seems totally alien to his image. 'Guillermo used to be warm and friendly', another player says. 'Now he has a singlemindedness that wasn't there before. He is all business, and cold. I wonder if he really enjoys the sacrifices he has had to make because of Tiriac. To reach the top, he has had to become less human, a lesser person. But to win, he had to be.'

A story under Vilas's byline in the Buenos Aires newspaper *La Opinion* last November had asked for Vilas's impressions of the earthquake in Argentina the day before in which some 80 people had been killed. Heavy tremors had been felt in parts of Buenos Aires. Vilas, who had been awakened from a sound sleep in his 17th floor apartment and who had rushed down the stairs and into the street where he had joined his frightened neighbours, wrote:

It [the earthquake] was most lamentable, but foreseeable. It's within the percentage of things which have to happen. Fervently, therefore, I think that many times one feels oneself to be secure, and suddenly, one's world falls down like a pack of cards in a matter of seconds. An earthquake belongs to natural law. Nature is irreversible just as much for physical and psychic phenomena. If reconstruction is necessary, I pledge to contribute my grain of sand, playing exhibitions gratis, always on condition that in the scheduling of them, the dates that tennis leaves me free are taken into account. This for me is a sacred pledge which I plan to honour.

Friends say the exhibitions were Vilas's idea, the proviso about free time was pure Tiriac.

For about as long as there has been an Argentina, there has

been football – soccer – in Argentina. Neighbouring Brazil has won the World Cup three times, and now Buenos Aires is preparing to host that event. There have also been renowned fighters from Argentina – Luis Angel Firpo, Oscar Bonavena, Carlos Monzon – but not until Guillermo Vilas arrived did sports take over in a big commercial way: T-shirts, sporting-goods stores, that sort of thing.

Vilas came out of Mar del Plata, a resort city of 350,000 on the south coast, from which he used to take seven-hour bus rides over bad roads to play in weekend tournaments in Buenos Aires. Vilas would play all day Saturday and all day Sunday, then board another bus for the seven-hour ride home. He would reach home at 4 a.m., barely in time to sleep before school the next day. An American TV announcer once said a player had to be dedicated to the game to do all that, and a viewer wrote in, 'either to the game or to school'. Vilas was both; he was a superior student.

Mar del Plata could probably exist forever on the beauty of its name (Sea of Silver), but the city has lost much of its elegance. The wealthy now vacation in Punta del Este, the chic Uruguayan resort, and the working classes and union leaders have taken over.

Though Vilas's father, an escribano (South America's version of the British solicitor), still lives in Mar de Plata, his mother long since moved away to live with Vilas's 22-year-old sister, Marcela, in Buenos Aires. Vilas has his own small penthouse apartment in a Buenos Aires suburb called Olivos, two blocks from where the Agentine presidents resided before the Peronistas were deposed in 1976. Everywhere one looks from Vilas's corner windows, there is water: swimming pools and yacht harbours and rivers. The mammoth Rio de la Plata, formed by the confluence of the Parana and the Uruguay, laps the banks of the city downtown, past the docks of the historic La Boca – a collections of rainbow-hued tenements comprising what must be the world's most charming slum – before flowing into the Atlantic Ocean 150 miles away. 'On a clear day you can see across to Uruguay – little hills, the tips of mountains,' says Vilas.

Last year Vilas purchased a condominium in Punta del Este. Moving from Mar del Plata to Punta del Este is analogous to leaving Atlantic City for Southampton. Given $300,000 bonus pool money, you'd move too. His apartment in Olivos is a study in eclectic taste. In the kitchen there is a lucite phone to which a girl friend is often attached. Arturo Romero, the former law school roommate and a zany who takes acting lessons and thrills everyone with his version of Dustin Hoffman as Ratso Rizzo, lives with Vilas. Tiriac, Tiriac's tall, blonde wife Mikette and their 18-month-old baby have an apartment in the same building.

Van Gogh reproductions, oriental tapestries, a spaghetti racket, fresh flowers, bongo drums, boxing headgear (Vilas and Romero often spar for exercise), a couple of trophies and the standard hi-fi-stereo-and-tape-deck monster machines decorate the penthouse. Cassettes are everywhere. One is a radio play-by-play of Vilas's victory over Roscoe Tanner in Washington DC; most are of Chuck Mangione, Chick Corea and all that jazz.

It is rumoured that Vilas will soon purchase a huge ranch in the provinces, but for now, during his brief moments in Argentina, this is the stopping-off place. It is where Vilas says he 'hangs'. Vilas does not even visit Mar del Plata any more. There is a reason.

'My old house was out in the country,' says Vilas. 'A quinta, a house with lots of land. Crops, gardens, fruits, vegetables. I used to play outside in the biggest tree in the world. Alone, just me. I didn't need anybody else. I was roaming a lot. Much time to think. The house is changed now. Everything is different. It is part of the town. No more crops. No dirt roads. No land. It is so sad. Once I wanted to show the big tree to a girl who was important to me, but it wasn't big anymore. Everything when you were young was so big, you know. Everything I was dreaming about was different. It was such a great experience. I wanted to relive it. It didn't work. I go back now to look and I get very depressed.'

Argentinians are mostly of Spanish or Italian origin and they have strong family ties: one for all, all for one. So, in the old days, did the family Vilas, which is of Basque descent. That feeling is gone now. Vilas's parents were separated for good about the time Guillermo went off to law school. Though he will not speak of it, friends say he was crushed and perhaps he has not recovered. His search for a surrogate family seems to continue. Or perhaps it has ended with Tiriac.

Vilas repeatedly grieves that he must endure long travel, airplanes, restaurant meals, strange beds and hotel rooms. Most of all, hotel rooms. The hotel room is not a home, and this is a man who greatly misses his home.

'We could see this from the beginning,' says Chilean player Jaime Fillol, who has known Vilas longer than most. 'Guillermo always seemed to need somebody else. He was close to me for a while, then to Manuel Orantes. Nobody lasted more than three or four weeks. He was always looking for something new, for some answers. When either of his parents was on tour with him, he was unsure, uneasy. He was morose and blue. Then he got into Buddhism and yoga and other Asian philosophies, which are nearly impossible to apply to your life if you were brought up in a Western society, in a Catholic style. Now he lets Tiriac worry about as many things as possible. He seems more settled. But also, more removed from the rest of us.'

For a time he and Borg became fast friends – Vilas bought an apartment in the same condominium in Monaco in which Borg lived, the two practised every day and they ate meals together. But Borg was on the verge of his engagement to Mariana Simionescu, while Vilas was surveying a field of international wonder women, including a 'Miss World Beauty', 32-year-old Mirta Massa. As Borg began to defeat Vilas regularly and Tiriac entered the picture, their friendship waned. Yet Borg's dominance in their matches – 12 wins to four, lifetime – while attributable in part to his greater consistency, is probably as much a result of Vilas's lack of a killer instinct against a friend. As Tiriac says of his ward, 'This guy is not capable in life to kill a fly.'

The hero worship that surrounds Vilas in Buenos Aires – one evening last winter his arrival at the restaurant Los Anos Locos (The Crazy Years) was accorded a standing ovation, after which a dozen waiters lined up for individual pictures with Vilas for the best part of an hour – is testimony to the depth of feeling Argentinians hold for their Numero Uno de Tenis. But for a better understanding of this national celebrity, it is necessary to travel with Vilas to a place such as Tandil, a hamlet some two-and-a-half hours south of Buenos Aires by prop plane. Tandil is in the flatlands, a green and fertile place with roads

lined by jacaranda trees and fields full of cattle. Vilas flew there
for an exhibition match with Tiriac and the inauguration of a
new indoor tennis club; his father, Jose Roque Vilas, met him at
the military airport. If 60-year-old Jose Roque could be
persuaded to wear a Peter Frampton hairpiece, he and
Guillermo could pass for twins. They have the same robust
energy, the magnetism, the same kind mannerly ways. And the
same eyes. At once soft and piercing – and clear, stark,
incredibly blue. Listings of tennis's best-looking men usually
begin with Adriano Panatta, the Italian: then comes Vilas.

As the three cars carrying Vilas, his father, Tiriac and local
officials headed from the airport through the farmlands into
Tandil, a strange scene developed. Every so often, there would
be a car parked alongside the road with one or two people inside.
As the Vilas caravan passed, the people in the cars would wave
wildly and honk their horns. Then the cars would get in line and
follow along. This continued for 10 miles, until the caravan
became a parade.

Just outside Tandil, Vilas's car stopped so Tiriac could pick up
some bandages at a drugstore. Within minutes the vehicle was
engulfed by dozens of people, mostly children who fought each
other to lean inside the window and kiss Vilas. 'Mucho gusto,
mucho gusto, Guillermo,' they would say politely. Then, 'Adios.'

In Tandil, hundreds of people lined the sidewalk to catch a
glimpse of Vilas. At the hotel another hundred rushed the car
which began to shake. Vilas forced his way out. 'No autographs
please,' he pleaded. 'I am sorry, but I am late.'

'We don't want autographs,' a girl said. 'we just want to touch
you.'

Tiriac, grumbling, said this happened all the time in the
provinces. 'Last month we were forced to have 20 police on
horseback guard him at exhibition. In Romania when I had
Nastase, there would be 200 people lined up, but only for
autographs. Here they are more aggressive. They want flesh.
Vilas, he is like Jesus Christ. He is prophet.'

Guillermo Vilas was not born in a manger – or on a tennis
court. Like any other Argentine kid, he grew up kicking a
football. Vilas's father, preferring that Guillermo play
something more white-collar, took him into the Club Nautico
Mar del Plata, of which he was the president, and hired a local

34

barber named Felipe Locicero to teach him tennis. Locicero remembers, 'On the face of the little boy were signs of deaf protest.' But the little boy learned the game. Later, when the elder Vilas wanted his son to become a lawyer, it was too late. Guillermo was hooked on tennis. He was playing in national and then international tournaments. And he was winning. In law school Vilas met the boisterous Romero, who came from the province of La Pampa. Of Romero, a notorious playboy, a friend once said, 'At 2 a.m., Arturo is not thinking the night is young, but, rather, the night is born.'

The two got along famously – talking for hours over bottles of sidra, Argentina's apple-champagne drink – when Romero's carousing did not interfere with Vilas's studying. Romero recalls Vilas coming home miserable from class every day. 'One night', Romero says, 'Guillermo came back to the room, threw down his books and nearly cried. "This is not my life," he said. "This is not my life."'

'The law was too square,' says Vilas. 'Rules, more rules. You had to have the same opinions as the professors. Nothing ever was flexible enough.'

But tennis. Well.

'I remember when I started tennis, it was considered a sissy game,' says Vilas. 'We used to walk down the street and hide the rackets in our bags. Everybody whistled at us and called us queers. But I liked the creativity of the game. A tennis player could create more than a painter. Create combinations of things. Nothing was secure. There were the variables of the racket, the surface, the weather, the opponent, the spin and speed of the ball. Where you were. Who you were. For me this was an unbelievable attraction. When someone said, "Come, go to court," it was like saying, "Come, paint." Only better.'

So Vilas left school forever. In 1973 he began his voyages around the tennis globe. The following summer there arrived on the American clay circuit a powerful, left-handed, fully fledged new star and anomaly: a flashing-eyed, head-banded South American who didn't moan and complain at line calls, didn't temperamentally quit at the slightest hint of trouble, and didn't ever seem to lose.

Vilas had played poorly on the WCT winter-spring tour that season, but in July he had won the Swiss and Dutch Opens and then in the US reached the finals at Washington. In August he won Louisville and made it to the quarters at Indianapolis. He defeated Borg, Tom Okker and Orantes to win Toronto before reaching the semi-finals in the US Pro at Brookline. In seven weeks, his record was 34–3 and he had earned $70,000. In short order he then won eight Grand Prix titles and jumped from No. 35 on the money list to No. 1.

The press did not know what to make of this scraggly-haired strongman who wore sash belts, POW bracelets and macaroni necklaces while quoting Neruda and Krishnamurti, whoever *they* were.

'I am the No. 1 sportsman in Argentina,' Vilas told everybody. 'Of course in Argentina we don't have many sportsmen.' But the Argentine magazine *Gente* soon abandoned its cover-girl format to feature Vilas, and a taped tennis match – Vilas vs. Fillol – was shown on Buenos Aires television for the first time.

At the end of 1974 Vilas pulled off the upset of the decade when he won the Masters on *grass* in Melbourne, sometimes playing in 125° heat as he ripped through John Newcombe, Onny Parun, Borg, Raul Ramirez and Nastase. In 1975, Vilas beat a fading Rod Laver at Boston by 6–3, 6–4, after which Laver said, 'I saw a great player out there.'

His press clippings made Vilas's countrymen expect too much. Because his baseline game had been born on red dirt, he was vulnerable to an aggressive charger, and he was still beset by familial problems. Vilas kept winning all his matches – except the big ones.

In 1974, Rome semi-finals: Vilas had put Borg away, but lost. In 1975, Rome semis: he was far ahead of Orantes, but lost again.

In 1975, Paris finals: Vilas was wiped out by Borg. In 1975, US Pro Finals: wiped out by Borg. In 1975, US Open semi-finals: having given up only 18 games in 12 sets at Forest Hills, Vilas led Orantes 2–1 in sets and 5–0 in games and had five match points. He lost all of them and the match, 4–6, in the fifth set.

In 1976, Rome finals: Vilas blew a one-set lead to lose to Panatta. In 1976, Paris semi-finals: Vilas blew a bigger lead to lose to Harold Solomon. In 1976, Masters semis: lost 6–8 in the fifth to Wojtek Fibak. In early 1977, Australian Open: wiped out by Tanner.

After his embarrassing loss to Orantes at Forest Hills in 1975, Vilas turned to Tiriac. For all his guff and bluster and Count Dracula's reputation, behind Tiriac's hirsute countenance is one of the game's most perceptive minds. Tiriac never got enough credit when he was honing Nastase's brilliance into marketable victories and he finally wearied of Nastase's selfishness. In Vilas he had a lesser talent but a more pliable student.

It took time. 'For Nastase, tennis was all a game, all play,' says Tiriac. 'For Vilas, it is all work.' Vilas worked hard, four, five, six hours a day of running and exercises and hitting balls. 'I make him run when he very tired,' says Tiriac, 'I make him stretch muscles when he very cold. Vilas strong? I play ice hockey. I think I am strong. If we arm wrestle, this guy snap my arm off quick. Laver strong? This guy snap Laver in two pieces.'

Vilas's strength is a source of wonderment to his fellow pros. Ashe says he was practising with Tiriac and Vilas in Australia once and had to stop out of sheer exhaustion. 'Guillermo trains like nobody I've ever seen,' says Ashe. 'Tiriac trampolines those balls to the corners and yells, "Run, run, run", and Vilas runs. He's not naturally gifted, you know. The kid is such a brute, he just muscles his way to the ball.'

Finally, in 1977, came the breakthrough, with his victories in the French Open, the US Open and his Grand Prix records. But some players consider Vilas's most impressive feat last year to be a *loss*. That was at Aix-en-Provence in October when Vilas defaulted and walked off the court, hopelessly behind 2–6, 5–7 to Nastase and the infamous spaghetti racket.

The ITLF had banned the use of the racket, the prohibition to take effect the day after the tournament ended. Nastase used it to drop and lob and run Vilas into the dusty clay as the crowd chanted, 'Take the racket off! Take the racket off!' Vilas had just completed a five-set semi-final against another spaghetti-wielder, Patrick Deblicker, which did not exactly help prepare him for Nastase.

Bjorn Borg in Retrospect

Nigel Clarke

It was one of those warm, velvet nights when the Via Veneto was at its most exciting. The bars were crowded, the traffic piled up in a familiar jam, and the beautiful people of Rome were posing. Music and laughter were everywhere, couples strolled slowly down one side of the Veneto and up the other, pausing to talk with friends, and to enjoy the great Italian habit of showing off to each other.

It was just outside Harry's Bar that I first spotted Bjorn Borg. He sat at a pavement cafe sipping wine, watching the world go by.

He wore blue jeans and a striped red and white shirt, and nobody took any notice of him whatsoever. His sweater was draped over his shoulders and already that expression of permanent gloom was beginning to settle over his youthful features.

Borg acknowledged my greeting and called me over for a drink. He pulled at the beard I was growing and asked me if I hid behind it. At his side was the bear-like Lennart Bergelin, the man who was already his constant companion, and was to master-mind the preparation that would see the Swede become a legend in his own tennis lifetime.

If Borg's handshake was firm, greeting Bergelin was like putting your fist into a crusher. You withdrew it and auto-matically counted the number of fingers left. A sudden explosion of noise, and flashbulbs, heralded the arrival at a nearby bar of football star Gianni Rivera with a lovely actress draped on his arm.

The swaggering playboy held court with much gesticulating and expansive gestures before being left alone. Borg watched, and smiled. 'Why come out and be bothered so much?' he enquired. 'Maybe he likes it that way,' I replied. 'A man must sometimes be seen to be a man,' smiled Bergelin. 'It's like being a book,' said Borg. 'Everyone is trying to read you.'

That was in 1975, and Borg was struggling his way through the Italian Championships with little of the charisma that was to catapult him to world stardom. I had first met him as a shy and nervous 16-year-old two years earlier at Wimbledon, in a shirt that seemed too big for his skinny frame, and shorts that definitely were on the large side.

He couldn't understand the fuss girls made of him. In his pensive, passive way he enjoyed it, yet was scared. It was almost as if he sensed that he was to become a pin-up figure, and was already beginning to back off. Borg was a nice man. He could shut people out, and yet give enough of himself to keep them interested.

That brief chat in Rome was the last time I ever saw him alone, the last time he was a teenager, the last time he could go unrecognised in one of the most sport-crazy cities in the world. Later I was to catch up with him in Barcelona. He was a star by now, but never coming out at night. He had lost a match to Sherwood Stewart that ended a 50-match unbeaten run. That night at his hotel he relaxed with a glass of white wine. He looked at the company around him, and half gave himself to us.

For a while he joined in a riotous sing-song, mouthing rather than shouting the words. Later he softly sang a Swedish ballad. He seemed so alone, a gentle man not quite knowing which path to take, wanting to join in, but always holding himself in check. You wondered why, and somehow felt for him.

As Borg dominated tennis so he changed. Often he was ashen-faced, not only with the five hours of practice he constantly put in, but from the tension and pressure to keep on winning. His eyes were old and tired, his shoulders had become stooped, he rarely looked up or at you. Greetings now were a nod of the head, or at the best a quiet hello. What was he doing to himself? The inner conflict and the discipline he always showed had clearly become a burden that was to ravage him. For a while he found a kind of peace and security with Mariana, the girl he was eventually to marry. I came across them one day canoodling in the back of a Saab in the public car park at Wimbledon. I was as astonished to see them cuddling as they were to see me. In embarrassment I pulled quickly away.

But Bjorn had seen me. He smiled and put a finger to his lips. I kept his secret safe from the pack of photographers out hunting for him and his lady. Borg's lifestyle was one of hard work and dedication. He would often be in bed by 7.30 p.m. watching his beloved sci-fi movies, or reading Captain Marvel. It was his way of relaxing, of not taxing his concentration or brain, to leave it free for the job of playing tennis.

He found it difficult to converse about life, the world, and its problems. His way would be to shrug his shoulders, but he listened a lot and those careful eyes missed nothing. In 1979 when he lost to Roscoe Tanner in the United States Open he was shattered. Mariana did his crying for him and told me, 'When he is hurt he goes away from me. Then I am hurt. He cannot talk to me, he shuts me out, he shuts everyone out. Only I know how he feels.'

A year later when he lost to John McEnroe I went round to his hotel the following morning. I was astounded to see how gaunt, tired and unwell he looked.

There were pimples in a cluster over one eye. Sores on his lip and cheek. He was bent over in a question mark of despair. Mariana had been crying again. 'I'm sorry,' I told him. 'Thanks for coming round,' he replied. 'Nobody else has. It's not a good time for me. I can't win in New York.'

Then there were death threats against him. He lost to McEnroe again and found the world lining up to tell him he was finished. That was a body blow and later he was to reveal that he would never go back to New York again. He didn't. In between the bitter disappointments were the triumphs of Wimbledon and Paris. I once asked him what it was like sitting in the waiting room with Jimmy Connors before going onto the Centre Court.

'Jimmy doesn't talk to me. I look at him, but he won't look at me. For him I am not there.'

His great friend has been Nastase. Together they've had their fun, but few people have seen the private life of Borg. That day in Rome eight years ago was such a contrast to his final appearance in Monte Carlo. The crowds cheered him all the way to the court, and all the way back again. It was a spontaneous appreciation of a great tennis player.

Borg liked a night out with the rest of us. He enjoyed a drink.

He loved ice hockey and football, and once asked me to introduce him to Bobby Moore, the former England captain.

He had his good times, but in the end tennis took its toll. Mariana admitted that had he not quit, he could have ended up in a mental hospital. Borg was not naturally stone-faced and severe. He made himself that way to get to the top. The millions came, and so too did the titles and the problems.

In Monte Carlo the difference in the man was amazing. The eyes, once clouded, were clear and sharp, there wasn't a spot to be seen on his face, he had a sheen of fitness about him, and looked 22 again.

Tennis had made him, but it almost cost him his marriage and his health. Now he had gone and the charisma with it. Borg was an enigmatic figure but also an exciting one. He could be stupidly stubborn and refused to talk to Swedish journalists in their own language.

But he could be incredibly kind, and gentle, and could act better than Greta Garbo. The last time I saw him he was laughing, yes, laughing, throwing back his head in a great gesture of delight.

We'll miss him . . . for sure. But I'm glad for his sake he's found peace of mind at last. Bjorn Borg was a remarkable sportsman. We will never see his like again.

He put tennis on the map for thousands of people who only associated it with the upper-class echelons of Wimbledon. For that we must all be grateful and wish him a happy retirement as he counts his millions, and his memories.

Jean Borotra

John Parsons

It was mid-afternoon on a bustling, sunny day in the first week of Wimbledon. All the courts were busy, the walkways an orderly pattern of human crocodiles edging their way almost aimlessly in search of the tastiest delight the tennis had to offer.

Within the guarded, rose-screened sanctuary of the Members' Enclosure at the All England Club, however, it was mainly quiet. Here and there were a few waitresses in their familiar royal blue uniforms, clearing the last remnants from an obviously hectic lunchtime invasion and starting to prepare for the next onslaught – the traditional British tea.

Yet tucked away in his favourite corner, oblivious to any other activity around him, except perhaps for the occasional outward glance after a particularly loud roar or cheer from the Centre Court, was Jean Borotra. On the table in front of him, a bottle of red wine, two or three clean glasses for any friend or acquaintance who might arrive to disturb him, and a mass of papers reflecting the endless business and other interests which still provide this remarkable man with at least a ten-hour working day.

'Borotra's corner' has become a well-established landmark within the Members' Enclosure. 'You'll usually find him there, working away every afternoon,' said the Commissionaire. On this occasion, however, he was still in his long white flannels, shirt and sweater, with, appropriately enough, a tennis racket resting against the side of his chair.

'I'm sorry, I haven't had time to change yet but Kitty Godfree, (then 88 years old and the star of the women's centenary celebrations at Wimbledon) and I have just popped away to a far distant court where there wouldn't be any fuss or bother to play a set or two as we always try to do at some stage during Wimbledon,' said this equally sprightly, amazingly fit hero of

42

tennis history who, at that stage, was a mere 86.

It is at a time such as this that I would love to have the opportunity somehow to see these former great champions as they truly were and not just the flickering black-and-white snippets from old newsreels. Thanks to the marvels of modern technology, future generations will forever be able to admire the full magic of John McEnroe and Martina Navratilova winning Wimbledon in such style.

For us, trying to conjure up visions of someone like Borotra, whose personality, like his tennis, has always been larger than life, great dependence is necessary on blending imagination with the facts gleaned from books and from the few of his tennis contemporaries who remain.

One fact not generally known or remembered about Borotra, one of 'The Four Musketeers' who will forever be part of tennis legend, is that it was not until he made his first trip to England that he held a racket in his hand for the very first time.

His mother, a widow, decided in the summer of 1912 that her son, then 13 and making excellent headway with his study of German, should also be able to converse fluently in English. Arrangements were accordingly made for him to spend some time with an English family in Kenley.

The lady of the house, Mrs Wildy, was, Jean remembers, 'very charming – so charming and welcoming in fact that after only a few days there I started calling her my holiday mother and she was very happy about that.'

Mrs Wildy, for her part, was anxious that Jean should have some suitable sporting pastime between his studies. He had participated in soccer, rugby and fencing back home in France. He was also a capable swimmer but when mention of lawn tennis was made he had to admit 'Sorry, I've never played it.'

One afternoon a few days later, Mrs Wildly spotted Jean watching tennis. 'Your eyes were glowing,' she told him. 'You can't tell me you aren't keen to start playing tennis as well.' She promptly provided him with a racket and within days everyone in the village of Kenley knew that there was a young Basque staying there who never seemed to miss a ball. A lifelong romance with tennis had begun.

Born at Arbonne, Basses-Pyrénées, on 13 August 1898, Jean Borotra's achievements and impact on the overall game of lawn tennis were considerable. He was a dominant personality from the time he made his first appearance for France in the Davis Cup in 1928 until he bowed out from the competition 25 years later in 1947. In all he played 26 Davis Cup ties, winning 44 of his 54 rubbers. At Wimbledon he was the singles champion twice, in 1924 and 1926, mens doubles champion three times and mixed doubles champion once. Also on grass, he won the Australian Championships in 1928. Indeed he did and still does love playing on grass, firmly believing that 'if Roland Garros had been grass instead of clay I'd have won it more than twice [1924 and 1931].

Looking back, it was so appropriate that this man who always played with such enthusiastic energy should have thrived so expertly on the faster surfaces and he emphasized this by winning the French covered courts title no less than 12 times between 1922 and 1947 and the British covered courts title, alas no longer in existence, 11 times between 1926 and 1949.

Borotra, a spectacular volleyer to support what by today's standards would be regarded as no more than an average serve, was part of the Golden Age of French tennis.

There were times, it seemed, when he and the other Musketeers, Henri Cochet, René Lacoste and the man who was regarded as the doyen of the quartet Jacques 'Toto' Brugnon, all great players in their own individual way, were more popular in Britain than in France, with Borotra loved most of all, especially at Wimbledon.

Long before the Bjorn Borg and McEnroe headbands became almost as familiar as the players who wore them – and generations before anyone had started to consider the commercial exploitation possible from such appendages – the dark blue Borotra beret was the best-known trademark in tennis. Borotra only had to pull it on to his head in the middle of a match to earn a standing ovation.

As my distinguished predecessor on the *Daily Telegraph*, Lance Tingay, wrote in his *100 years of Wimbledon*, 'When he donned it, it was a signal that he was hard pressed and about to launch his major effort. It was also a signal for the crowd to rise to their feet and applaud him, even if he were opposed to a British player.'

Jean Borotra's game consisted of a fearless net attack and

there are those still around from those days who will swear to this day that no one has come up with a superior backhand volley or possibly even a better smash. Above all, Borotra was both a great strategist and an unrivalled showman, in a sporting manner, which the crowds adore.

'The Bounding Basque' he was called. And to the obvious, affectionate delight of all those who attended the Awards Dinner held by the British Lawn Tennis Association in December 1983, the Basque was still bounding with youthful exuberance and zest as he leapt upon the stage to greet members of the British Davis Cup team which had defeated the French team, of which he was a member, 50 years earlier.

Not all of Borotra's Wimbledon experiences were triumphant, of course. In 1927, in the third all-French final in four years, Borotra's defeat by Cochet, 4–6, 4–6, 6–3, 6–4, 7–5 was after a match which not only brought the Championships to a thrilling climax but also involved, by Cochet, one of the greatest comebacks of all time.

In both the quarter- and semi-finals, this player with a masterly touch and, as history shows, a record of astonishing brinkmanship, had survived quite remarkably. He had lost the first two sets in both matches and, in addition, recovered from 1–5 in the third set of the semi-final. Against Borotra, where he was also two sets down, Cochet also slipped to 2–5 in the final set.

Again I am indebted to Lance Tingay's official history of The Championships for this detailed account of the climax:

Cochet, serving, was advantage point down in the next game but on this match point Borotra netted his service return a little lamely. At 5–3 Borotra served for the match. At 40–30, he double faulted. Then he reached advantage for a third match point. A volleying exchange ensued and Cochet's first shot, a backhand, was thought by some to be a double hit. The umpire quickly ruled that the ball was good. But a dramatic game was not yet down. Borotra had three more advantage points. He put a volley out. A forehand passing shot from Cochet clipped the line. Borotra volleyed out again. That was six chances Borotra had held in all. He had no more. His momentum slackened. Cochet took the next three games for the loss of three points to win the match.

Borotra was, and still is, a great sportsman. Much of his time, between still working for the petroleum equipment distribution company he joined in the early 1920s is taken up by his duties as a member of the International Committee for Fair Play. 'Fair play is so threatened nowadays,' he says. 'Too great a degree of importance is placed on victory, either for the money, the prestige, the club or the country. There is a temptation to win by any means and when that happens it is the finish of sport.

'For 20 years I've been President of that committee which really is trying to save sport. Sport has done so much for me that I consider it my duty to give almost a half of my time to the defence of fair play.'

At an earlier meeting it was close to midnight as Monsieur Borotra and I chatted. He had to rise at 5 a.m. the next morning to fly from London to Paris for several business meetings, so one could readily understand when he said he did not have a great deal of time to watch modern tennis.

'I don't find I have enough time to play tennis, which I try very hard to do two or three times a week, but I can't always because I have too much to do so I'm not going to spend my time watching tennis,' said this enviably sprightly octogenarian.

One event he does attend every year is the French Champion-ships. 'I was very worried when I saw, for instance, Vilas and Borg playing for several hours with only seven volleys in all because that was really so dull. Mind you some people say "Ah, that's wonderful, that's precision, that's tenacity that's physical strain and all that . . ." One day there was a charming lady saying all that in front of Budge Patty. Budge won Roland Garros – but by going to the net – and he replied to the charming lady, "That's true – fantastic accuracy, wonderful driving, beautiful lobs and so on," and then he added "But what a terrible bore."

'So I was very worried for Roland Garros, for despite what some may say there the volley is so important. Each year I was counting the volleys. Now we have a certain number of players, even at Roland Garros, who are able to go to the net and not only on the first serve, so things are much better.'

Borotra's other great concern for the game in recent years has been the dominance of the serve. Back in the 1970s when he felt it had reached a degree where naked power on grass was taking all the subtlety and spectacle out of the game, he persuaded the French Federation to put forward a proposal to the International

Lawn Tennis Federation, as it was then (before dropping the Lawn from its title), whereby in men's tennis the serve should be delivered from three feet behind the line.

He resurrected the idea at the end of Wimbledon 1984 after John McEnroe had won more than 60 per cent of his points against Jimmy Connors directly or indirectly on the influence of the serve, although he also acknowledges that the extra skill which many players have developed in recent years in returning the serve must be set against that and placed on the credit side of the game's appeal.

Lawn tennis for Jean Borotra was always a strictly amateur game to be played for love. He does not envy or condemn the changes which, in the normal passage of time and progress, have transformed so much of the game into a commercial, highly profitable jungle.

But would he like to have been born 60 years later to share the benefits and fortunes now available to his successors?

'Tennis has given me so many joys that I have always been content,' he said. 'I don't need all that money. I was happy when I was playing and also working for my business. The only possible regret I have is the feeling that I will die without having played tennis enough!'

"I'll Play my own Sweet Game"
Frank Deford

With any artist who attains the ultimate in his craft, there must
be one moment, an instant, when genius is first realized, when a
confluence of God's natural gifts at last swirl together with the
full powers of endeavour and devotion in the man to bear him to
greatness. Virtually always, of course, that moment cannot be
perceived, and it passes unnoticed, but with Big Bill Tilden it
was isolated, forever frozen in time. He knew precisely when he
had arrived, and, thoughtfully, he revealed it.

This happened on Centre Court at Wimbledon in 1920. Tilden
was already 27, and although he had never won a major
championship, he had reached the final. It was his first trip
abroad, and to his delight the British, unlike his own
countrymen, had taken to him right away. Americans always
only grudgingly granted Tilden recognition, never mind
respect, largely because they were emotionally hung up on Big
Bill's main rival, Bill Johnston, who was affectionately known
as Little Bill, or even, in the soupiest moments, Wee Willie
Winkie. Johnston was five feet eight, a wonderful cute doll-
person from the California middle class, and all Americans
(Tilden prominently included) were absolutely nuts about him:
the little underdog with the big heart who cut larger fellows
down to size.

By contrast, at six feet one and a half inches tall, 155 pounds,
angular and overbearing, a Philadelphia patrician of
intellectual pretension, Big Bill was the perfect foil for Little
Bill, and the great American villain. Until 1920 he had also
co-operated by remaining a loser with a healthy reputation for
choking in important matches. The year before, in the final at
Forest Hills, Johnston had defeated Tilden in straight sets, and
so it was assumed that Wimbledon would serve as the stage
where Johnston, the American champion, would duel Gerald

Patterson, the Wimbledon defender, for the undisputed championship of the world.

Unfortunately for hopes for this classic confrontation, Johnston was waylaid in an early round by a steady English player named J. C. Parke. Not until the next day, when Tilden routed Parke, avenging Little Bill's defeat, did Big Bill move front and centre as Patterson's most conspicuous challenger. Of course, from the moment Tilden strode upon their grass that summer, the British had been enchanted with him – his game, his manner, his idiosyncrasies: 'this smiling youth, so different from other Americans.' A woolly blue sweater Tilden wore seems to have positively enthralled the entire nation, and *The Times* exclaimed that 'his jumpers are the topic of the teatable.'

While little Johnston struck the· British as just that, a pleasant little sort, the lean giant caused them admiration and wonder: 'Of great stature, he is loosely built with slender hips and very broad shoulders . . . in figure, an ideal lawn tennis player.' His game they found so arresting – 'There is no stroke Mr Tilden cannot do at full speed, and his is undoubtedly the fastest serve seen' – that one of the more poetic observers even rhapsodized, 'His silhouette as he prepares to serve suggests an Egyptian pyramid king about to administer punishment.'

Seeing Tilden for the first time, unprepared for that sight, was obviously a striking experience. Not so much in what exactly they said but in their evident astonishment and determined hyperbolic reach do the British of 1920 best intimate what an extraordinary presence Big Bill Tilden must have been. Yet perhaps even more important, the British understood immediately that here was a different sort of athletic temperament. The Americans were not to fathom this in Tilden for years, if indeed many of them ever did. But Tilden had played only a handful of matches in England that summer before he was assessed perfectly in the sporting press: 'He gives the impression that he regards lawn tennis as a game – a game which enables him to do fascinating things, but still a game . . . When he has something in hand he indulges his taste for the varied at the expense of the commercial.'

Pleased at the attention given him, even more gratified that his playing philosophy was appreciated, Tilden grew assured, and, boldly and not without some conceit, he began to enunciate his theories of the game. When not at the courts or attending the theatre, he spent all his time writing in his hotel room, and within three weeks he had completed his first book, *The Art of Tennis*. 'The primary object in match tennis is to break up the other man's game' was, significantly, the point he most emphasized.

Patterson, meanwhile, remained quite confident. An Australian, the nephew of the great opera star Nellie Melba, he was not only the defending Wimbledon champion but star of the team which held the Davis Cup. He was at his peak and generally recognized above Johnston as the ranking player in the world. At Wimbledon Patterson had only to bide his time scouting the opposition and practise at his leisure, for in those days the defender did not play in the regular tournament but was obliged only to meet the 'all-comers' winner in a special challenge round.

Patterson's supremacy seemed all the more obvious after Tilden appeared to struggle in the all-comers final against the Japanese, Zenzo Shimizu. In each set Tilden fell far behind: 1–4 in the first, 2–4 in the second, 2–5 in the third. He won 6–4, 6–4, 13–11. Nobody realized it at the time, but it was one of Tilden's amusements, a favour to the crowd, to give lesser opponents a head start. Tilden had whipped Shimizu 6–1, 6–1 in a preliminary tournament the week before Wimbledon, and he certainly had no intention of cheating his Centre Court fans with that same sort of lopsided display. In the final set Big Bill tested himself and kept things going, largely just by hitting backhands and nothing much else.

'The player owes the gallery as much as an actor owes the audience,' he wrote once; and Paul Gallico summed it up: 'To his opponents it was a contest; with Tilden it was an expression of his own tremendous and overwhelming ego, coupled with feminine vanity.' Big Bill never really creamed anybody unless he hated them or was in a particular hurry to get somewhere else.

Certainly he was not ever anxious to hastily depart Centre Court at Wimbledon, and he returned for the championship against Patterson on Saturday, 3 July. Big Bill found this date especially felicitous; an obsessive patriot, he noted that, for an American, 3 July was the next best thing to 4 July. He further buttressed this omen by somehow obtaining a four-leaf clover that he was assured had once grown under the chair that Abraham Lincoln used to sit in on the White House lawn. And so, with that talisman safely ensconced in his pocket, he set out to become the first American ever to win the Wimbledon men's championship.

Patterson had a strong serve and forehand, but his weakness was an odd corkscrew backhand that he hit sort of inside out. And so, curiously it seemed, Tilden began by playing to Patterson's powerful forehand. The champion ran off the first four games with dispatch and won the set 6–2. But then, as Tilden changed sides for the first time in the second set, he spotted a good friend, the actress Peggy Wood, sitting in the first row with a ticket he had provided her, and he looked straight at Miss Wood, and with a reassuring nod, that kind delivered with lips screwed up in smug confidence, he signalled to her that all was quite well, that it was in the bag, that finally, at the age of 27, he was about to become the champion of the world.

Miss Wood, of course, had no notion that she would be used as a conduit for history; nor, for that matter, could she understand Tilden's cockiness. He had lost the first set 6–2; he was getting clobbered by the best player in the world. But down the five full decades, and more, that have passed, she cannot forget that expression of his, nor what followed. 'Immediately,' she says, as if magic were involved, 'Bill proceeded to play.'

In that instant he had solved Patterson's forehand, and the champion, his strength ravaged, had nothing but his weakness to fall back upon. *The primary object in match tennis is to break up the other man's game.* 'A subtle change came over Patterson's game,' the *Guardian* correspondent wrote in some evident confusion. 'Things that looked easy went out, volleys that ought to have been crisply negotiated ended up in the net.' Tilden swept the next three sets at his convenience, losing only nine games, and toward the end it was noted for the record that 'the Philadelphian made rather an exhibition of his opponent.'

Big Bill did not lose another match of any significance anywhere in the world until a knee injury cost him a victory more than six years later. Playing for himself, for his country, for posterity, he was invincible. No man ever bestrode his sport as Tilden did for those years. It was not just that he could not be

51

beaten, it was nearly as if he had invented the sport he conquered. Babe Ruth, Jack Dempsey, Red Grange and the other fabled American sweat lords of the times stood at the head of more popular games, but Tilden simply was tennis in the public mind: *Tilden and tennis*, it was said, in that order. He ruled the game as much by force of his curious, contradictory, often abrasive personality as by his proficiency. But he was not merely eccentric. He was the greatest irony in sport: to a game that then suffered a 'fairy' reputation, Tilden gave a lithe, swashbuckling, athletic image – although he was in fact a homosexual, the only great male athlete we know to have been one.

Alone in the world of athletics, nearly friendless and, it seems, even ashamed of himself, there was seldom any joy for the man, even amidst his greatest tennis triumphs. It's quite likely that in his whole life Tilden never spent a night alone with an adult, man or woman. And his every day was shadowed by the bizarre and melancholy circumstances surrounding a childhood he tried to forget; certainly it is no coincidence that he did not blossom as a champion until just after he discarded the name of his youth.

He had been born on 10 February 1893, and christened William Tatem Tilden Jr, which he came to hate because everyone called him Junior or June. Finally, arbitrarily, around the time of his twenty-fifth birthday, he changed the Junior to the Second, II. That onus officially disposed of, June became Bill and then, even better, Big Bill.

He had been introduced to tennis early. It was an upper-class game, and the family he was born into was rich, of ascending social prominence, and even greater civic presence. The family mansion, Overleigh, was located in the wealthy Germantown section of Philadelphia, only a block or so from the Germantown Cricket Club. The Tildens belonged, of course, and the club was indeed to be the site of many Big Bill triumphs, but the family summered at a fashionable Catskill resort, Onteora, and it was there that young June learned the game of tennis, in the last year of the nineteenth century.

The first clear vision of him as a player does not arise, however, until about a decade later, when Tilden was playing, with litte distinction, for the team at his small private school,

Germantown Academy. This day he was struggling on the court, slugging everything, all cannonballs, when Frank Deacon, one of his younger friends, came by. Even then, as a schoolboy, Tilden was always closest to children years younger than he. At the end of a point, which, typically, Tilden had violently overplayed, hitting way out, Deacon hollered to him in enouragement, 'Hey, June, take it easy.'

Tilden stopped dead, and with what became a characteristic gesture, he swirled to face the boy, placing his hands on his hips and glaring at him. 'Deacon,' he snapped, 'I'll play my own sweet game.'

And so he did, every day of his life. He was the proudest of men and the saddest, pitifully alone and shy, but never so happy as when he brought his armful of rackets into the limelight or walked into a crowded room and contentiously took it over. George Lott, a Davis Cup colleague and a man who actively disliked Tilden, was none the less mesmerized by him: 'When he came into the room it was like a bolt of electricity hit the place. Immediately, there was a feeling of awe, as though you were in the presence of royalty. You knew you were in contact with greatness, even if only remotely. The atmosphere became charged, and there was almost a sensation of lightness when he left. You felt completely dominated and breathed a sigh of relief for not having ventured an opinion of any sort.'

Tilden himself, said, 'I can stand crowds only when I am working in front of them, but then I love them.' Obviously the crowds and the game were his sex. For a large part of his life, the glory years, all the evidence suggests that he was primarily asexual; it was not until he began to fade as a player and there were not enough crowds to play to that his homosexual proclivities really took over. But ahh, when he was king, he would often appear to trap himself in defeat, as he had against Shimizu, so that he could play the better role, prolonging his afternoon as the cynosure in the sun, prancing and stalking upon his chalked stage, staring at officials, fuming at the crowd, now toying with his opponent, then saluting him grandly, spinning, floating, jumping, playing his own sweet game, revelling in the game.

And yet, for all these excesses of drama and melodrama, his passion for competition was itself even superseded by another higher sense: sportsmanship. Tilden was utterly scrupulous, obsessed with honour, and he would throw points (albeit with grandeur, Pharisee more than Samaritan) if he felt that a linesman had cheated his opponent. Big Bill was the magistrate of every match he played, and the critic as well. 'Peach!' he would cry in delight, lauding any opponent who beat him with a good shot. And, if inspired or mad enough at the crowd or at his rival, he would serve out the match by somehow holding five balls in one huge hand and then tossing four of them up, one after another, and pounding out four cannonball aces – bam, bam, bam, bam; 15–30–40–game – then throwing the fifth ball away with disdain. That was the style to it. Only the consummate showman would think of the extra ball as the closing fillip to the act.

'He is an artist,' Franklin P. Adams wrote at Big Bill's peak. 'He is more of an artist than nine-tenths of the artists I know. It is the beauty of the game that Tilden loves; it is the chase always, rather than the quarry.'

Further, even more unlike almost all great champions in every sport, whose brilliance is early recognized, early achieved, Tilden was required to make himself great. Very nearly he created himself. Only a few years before he became champion of the world, he could not make the college varsity at the University of Pennsylvania. He taught himself, inspired himself, fashioning a whole new level for the game in the bargain.

Withal, it is probable that the very fact that he was homosexual was largely responsible for the real success he achieved in tennis; he had none elsewhere. Urbane, well read, a master bridge player, a connoisseur of fine music, he held pretensions to writing and acting as well as tennis, but these gossamer vanities only cost him great amounts of stature and money, and even held him up to mockery. For all his intelligence, tennis was the only venture that June Tilden could ever succeed at, until the day he died in his cramped walk-up room near Hollywood and Vine, where he lived out his tragedy, a penniless ex-con, scorned or forgotten, alone as always, and desperately in need of love from a world that had tolerated him only for its amusement. 'He felt things so very deeply,' Peggy Wood says. 'He was not a frivolous person. And yet, I never saw him with anybody who could have been his confidant. How must it be like that? There must have been so many things deep within him that he could never talk about. I suppose he died of a broken heart.' It seems he did.

To the end, in the good times and the bad, he searched for one thing above all: a son. He could not have one, and so he would find one for himself, make one, as he made himself a great player to honour the dead mother he worshipped. But the boys he found, whom he loved and taught, would grow up and put away childish things, which is what any game is, what tennis is, and ultimately, what Big Bill Tilden was. He was the child of his own dreams, always, until the day he died, age sixty, his bags packed, ready once again to leave for a tennis tournament.

Come Back to Centre Court, Billie Jean, Billie Jean

Bud Collins

For one who was called 'Old Lady' by her greener colleagues when she was only 23, the subject of age, nearly 17 years later, is obviously touchier. The nickname 'Old Lady' has been out of fashion for a long time, but I must ask whether she thinks a champion should get out at the top, quit before the inevitable decline sets in.

'Oh yes,' replies the former Old Lady. 'I've done that. I did retire in 1975.'

So Old Lady may be buried somewhere in 1975, enshrouded in a retirement announcement, but her successor, still very much in vogue, carries on as . . . what?

First Living Ancestor of Tennis?

Or, at the very least, First Lady.

Although some see her as a tormented 39-year-old Flying Dutchman who doesn't know how to get off the road, Billie Jean King is nothing less than Saint Billie Jean to others who pray she'll keep striking blows on behalf of working women eternally. Says one front-line feminist, not wishing to be identified because she has been burned by the saint's ire: 'Billie Jean is an inspiration to all of us – the bitch!'

Julie Anthony, at 35 a used-up pro whose name is preserved in bylines and commentary jobs, recounts her latest meeting with King, six months ago in Philadelphia at the National Women's Indoor Championships. 'It was *déjà vu*. I walked into the dressing room, and there was Billie Jean. She was probably in the first pro dressing room I ever entered, years before, and she's still there. It struck me that nothing had changed – only the surrounding cast. But Billie Jean was babbling happily, the centre, as always. She's a good friend, but still it was eerie coming on her there – like visiting someone in her home that you thought she'd moved out of some time ago.'

This week's address is the Boston University hockey team's locker room at Walter Brown Arena, where Billie Jean Moffitt King, the First Living Ancestor, has set up the itinerant shrine. She reappears in our province, which she first visited in 1960, as one of the elite on the Virginia Slims tour. Among the tour's population are several schoolgirl competitors whose parents were romantically inclined toward each other about the time (1961) that King won the first of her bagful of Wimbledon titles.

'I guess I hit some balls with her when I was two. There are pictures,' says twice-US Open champ Tracy Austin, 20. 'I don't remember it.' But she will never forget losing to King in the Wimbledon quarter-finals last summer. Says Austin, 'I wasn't at my best, and she's still dangerous.'

Still dangerous after all these years, this woman whose big-time tennis career began when the abdicating Bjorn Borg was two years old, carries on with no signs of burn-out. In business, a newly inducted member of a quarter-century club often gets a watch, a free dinner, and a spatter of obligatory applause. Embarked on her 25th season in big-time tennis (16th as a professional), King will be content if people watch and she earns their handclaps. She has always preferred to buy her own dinner.

Retirements, comebacks, championships, injuries, celebrity, notoriety, heavy money, light comedy, there's nothing in tennis that Billie Jean hasn't reaped or endured. In fact, millions of Americans, unaware of the sport before 20 September 1973, will swear that Billie Jean invented tennis that night, when she collided with His Piggishness, Bobby Riggs, in their televised sextravaganza at the Houston Astrodome. Those people, for whom Wimbledon and the US Open and the French Open hold no meaning, will recall eternally that match – in which the spunky woman silenced the boasts and japes of dirty old man Riggs and won it for womankind – as her biggest day in court. Her biggest day, that is, until 15 months ago, when the King found herself in a real-world court in Los Angeles, defending herself against a foe more threatening than the ancient Riggs, whippersnappers Andrea Jaeger and Tracy Austin, or age itself.

This wasn't just another career-threatening knee operation, as agonizing as the four of those had been. This time the foe was an ex-lover, a slight blonde, Marilyn Barnett, and the stakes were the highest: Billie Jean's glowing reputation, built and burnished over decades. King was renowned not only as an all-time champ, but also as Mother Freedom of tennis (perhaps of all female sport), a prophet in sneakers who led her flock into the promised land of golden paydays, a beacon for feminists as well as little girls with a yen to be jocks.

Esquire magazine asserted in 1974 that the two most internationally recognizable US athletes were Muhammad Ali and Billie Jean King. And there were similarities: they were fighters from working-class backgrounds who did it on their own in ring and rectangle, glorifying themselves as much with palaver as punch. And Ali was an idol of King's, although she is 'disappointed he wouldn't pay the price to stay fit as he got older', a price that becomes higher for her almost by the minute.

'Billie Jean has to work three times as hard as the rest of us to stay even,' says 28-year-old Chris Evert Lloyd. 'When I get out of bed stiff the morning after a long, tough match, I can't imagine what it must be like for her.'

King, who describes herself as 'a Southern Californian raised as a middle American in Long Beach' by parents who believe in God and Horatio Alger success stories, has rejoiced in a devastating backhand, a handsome, caring husband, and the thought that she was paving the way 'for young girls who can see that it's now acceptable to aspire to be professional athletes'.

But Barnett, a former hairstylist greatly in evidence during the summer leading to the Riggs match, was depicting Billie Jean somewhat differently, as a woman turning her back on alleged promises and obligations to Barnett, with whom she shared a romance and road trips over several years during the 1970s. In May 1981, Barnett brought suit for lifetime support and, more menacingly, threatened to welcome the world to a juicy scandal, revealing the details of her affair with King.

In typical strong-hearted style, however, Billie Jean went on the attack, volleying regardless of her opponent. King called for the press. Bring notebooks and cameras, she said, she would tell all – or at least admit a lesbian affair – before the case came to judgement. It was a stunning manoeuvre to defuse Barnett's strategies. Bold, calculating, or just plain honest, King won public support, despite some who smirked when King characterized that romance as an isolated mistake. Seven months later, Judge Julius Title found in King's favour and censured Barnett in the process, branding her claims as bordering on extortion.

'We won,' says King, 'but there was no joy in so-called victory. The fact is, I could never win. I'll never be the same. I'll never recover from the damage I suffered, the emotional damage to me and Larry [husband Larry King] and my folks. But . . . you have to go on.'

Go on to what? wondered friends and observers. Certainly not to the Wimbledon semi-finals – yet there she was, at the high point of a season that returned her for a record 18th time to a place in the US top ten (she was number six). A year before, ostensibly retired again, she had shunned an invitation to be among champions saluted at the centennial observance of the US championships at Flushing Meadow, New York. What champ more deserving than she, holder of 13 US titles? 'I was in New York, but I couldn't bring myself to go,' she says. 'I just didn't want to be seen in public. I was so down about the Marilyn thing. And scared. The trial still hadn't been set.'

Frank Deford, who at the time was collaborating with King on her latest autobiography, *Billie Jean*, remembers the period. 'It was clear the last thing she wanted to talk about was the upcoming trial or anything about her private life . . . But I'd show up and she'd grit her teeth and begin talking about . . . everything personal.'

Late revisions, however, kept much of that talk out of print and killed the title the two of them had agreed on: 'Misfit'. 'Both of us thought "Misfit" fitted her perfectly – a unique person, something of an eccentric, a visionary, but with a distinct, telling view,' said Deford. 'There were so many changes that it isn't the book it should be, not the book she told me freely.' According to Billie Jean, 'There were misunderstandings; Frank got some things wrong.'

'What I'm sure I got right', says Deford, 'was the relationship with Marilyn, and it doesn't show in the book now. Billie Jean led me, a heterosexual male, to understand how a homosexual love affair could be beautiful and very tender . . . Despite my problems with Billie Jean and her lawyers and agents in getting the book out at all, my admiration for the woman remains high.'

Though apparently through as a player, King was at her

customary stand, Wimbledon, as a journalist in June 1981, a somewhat shell-shocked kibitzer in the NBC commentators' booth. 'I was a zombie then,' she remembers, a statement confirmed by those who saw her at the time. 'I would wake up every morning depressed. I didn't want to be there. I didn't want to see anybody. I wanted to hide from the public. But Don Ohlmeyer, the boss then at NBC, had stuck by me through all the publicity furore in May, and I appreciated his loyalty and the opportunity to work.'

'Do you know the only place Billie Jean can hide and find real peace?' says another pro, Ilana Kloss, a close friend and frequent doubles partner. 'A tennis court. There may be thousands there watching, but she's alone in her own world, immersed in what she loves best, tennis. Nobody can bother her there. Whenever there's trouble, Billie Jean runs for a tennis court.'

So King, who long ago made the comeback her motif, rebounding from painful defeats (financial and athletic), from debilitating illnesses and injuries, and from two or three retirements, has returned from 'the worst beating of my life'. She has survived love's labour litigated and all those other traumas and birthdays not merely to reappear as a geriatric curiosity, but to compete at the uppermost level once more.

'It's like Sinatra,' says her pre-eminent booster, her husband Larry, a tennis promoter and president of Team Tennis, the city league of which the Los Angeles Strings' Ms King is the foremost ornament. 'She was born to be an entertainer. Money has nothing to do with it; we don't need it [although he says legal costs in the Barnett case have exceeded $250,000]. But she has to perform for a crowd, and she will as long as people clap. I'm afraid, though, that people like this sometimes equate adulation with love.'

She is a lady hurting, but not singing the blues. Her psyche is as black and blue as her body used to be when she was a teenager training under fire, and another old great, Alice Marble, a 1930s champion, would blast balls at Billie Jean at point-blank range to toughen her and hone her volleying reflexes.

'I'm just working harder than ever these days because I know now I can still do it, that I still have more to give,' King says.

And more to get? 'It's a two-way street with Billie Jean,' says one of her friends of long standing, Karen Hantze Susman, doubles accomplice in the Wimbledon championship of 1961. 'She loves the attention, the hype, the media. She needs it. It feeds her ego. And she handles it so well even though Billie Jean is basically very shy. She has the need to compete, the need to perform. But she gives the audience as much or more than she gets, and that's important. She has to give.'

Billie Jean grins. 'The ultimate power trip for me, for any athlete, is to give to those watching, to inspire, motivate, bring joy,' she says. 'And if you want to know about my ego, which is obviously big, it operates this way: every time you tell me I can't do something, that ego tells me I not only can, but must. Even my agent, Barry Frank, keeps telling me, "Don't embarrass yourself. If you were 22 it wouldn't be so bad to take some of the losses to lesser players, but now you don't need it." '

Larry King says Billie Jean 'cares very much what people think of her, and that's the principal reason she's still at it now. She's trying to build up new last memories of her for the public. It bothers her terribly that the last impression – the lasting impression – would be the trial and the affair. Wimbledon was a wonderful start in that direction, although I don't agree with her, and I kept telling her that her reputation was too secure for Marilyn to hurt.'

At Wimbledon last summer, her daily resurrections dazzled opponents and millions of viewers. Bursting from a three-match-point trap set by Tanya Harford, or slickering heavily favoured Tracy Austin, or stretching Chris Evert Lloyd to the limit in the semi-finals, King upstaged everything during the illustrious fortnight except for Jimmy Connors's jolting of John McEnroe in the men's final.

But success at Wimbledon is dancing in full view as winner at the top of the pyramid of players. 'What amazes me', says Susman, 'is the way she could come down off the pyramid and, after where she'd been for years, take the degrading losses to players ranked down in the forties and fifties as she tried to re-elevate herself. Especially after the way she's been buffeted by the lawsuit.'

The losses weren't all that was degrading. 'I tell you, I was a little crazy when the year began,' says Billie Jean. 'It wasn't too great a year for the King family.' (Along with the Barnett case came a horrendous skiing accident for Larry King, a fractured leg that incapacitated him for months, and a punctured colon for King's brother, Randy Moffitt.) 'But, no excuses, I behaved badly, terribly at times. I can really be a poor sport, and I know that disappoints some of the young kids on the tour.'

Her tempestuous scenes included hurling a racket at the umpire in Boston, screaming at opponent Jo Durie in Berlin, and loudly calling a Parisian line judge a name that would uncurl McEnroe's hair. But the nadir was a February 1982 misdeed in Detroit: 'So unprofessional, so unfair to the crowd: I walked out. Quit.' She had split sets with Anne Kiyomura in a first-round match. Kiyomura held serve to start the third set, and King picked up her rackets and departed. 'I don't know why. Everything was getting to me then. It was my third tournament back on the tour, and I still didn't have my attitude straight. Was I really supposed to be out here again? And I was still uneasy in public. I went a little crazy. Every day since I've told myself, "Don't ever let that happen again."'

Chris Evert Lloyd, a staunch King supporter, was bothered by what she considers the deadliest tennis sin: 'I saw Billie Jean quitting . . . Even when she played out a match, and against players who were in diapers when she was great, I didn't like it. If she wasn't willing to give 100 per cent, then it was time to get out. Forever. Her competitive standard was too high for her to tear it down like that.'

'It was attitude, and letting myself be satisfied with less than the best effort,' explains King. 'You can fall into that sort of habit and justify it because I said I was just playing to help out. The Women's Tennis Association had asked me to go on tour again because I was a name. Injuries to Austin and Jaeger, and the fact that Evert Lloyd wasn't playing the winter tour, had weakened the box-office appeal. They just wanted me to show up, regardless of how I played.

'So I could rationalize. I was just seeing what would happen, and I didn't have to make a full commitment, to say that Billie Jean King was back to win. So if things weren't going well, I could tell myself it didn't mean anything, my career was behind me.' She smiles. 'But that wasn't me, and I knew it.'

Evert Lloyd believes 'the turning point came in Perugia at the Italian Open in May. Billie Jean was playing an ordinary player, Pat Medrado, in her first round. She had to save a lot of match points to win, and then she went on to the semis where she almost beat Hana Mandlikova. It would have been easy to give up against Medrado. It was a lousy, rainy day, and nobody was watching. But I think that turned it around for her, and she knew she might have a good year.'

Billie Jean nods. 'That tournament made me re-evaluate,' she says. By then she had won only six of 12 matches, following up on but four of ten during the 'phase-out' campaign of 1981. She hadn't come close to winning a tournament in two years, a deficiency to be rectified through the triumph at Birmingham, England, preceding Wimbledon. 'Perugia showed me I could still guts it out and was strong enough to play a full tournament – I got to the doubles final, too – with good players on not my best surface, slow clay. Poor Medrado. She had six match points, the last one on a second serve. I got lucky, the ball hit a hole and didn't bounce, just stayed down like a ground ball. If I hadn't won that point it would have been a very discouraging loss. Who knows what I would have done after that?'

Was a good season (winning 67 of 117 singles and doubles matches) predicated on a bad bounce in an obscure Italian city? Had she received timely adulation that week from Italian male spectators, traditionally disdainful of female tennis, who constantly bellowed, 'Dai, dai, Guglielmina.' ('Come on, Little Bill!')? Maybe she was rehearsing in an out-of-town limbo for the worldwide Wimbledon drama of match-point rescues against Tanya Harford.

But can it really be worth all the time, tedium, and discomfort? Does a woman on the far side of 39 wish so desperately to avoid growing up that she will pack herself in ice for hours at a time, praying that antique, workaday knees won't become swollen beyond game-playing dimensions? Or lift leg weights practically as unfailingly as brushing her teeth to strengthen those suspect joints hinging thighs and calves? Hasn't she won enough titles, money, acclaim, eminence, and pain?

The answer to the first three questions is a fervent yes. To the last, a determined no.

Thus King, a fireman's inextinguishable daughter and the longest-running show in major tennis, begins another season. This is no cameo on the order of such other former champs of her vintage as Stan Smith, Fred Stolle, or John Newcombe. No, Billie Jean – ever chilled in all those ice packs but still possessed of chilling will and volley – returns as a legitimate contender, playing not only the Slims circuit but the Women's Tennis Classic, a new category for players over 30, as well as Team Tennis.

Is Billie Jean, in plunging once again into the pro tour, simply fleeing the shadow of Marilyn Barnett, the woman who tried to take away something from her? 'One thing,' says Arthur Ashe, an ex-Wimbledon champion and current US Davis Cup captain, 'with that Wimbledon performance Billie Jean pushed the Barnett fire to a back burner and maybe, hopefully, put it out for good. But how long can she keep this up? Tennis is individual; Billie Jean has to do all her own running and playing. No substitutes.'

There is no substitute for King anywhere. Who can imagine tennis without her?

'What was my first impression of Billie Jean?' muses 26-year-old Mary Carillo, a former player who works as a writer and commentator. 'I can't pin-point it; she's just always been there.'

Right. Always. She was a chubby-yet-agile 'sweet 16' – hooked on candy bars and ice cream – at a small tournament at the Essex County Club north of Boston when I first saw her in 1960. Billie Jean Moffitt then, she got a set from that year's Number 1, Darlene Hard. Extraordinary vision wasn't required to see her as a future champion, but there weren't many watching in those days, and it was fun to consider her a discovery. I saw her win her first Wimbledon final a year later, and since then I have covered most of her 38 major championships. I can think of no player whose play gave me greater joy.

Her rage to win, blended with superb reflexes and athleticism, made it easy for audiences and reporters to overlook the defects of terrible eyesight and a body too small (five feet four, 140 pounds) for an attacking player, a body susceptible to infirmities ranging from hay fever and bronchitis to the over-taxed, much decorated (with scars) knees.

Nevertheless, it was damn the defects, full speed ahead to the heights as probably the greatest all-round female player.

After her unlikely 1961 Wimbledon victory – she and Karen

Hantze were unseeded, the most precocious team ever to win – King was on her way. Knowing she had to make this game her life, she wished there were a respectable means of making it pay so she could be a proud professional rather than a frequently busted-out amateur, beholden to a fraudulent system of clandestine underpayments.

Speaking her piece, she called herself a 'professional' in amateur's clothing, vexing and sometimes infuriating the men in charge of the American amateur game. However, her way became clearer and cleaner in 1968 when Billie Jean, younger Californian Rosie Casals, Englishwoman Ann Haydon Jones, and Frenchwoman Françoise Durr, accepted a promoter's offer to become the first women's professional troupe. Shortly, the dawn of open tennis (the integration of pros and amateurs in prize money tournaments) was an answer to King's pleas. But it quickly became apparent that the bulk of prize money would go to the men, with the women regarded as excess baggage.

The crusade for genuine professionalism for women was yet to begin. When it did, in 1970, the atmosphere crackled with the excitement of the ringleader, King, waging war with racket strings and vocal cords. 'I had to be the spokesperson because nobody else was either willing or able,' she says. 'Maybe nobody wanted or believed as much as I did, or if they did they didn't play well enough. People weren't going to listen unless a champion talked.'

The champion talked and played majestically as the Virginia Slims circuit came into being and prospered. During 1971, a season that seems beyond Saturn to today's pros, she ran rings around anything they could envision and won 33 titles (19 in singles) and $117,000 in prize money, a landmark for female athletes and a staggering seasonal prize figure for anyone, male or female, in that day.

Even though she is not on good terms with King, Martina Navratilova, who won $1,475,055 in prize money for 29 titles in 1982, readily declares, 'We wouldn't be where we are without her.' And Arthur Ashe now appraises King as 'the most important player of the open era', although he was not in her corner when she pushed for, and attained, partly of prize money for the women at the US Open.

By autumn of 1981, after all the misery brought on by

Barnett, it occurred to King that it was time 'to stop feeling sorry for myself, to kick myself in my behind and start getting well. I was fat, at least 160 – my best weight is 135 – and I could see myself ballooning to 200. I couldn't even run a quarter-mile, I wasn't doing anything but brooding, and when I'm not in shape nothing is right. So I started working out again, hitting some balls. I had no intention of returning to competition then,' she recalls, but she discovered that there was less pain than she expected in her knees. 'There was definitely less pain, less than there'd been in years. I was able to lift heavier weights and I could feel myself getting stronger. In November, I began getting repeated calls from Peachy Kellmeyer at the WTA, almost begging me to play again. Here I was, thinking I was making a transition out of playing, but they needed me, and I thought, if the pain stays away, why not? Just getting in shape put me in a very joyful mood. That's what tennis gives me: joy. It helps me keep my sanity. I just love to play,' she says. 'I can live without the crowds, no matter what anybody says, and the publicity. But I have to play, and I always will, even if it's at a public park with nobody watching.'

'It's because that's all she's got,' says a contemporary who, though highly ranked, dropped from the circuit years ago. Following college, as was expected of the young women in the amateur days, she married and had children. 'Billie Jean's marriage isn't a marriage. She has no children. Tennis is her family.'

King scoffs at this notion and 'all the psychoanalysing of me. It's easy to try to make it complicated, but the simple fact is: I love tennis. I have to play as long as I can. I know the young girls in the Wimblebon locker rooms were cheering against me when I played Harford [last year]. Sure, they can't understand me, and I'd be the same, seeing this 38-year-old out there and saying, "No way! You won't catch me playing at 38." I said the same things about older players when I was a kid. But they don't know the hold on my soul this game has. The reason I've been able to do so well – who knows how long this will last, the absence of pain, the will to make myself work out so hard every day – is that I've been able to isolate points. Each point I play is the "now moment"; the last point means nothing, the next point means nothing. All that counts in the whole world is this now point, and that's where I'm living for all I'm worth. Now.'

She has frequently said she will know the 'now' to say no, and that 'they won't have to drag me from tennis screaming'. Hang on to your earplugs just in case.

Ashe, for one, says he is 'amazed, somewhat dismayed, that Billie Jean, with the incredible vision she had for pro tennis, and how she worked to realize it, is apparently unable to plan ahead for her own life.'

Those plans may not be routinely formulated if, as Martina Navratilova asserts, Billie Jean 'has to be the big cheese. That's why I broke up our doubles partnership. I was tired of her wanting to be in the spotlight all the time, playing to the crowd. After all, I had become the better player. I wanted to play with someone as an equal . . . I'm surprised there are still hard feelings, but I know she knocks me. I could say plenty about her, too, but I won't. She's a legend.'

Ted Tinling, a septuagenarian tennis courtier and historian, feels 'Madame Superstar is too susceptible to moods, too turbulent to ever be very happy for very long . . . She self-destructs. Scorpios [King's birthday is 22 November] are emotional, manipulative, energetic, but devoted and committed – that's Billie Jean. She is capable of intolerance, destructive impetuosity – even 'tanking' – but she reaches a high level of dynamism. Her exuberance is contagious, and you find yourself in her company wanting to do better. In coming out in public about her abortion [in 1971] and the Barnett affair, she displayed both honesty and courage. I believe she's a better person because of the Barnett affair.'

King does not concur. 'Maybe someday I'll be able to say I gutsed it out, but I can't be Pollyanna now and say it was a strengthening experience. It was a nightmare. I'd be sitting in court those four days, wanting to scream. It was so unfair, such a waste. And it's not over. It's never going to end. Even though the judge dismissed Marilyn's first suit for lifetime support and another for palimony, she can still appeal. I'm a prisoner of the process of law."

'Forty-eight hours before the suit was filed,' says Billie Jean, 'when I knew it was going to happen, and there was no way to prevent it, I felt as though a cloud was now over my life. A cloud that could never be removed. I knew my life had changed forever, that for the first time it was out of my control. I was constantly in tears for a while but, no – she replies to a question – 'never suicidal, nothing like that. But I could see how that could cross some people's minds.'

Larry King says, 'The trial was life and death to Billie Jean, match point in a Wimbledon final, and I'm proud of the way she rose to the occasion, like always. Even though she knows I love her no matter what, and she loves me, and she was mad at me during the trial because I was telling her we couldn't lose. It was a sham, and I told her to believe in the judge and justice.'

Usually Billie Jean has no difficulty believing in Larry. 'She took my advice from the beginning when I urged her to get the most from her talents in tennis, which meant going on the road, long separations. That changed our relationship, but not our love. I don't satisfy all her needs, and she doesn't satisfy all mine, and we've come close to divorce several times. But we believe in each other and value each other's opinions.'

It is a marriage with area codes as bonds, refreshed periodically by connections at their hideaways, a house in Hawaii, and an apartment in Manhattan. That's as materialistic as the Kings get. 'You can look at us,' she says, laughing, 'and tell we don't spend on clothes. We've spent, and lost, a lot on things we believe in, *WomenSports* magazine, Team Tennis, tennis camps. But I'm not broke. I'm not playing because I need the money, but a lot of people don't believe that.'

She says people guffaw if she suggests she might win Wimbledon again. 'I could have this [last] time. I was *soooo* close. But instead of being annoyed by missing my chances in the semis against Chrissie, I'm encouraged for this year.'

This year? This is part of what charms and infuriates about Billie Jean King – the swings from one direction to another, even within a sentence. From 'How can I tell how long I can go without pain? – every tournament could be my last' to 'I'm thinking about Wimbledon '83 already. You set a goal and go after it, rung by rung.'

Up and down. From saying nobody believes her to saying the public is solidly behind her. 'I know I'm high strung and flit about,' she shrieks in a voice reminiscent of the 16-year-old of an eon ago. Then, lowered and scratchy, the tone conveys anguish as she talks about 'betrayals'.

'Not the genuine friends. They stuck by me. And God knows my parents did, even though the case was such a shock to them, so out of their world, that I can't even discuss it with them today. But I could tell by the way they hugged and kissed me that I had their love, and they were with me even though they may have disapproved. That was so important. My folks are so middle America it's unbelievable. How did they ever get me? But if they'd been bohemians I wouldn't have any touch with sanity. It was the strength I got from them that pulled me through. It may sound corny, but they taught me nobody's perfect. You have to live with yourself, everything is relative, and no matter how bad off I was, I was still a lot better off than most people."

Betty Moffitt, the perky, white-haired lady who shared those vitamin commercials with Billie Jean before the sponsor pulled out, maintains the only real home her daughter has ever known, a three-bedroom house painted beige on Thirty-sixth Street in Long Beach. The Moffitts moved there in 1946. The fence Billie Jean destroyed as a child with a stream of tennis balls has been rebuilt. Behind it is a small garden featuring strawberries, tomatoes, peppers, and zucchini, and in the family room are two trophies, one from Wimbledon, the other the Babe Zaharias Award for Outstanding Woman Athlete of 1973. 'We aren't too much for trophy display,' says Betty Moffitt. 'The rest, I think, are in the garage. This hasn't been an easy time for Billie Jean, and I think it helps her to play well again. We always figured our children's business was their own after they'd grown up. We'd keep the faith. We believe if the kids know they're really loved, they can pull themselves up by their bootstraps.'

Bill Moffitt, a strapping lifelong athlete, retired from the fire department and scouting for the Milwaukee Brewers, is 'pleased to see that Billie Jean is accepted despite her problems. People are for her.'

No anger or bitterness cloaks his voice as he refers to the Barnett case. 'Talk about the props being knocked from under you! And coming at the time Randy was sick and we didn't know what it was. It was rough for a while, but I told Betty, "Look, people have forgiven Nixon. They'll forgive Billie Jean, too."'

Though the Moffitts may wish Billie Jean would settle down and raise a family – she talks about that herself, 'with natural or adopted children' – her father says, 'Everybody's different. They face different pressures. But I'm proud of my "elderly daughter" – she'd hit me if I called her that to her face – I didn't think she'd play so well again.'

No betrayals from within the family circle, 'but I've been hurt elsewhere', says Billie Jean. 'Marilyn and her lawyers, of course. They tried to get something for nothing, and they may still try.'

Had there been any redeeming qualities to their love? 'None,' rasps Billie Jean. 'I regret we ever met. No saving graces whatsoever. I was patient with her, I was a friend, tried to help her get settled in life with $125,000. They wanted more – for nothing. She's a fake, not a good person.'

King estimates that those in the business world who deserted in her hours of stress cost her 'at least a million dollars over three years. I have no idea what it cost Larry in deals that fell through – plenty, and just because a lot of people we trusted had no guts. They ran when the bad publicity began. And they kept running even though the consumers, the public, have been encouraging and sympathetic. But for businessmen, the easy way out is indifference. The Yonex racket people, Nike shoes, and Power Grip stayed with me. They were terrific, but I lost several endorsements that were pending, and one of the contracts I had wasn't honoured because the company said I was a bad person. Imagine weaseling out like that. I don't think the case had anything to do with Squibb dropping me on the vitamin endorsement. But what got me was at the time of the suit they made a big deal of announcing they weren't gonna renew, instead of just saying nothing. They were trying to look good at my expense. I wish I could tell you that Wimbledon improved my business possibilities. It hasn't, although I've had some feelers lately and that makes me feel good.' She spreads her hands: 'So I'm writing that stuff off. I'm not counting on it. I'm just counting on me, and Larry.' She smiles. The smile may bring out more wrinkles than the first time we saw it, on a face more weathered, yet it remains a great smile, the emblem of a woman not always sure where she's going, but certain she's going there like Hurricane Billie.

'I'm 39, I'm tired, it's so easy to cheat and let my weight and my legs go, stop working hard and eat everything I like, all the ice cream and chocolate and junk food. But then I couldn't play, and I'm *sooo haaappy* when I play. Who am I hurting? Why do people keep asking if I'm going to quit? Did anybody ask Rubinstein when he was going to stop playing?'

It's a good point, but on the other hand, the only legs Rubinstein had to worry about were the piano's.

Little Mo

Laurie Pignon

'Maple syrup? . . . No Madam, I'm sorry. We have Chunky Oxford marmalade, Robinsons Golden Shred, or strawberry jam, but no maple syrup.'

To his everlasting credit the waiter, tall and gaunt and looking as happy as an undertaker in Shangri-La, did not lift a bushy eyebrow or show an iota of emotion as the young lady proceeded to add spoonfuls of Tiptree's best to her scrambled eggs, bacon and grilled tomatoes. (After all she was not English.)

Expense account businessmen busy with their boiled eggs and studying form in the *Financial Times* or the *Sporting Chronicle* had no idea that the chummy, chattering little American in a pinafore dress and a turtle neck sweater – this was before the age of track-suits – was to become the most feared woman in lawn tennis, whose pictures were to fill the sports pages of the world for the next three years, and our hearts forever.

This was my first breakfast with Maureen Connolly, and the strawberry jam was the only time I saw her compromise with anything, on or off court. But this was Manchester 1952, and housewives and hotels were still having to wrestle with the problems of food rationing.

Youth is a beautiful thing, so beautiful that at times I am driven to believe that it is wasted on the young. They keep carrying on as if they invented it . . . But not Maureen Connolly, she accepted it for what it is, then disregarded it. She never used her age as an ally or an alibi, everything in her life was inconsequential except her relentless hunger for success.

She was a girl in a hurry, but it would be wrong in retrospect and quite alien to her irrepressible get-up-and-go-character to suppose that nature had given her some sort of warning that her time was to be painfully short. Her remarkable success was based on the simple fact that her fear of failure was always bigger than her opponent's will to win.

On court she was quite ruthless, off court she was fun to be around with, and her laughter was as infectious as measles, as I learned on the day we played a mixed doubles. She was American champion, favourite to win Wimbledon, and the grass at the West Didsbury Club, Manchester, was damp, but none of this had the slightest effect on Little Mo. She always believed, and later wrote, that top players should unwind by playing 'relaxed but not lackadaisical' fun matches. So it was that Bill Martin, who reports lawn tennis for the Press Association a good deal better than he can play, and I were invited to join her in a mixed doubles.

Martin won the toss and chose Maureen as a partner, and I refused to play unless Maureen handicapped herself by playing left-handed, which she proceeded to do with tremendous effect. After she had won – by telling Martin to stay at the net and keep out of her way – I discovered that she had started her climb to stardom as a left-hander and only changed when her first coach Wilbur Folsom had told her that no left-handed woman had yet won Wimbledon. 'O.K. I'll be a right-hander,' said the 11-year-old on the court in San Diego.

Nothing it seemed could stop Maureen, and when her coach the hatchet-faced but inspired Eleanor 'Teach' Tennant who had helped produce such contrasting champions as Bobby Riggs and Alice Marble told her to scratch from her first Wimbledon to nurse an injured shoulder, Maureen refused. 'You have got plenty of time, don't risk your career,' advised Miss Tennant. Maureen's response was to call a press conference at Wimbledon, something that was not done in those days, and announce that she had sacked probably the greatest coach of that time.

An act of precocity possibly, defiance certainly, but in either case Maureen knew that the only way to silence her critics was to win the Championships.

She won three Wimbledons, only twice dropping a set (in her first year), three US, two French and one Australian title and the Grand Slam in 1953, and did not play another competitive match after the age of 19.

Today the game is full of youngsters, some of whom have become millionairesses before they are old enough to leave the class room. Most of them have a rough idea that Maureen Connolly was a bit special in her time, but consider they are survivors in a tougher, more professional game than was played in the 1950s. But they would be kidding themselves if they thought that Miss Connolly's contemporaries such as Margaret du Pont, Louise Brough, Doris Hart, Althea Gibson and Shirley Fry – all Wimbledon Champions – could not have got into today's top ten.

A fall from her horse ended her playing career before her 20th birthday, cancer ended her life on the eve of the 1969 Wimbledon, and if she had taken her place in the centenary celebration parade of Champions she would have been 49. But her laughter and those sparkling eyes live on in her two beautiful daughters, Cindy and Brenda. Having dinner in their Dallas home last spring reminded me of breakfast with their mother: we had fresh strawberries with our lamb curry.

Virginia's 20th Wimbledon

Ronald Atkin

Heads turn as Virginia Wade, immaculate in a light skirt and
check jacket and toting an umbrella against New York's
uncertain skies, saunters into Rumpelmeyer's (purveyors of the
world's greatest cup of hot chocolate) on Central Park South.
Ain't that the gal who won Wimbledon once? Didn't she play
Team Tennis for New York Apples way back? Surely she's the
one we see on TV advertising furs, credit cards and pens?

The very same, folks . . . Britain's own, Britain's very own
Virginia Wade, darling Ginny of the Centre Court, or as
Wimbledon officially and formally refers to her in programme
and on scoreboard Miss S. V. Wade (the S. stands for Sarah but
it's a name she never uses).

This month Virginia celebrates two landmarks: her 20th
consecutive Wimbledon and her 36th birthday. The latter
should in the politest circles be dismissed with a quiet murmur
but the former merits much praise and comment.

In these days of jet-paced, year-round tennis the wear on
bodies and the pressure on minds is enormous – and growing.
The casualty rate, among both men and women on the professional circuits is impressive – or depressing if you happen to
become one of the wounded.

But through it all has sailed Miss S. V. Wade, shoulders still
firm and smile still wide despite the burden of having carried
the hopes of Britain for more years than is decent. How on earth
has she stayed around at the top for all that time?

One of the reasons is that she has rarely been injured, because
she simply refuses any longer to believe in injury. 'I used to have
a bad back,' she explains amid the late morning clatter and
swirl of Rumpelmeyer's. 'Then I suddenly realized that it was
always at 2-all in the third set that my back would pack up and
that it had to be purely tension, and that I was probably just

imagining it. I have never believed in being injured since then, though you can't help twisting the odd ankle, having that sort of accident occasionally.'

Another reason is that she has nurtured the determination to support those sort of beliefs since taking up the game as a child in South Africa, where her family had moved – from Bournemouth – at the end of the last war when her clergyman father was appointed Archdeacon of Durban.

Virginia has also marked up a remarkable list of achievements for consistency, while remaining maddeningly (or as some would have it, endearingly) inconsistent in her performances. She has been ranked No. 1 in Britain for ten years now, a member of our Wightman Cup team for 15 years and its captain for the past eight. She has beaten all the world's best women on her day. She has also lost to quite a few of the worst ones.

Since the pinnacle year of 1977 when she lifted the Wimbledon crown right on cue in the tournament's centenary year and watched by the Queen, who was celebrating her Jubilee, Virginia has trodden the stony path down from the summit. In 1977 she was the world's No. 2 behind Chris Evert. Last year she wasn't ranked in the top 10, for the first time in 13 years.

Last year, also, she became one of the handful of women in the tennis world to exceed the million dollar earnings mark. She had made her point – made her pile, too – and there wasn't much more to prove. Apartment in New York, flat in London, impressive family home in Kent . . . she was perhaps Britain's wealthiest, and certainly best-known, female athlete.

Increasingly, Virginia has been looking towards the world of television as an alternative career when her playing days are over, and she came close to that moment a year ago.

'I had only geared myself mentally to carry on playing until the end of last year's Wimbledon,' she said, sampling that exquisite hot chocolate. 'Last year was going to be my final one on the circuit. Then I found out that 1981 would be my 20th Wimbledon. There was no way I was going to miss that. And the 20th Wimbledon has dominated my thinking ever since.'

Her plan to leave the women's circuit centred around an offer from ITV to commentate on the Moscow Olympics, the sort of opportunity she had been angling for. 'Then the Olympics became such a shambles because of the boycott. Moscow was out. I felt disappointed and I didn't even feel like playing tennis. I was very close to packing up at that point because the whole point of my tennis is that I have always loved playing the game.'

Virginia claims the low point of her career was reached in the Daihatsu tournament at Brighton last October when she was beaten by the 19-year-old American Barbara Potter. 'All I wanted to do was just get off court,' she admitted.

'It was then in Brighton that I realized I had a choice. I could mess around until my 20th Wimbledon or put in a really big effort for six months.'

In effect she has fallen somewhere between the two options. She could never be accused of having messed around during the winter and spring but neither was the effort as consistent as it might have been particularly on the Avon tour. Places like Detroit, Cincinnati and Kansas City possess less than irresistible appeal in the depths of an American winter.

Virginia's high point was in reaching the final of the Avon tournament of San Francisco only to lose to her pigtailed gremlin, Andrea Jaeger. But she has stayed fit and keen, as feline, arrogant, predatory, sleek and eye-catching as ever.

She acknowledges that the 20th Wimbledon will be her last big effort to lift the title again, but the word retirement is allowed no dwelling place in the Wade vocabulary.

'There are several reasons why I don't like the word,' she said. 'One of them, though I'm not particularly proud of it, is that the companies for which I have endorsements are not too happy about the word 'retire'. Another reason is that I've always hated this bit about people saying they're retiring. I am allergic to that particular terminology. They all retire and then come back. Billie Jean three times, Margaret Court, Chris Evert Lloyd. Why don't they just say they aren't going to play for a while?'

It's far more likely that Virginia will ease out of tennis with the same grace she has brought to her playing career. She certainly intends to lead Britain into the Wightman Cup match against the United States in Chicago two weeks after Wimbledon, and will possibly compete in the Centenary US Open as a distinguished former champion (she won the title in its first full, open year, 1968).

She makes no secret of her interest in a TV career – 'and not just sports commentating either,' she point out. She has done quite a bit of this already in America, including work during the US Open last year, where she was always either hurrying onto court for a match or into the commentary box to air her opinions.

Though it seems a pity that Britain's best-ever woman player will be lost to this country as a coach, Virginia Wade has no plans to return to Britain for at least three more years. She is content to make New York her home for the time being, especially since it constitutes a more-than-tolerable haven from the savagery of the gentlemen from Inland Revenue.

Severely critical of the fact that there is no natural successor among British girls – 'It's absurd, there is no one who looks remotely as if she can play the game the way it is played in this modern day' – she does not feel her future lies in helping to pull British tennis out of its abysmal condition.

'I could never undertake straightforward tennis teaching,' she said. 'I would be interested in having a coaching school, but more along the American lines with children "living in". I might be able to do some good being in charge of a small group of talented youngsters, giving them specialized coaching, but I just couldn't go out and do that sort of thing six hours a day every day.'

For the time being, however, TV amibitions and coaching opinions can wait. Once more the name Miss S. V. Wade is going to be slotted into the Centre Court scoreboard, and the nation's viewers can settle back to agonize the day away with their favourite.

It's more unlikely that Virginia Wade will win, as she did in 1977. But, given a clear mind, a following wind and a friendly draw, she may topple an opponent or two. Alternatively, she may make a swift exit, to the acompaniment of headlines like 'Ginny Shock'. But then, that's the way she has always been, 20th Wimbledon or not.

Suzanne Lenglen

John Ballantine

On the morning of Tuesday 16 February, 1926, a match took place in Cannes in the South of France which hundreds of Americans crossed the Atlantic to watch.

Helen Wills, a fresh-faced 19-year-old college girl from California and, for three years, the United States singles champion, threw down a soft white gove, beneath which everyone knew lay a remorseless iron fist, at the dainty feet of Suzanne Lenglen, then 26 and the unquestioned queen of tennis.

Suzanne Lenglen opened her eyes slowly in her first-floor suite in the Gallia hotel in Nice. Pale sunlight filtered through the white chintz curtains. She glaced through the window while stretching her ballet dancer's limbs languorously across silk sheets.

Bien. So the horrid rain had ceased. Today was a day of reckoning on which, in the final of the Carlton hotel tournament in nearby Cannes, she would pit the wiles, skills and speed of France against the youth, enthusiasm and confidence of the New World in the strong physique and coldly unnerving manner of the Californian prodigy, Helen Wills.

Several weeks earlier Helen, accompanied by her formidable mother and a host of supporters and writers, including the humorist James Thurber, had arrived unexpectedly on the Côte d'Azur. To the logical French, her aim was unequivocal; to beard their acknowledged empress, no less, in her own Mediterranean fastness.

Suzanne's total dominance endured. She had won six Wimbledon singles titles, four of them in the previous four years and, on the last occasion she had conceded only five games in her five matches.

The diva, in fact, had not lost a singles since 1919 when she had defeated the 40-year-old English player, Dorothea Lambert Chambers, the holder of seven Wimbledon titles, at Old Worple Road, unless you count the time she retired, allegedly sick, against Molla Mallory in the first round of the US championships in 1921.

It was rare for her to lose even a single game on the Riviera. Most 'exhibitions', for you could hardly call them contests, took only 20 minutes or so, after which fascinated visitors were frequently taken out on to the smooth red shale to see where her deadly placements had dug grouped targets of marks in the backhand corners or just inside the service court corners.

Very occasionally, guests in club restaurants having early lunch dropped a crumb or two on to the white damask when disturbed by a red-faced messenger: 'I say everyone, Suzanne's just lost a game.'

'Lenglen dropped a game? Golly, who to?'

'Miss Everett-Dunne of London got one in the second set. She had a bit of luck of course with a couple of net cords.'

The Riviera was crowded always in the winters of those Roaring Twenties with the rich and famous basking in the warm midday sun, enjoying wine and small talk. 'Well, my dear,' a new comer was told, 'Suzanne is inflicting her usual annihilations and Tilden arrived at the end. Big Bill is so handsome in his teddy bear coat but, oh, you know, so Oscar Wilde-ish.'

One legend had Tilden supposedly playing Suzanne and deliberately giving her the first three points of each game before beating her 6–0. No such set ever took place although the flamboyant superstars, both so typical of those socially conscious days, had practised together harmoniously.

Most Americans expected Helen to win, a belief which, in the crisis of six-all in the second set, caused one Yankee to roar out: 'Two thousand dollars say Wills wins.' An English aristocrat took the bet. After all, Helen had been as dominant in North America as Suzanne had in Europe and, in addition, she had won the Olympic title at St Cloud, Paris, in the 'Chariots of Fire' year of 1924, admittedly in Lenglen's absence.

'The Americans have agreed to have English officials', Suzanne's mother said through the gilt door. 'Commander Hillyard is in the chair and on the lines are others you know, Mr

Cyril Tolley and Lord Charles Hope. Now *fais vite*, shortly I'll come in to help you with your hair.'

Suzanne had never watched Helen play although, recently, in Nice, she had been unable to avoid witnessing the American, distinctive even on a distant court in her white sunshade, hit a few forehands. The power of the stroke shook Suzanne out of her earlier conviction that Helen was just more cannon fodder for her accurate barrages. So that, when the Californian instinctively glaced across to see the reaction of the world champion, Suzanne made a typical gesture.

Bending her supple body forwards slightly, she kicked her right leg up behind her until her foot rested upon her right shoulder. She glanced sideways at the exposed sole to see whether a pebble was lodged there before pushing the shoe nonchalantly back down to the ground. Tossing her jet-black hair defiantly, and uttering screams of delight as her acolytes buzzed about this body language, she extended her arms theatrically and flounced into the clubhouse like one of the Hollywood movie queens she so much admired.

Only when she lay down briefly on a *chaise-longue* did she permit herself to consider the forthcoming meeting. *Oui*, she would play this little Wills like a salmon, a strong and vigorous fish no doubt but one who would finally have to yield.

Helen Newington Wills was born at Centerville, California, on 6 October 1906, seven years after Suzanne first saw the light at Compiègne in Picardy. Educated at the Anna Head school and at the University of California she took up tennis, aged 11, at a Berkeley club. It was not long before she began to make the elderly coach wish for a less demanding pupil for, as she later told an enquirer about her resolution, 'In our home, we were all taught, and indeed expected, to succeed in all we did.' To another friend, she confided: 'When I was little, my mother made me repeat several times at night, "I can, *and I will!*" '

She copied her famous forehand from that of her fellow-Californian, 'Little Bill' Johnston and, while doing so, went about for months repeating, 'I *am* Johnston.'

Ellsworth Vines, who is now a golf professional at a club in Palm Springs, was then the Californian junior champion of tennis and he recalls playing a match against her in Los Angeles for charity. 'It didn't take me long while warming up to

81

realize I'd have an awful lot of trouble if I attempted to slug it out with her. So from the first ball, I rushed the net, serving or receiving. When I reached 5–love, Miss Wills left the court saying she didn't feel very well.'

Mid-morning, and Helen was whisked away by her mother to change into her usual white one-piece dress, heavily pleated at the hem, below which, like Suzanne, she wore the fashionable white stockings. About her chances, she had few reservations. Unaccustomed to losing at any level, she felt well able to take care of an ageing French player who, admittedly, had been great in her day, but in an earlier age. Repeatedly she had been assured by friends and backers that Suzanne had been deliberately avoiding her, which was true.

After driving to the court, the Americans were shepherded by French officials to the gate where Mrs Wills kissed her daughter and told her firmly, 'Just do your very best, dear, but make sure you win.'

Spectators clambered over the rickety, temporary stands. Others stood on the roofs of motor cars or perched in tree branches, and tiles had been removed from nearby houses. Every few yards, a head stuck through like a surrealistic drawing by Dali.

Commander George Hillyard, the leading Wimbledon umpire, busied himself at the chair while other English notables were in position on the lines. Suzanne already sat five or six yards away on an ornate red plush hotel chair.

She looked to Helen a canny old pro. She had a sheaf of four or five rackets on her lap. Holding one up to her ear, she twanged the gut to make sure it had the right pressure sound. Her young admirers, banished for once from her immediate presence, sat in the front row.

Helen laid her own three rackets, together with a napkin of fine linen which she used to mop beneath her eyeshade, on her own chair. To her surprise, Suzanne, to whom she had not been formally introduced, immediately rose to her feet and walked across with a friendly smile.

Although with her heavy Gallic features and sallow complexion, she was far from beautiful in any accepted sense, Suzanne's appearance and manner was animated, exotic even, and Helen could see at once why she eclipsed far prettier women.

Her dark eyes, large and luminous, were enlarged with mascara. She wore a well-cut white silk dress with cutaway arms and a neckline that was, in those days, regarded as far too revealing to be respectable. Tantalising glimpses of flesh showed above her stockings whenever she moved (there is a picture in existence in which she is diving for a low volley with one breast fully exposed). Short hemlines framed her shapely calves.

'*Ma chère* Mademoiselle Wills, permit me to welcome you to France and to wish you the best of fortune,' she volunteered.

'That is exceedingly kind of you, Mademoiselle,' murmured Helen 'And may I, as a stranger to your country, also wish you the best of luck.' They touched hands and Helen, after a slight hesitation, added: 'It is an honour to play you, Mademoiselle.'

Suzanne glanced enigmatically at her young rival, after which the combatants, so different in manner, breeding and race, took the court. Suzanne called successfully to Hillyard's spun coin and elected to serve. Helen chose the shady end and reflected that, even had she won the toss, she would have given her rival service in the hope of breaking through before she had fully warmed up.

Men living today who knew Suzanne well over the crucial eights years since she first amazed Wimbledon in 1919 until the time in 1926 when she left it in disgrace, having been accused, unjustly some believe, of keeping Queen Mary waiting, make it clear that Suzanne possessed a strong open nature with no malice in it.

On the contrary, Dan Maskell, Ted Tinling and Jean Borotra remember her as exceptionally level-headed, kind and loyal. As a model daughter brought up by a demanding father, Charles, who saw in her talent a chance to realize the fulfilment denied to him as a potential cycling champion, she was modest and forthright.

Her feline grace was that of a ballerina and some spectators said that they would much rather watch Suzanne simply walk about a court than others play upon it. Her parents brought her up to regard herself as the supreme star she undoubtedly was, and she regarded each match as a gala performance. Her high leaps, particularly on the backhand, were, Maskell believes, just *joie de vivre*.

Helen, in contrast, was a handsome college girl with large hips. She was taciturn to the point of arrogance, thought the French, but she had little to say also to the American press because she was under contract to the United News Service agency.

She could be waspish. At Wimbledon, in 1934, when hurt and forced to retire to her great rival Helen Jacobs, she reacted coldly when her opponent sympathetically touched her and asked if she would like to continue after a rest.

'Take your hand off my shoulder,' Wills is reported to have snapped, before gathering up her rackets and walking off. On another occasion, when asked her opinion of a writer who, unable to get an interview with her, simply used his imagination, she said icily: 'He appears the kind of fellow who would steal anything not actually nailed down.'

As the champions took up their respective positions, a sound arose from the crowd like the murmur of the distant sea. Suzanne wore a pink turban which accentuated her pallor and taut expression, while Wills donned her white visor beneath which her lips pursed in a thin line.

During the warm-up, Suzanne sent several drives rocketing over the baseline. She preferred to range long before shortening her trajectory rather than be timorous and short when it didn't matter. To some watchers, she seemed to be having trouble fully stretching her racket arm, but this probably psychosomatic, for it quickly disappeared.

When play began, Suzanne's technique, born of thousands of hours of baseline drudgery insisted on by her perfectionist father, made Wills look clumsy and erratic. The Californian struck some tremendous blows with her forehand but, after leading by 2–1, she fell behind and, unable to raise her game to cope with the flitting Frenchwoman, she lost the first set 6–3.

To the intent audience, however, it was obvious that there was very little to choose between them. In the long rallies, Helen's occassional whizbangs cancelled out the relentless steady chiselling away of Suzanne's long-short-short-long technique. Essentially a tactician of medium pace, Lenglen's accuracy enabled her to move the heavier Wills around like a bell-bottomed piece on a chessboard.

By angling her short drives, Lenglen forced her young rival to come into the forecourt from where she either overhit or else was easily passed. The American was surprised and alarmed. Never before had she met an opponent whom she could not hit through by sheer pace and to have the ball constantly returned to a perfect length and then immediately to irritating short angles which forced her to rush forward and overhit was both humiliating and puzzling.

In the long interval before the second set (for Hillyard never dreamed of calling either lady forward before she was completely ready) Helen recalled the words of her old coach: 'always change a losing game.' So early in the second set a marked change came over the match. Wills's errors grew fewer. She launched herself off her feet to get more pace. This determined long-range assault took toll of Suzanne's notoriously limited energies. She took frequent nips at a small silver brandy bottle, even between points.

Helen broke through to lead 3–1. The crowd grew noisier as it was treated to the unique spectacle of watching its unparalleled champion decisively outplayed. No one could ever recall seeing the ball being hit so hard.

The unthinkable was happening. The great diva had, at last, met her match, both in strokes and in will. She seemed strained and shot apprehensive glances at her distressed mother, who was beginning bitterly to regret that she had not insisted on the presence of Monsieur Charles.

Helen served for a 4–1 lead which, in that set at least, might have proved decisive. But suddenly she made a fatal alteration to her strategy. Instead of persevering with her all-out attack, she began to trade slower baseline strokes. Perhaps she was so sure she had the veteran on the run that she wanted to show she could beat her every which way, including by the French player's own favourite tactics.

The plan went disastrously wrong and Suzanne swiftly turned things back her way, reaching 3–3 with the loss of only two points. With the Californian serving, there ensued the longest game of the contest. Suzanne held a 40–15 lead, but Helen resisted stubbornly and won the game after ten more points.

With America leading 4–3 the next few games were crucial. At 30–30, Suzanne, now looking very much the weaker player and swigging brandy regularly, hit a forehand drive towards Wills's forehand line. No immediate call came and Helen glanced at the linesman, Tolley. The famous golfer sat impassively, briar pipe clenched firmly between his teeth.

Clearly Helen had thought the ball out, for a shudder of disapproval ran through her. She reacted by netting the next ball. Four all, five all, then came the vital break. Suzanne, from 30–30, hit two winners to lead 6–5. Seeing her chance to end the affair, she served firmly, keeping the ball on the American's more vulnerable backhand, and she reached 40–15 – two match points.

A long rally. Spectators' heads nodded like metronomes and, for once, there was total silence. Finally, Wills saw a chance, rose on to her toes and threw everything into a furious drive across court. Suzanne was nowhere near the ball when it landed on or near the line, but she gave a shrill cry of truimph when a cry came "Out!"

Throwing the ball she carried in her left hand high in the air, she danced theatrically, but with obvious relief, towards the net. Helen walked forwards more slowly and this was thought to be from sheer disappointment. Or perhaps she was claiming that her shot was in?

But she smiled pleasantly and shook hands like a good sport and the court was besieged instantly with scores of Lenglen admirers thankful that the ordeal was over and handing her bouquets of flowers.

But what was this? Someone was holding a hand in front of the lens of a newspaper photographer who was attempting to record the historic scene. A fearful apprehension arose, especially when it was seen that there was a commotion near the umpire's chair.

A linesman, Lord Charles Hope, a keen player whose reputation rested upon his being able to play equally badly with either hand, and who had been in charge of the line in question, was engaging Hillyard in earnest conversation.

'Sorry Georgie, but that call didn't come from me. Some Frog anticipated the call. The ball was clearly good.'

The commander nodded firmly and did not hesitate. Picking

up a speaking trumpet, he roared: 'Ladies and gentlemen, please resume your seats. The match must continue. The last ball was unfairly called out. Fair play dictates we must resume. Will the players return to court and take up their positions? The score is 40–30 in Miss Lenglen's favour.'

Had a bomb exploded at the net there could hardly have been greater consternation. The truimphant French at first could not believe it, and flatly refused to face the unpalatable change in their champion's fortunes. Initial reaction was that it was all some damnable Anglo-American plot to cheat their beloved Suzanne of her well-deserved victory, and the fact that Hillyard throughout had never used a single word of French reinforced this conviction.

Some stood stock still as if shell-shocked, while others ran wildly about the court looking for friends who, when found, joined in the general condemnation of the startling announcement. There had been no mistake, *absolutement non*, the ball had been out by all distances up to a metre.

None of this incredulity and rage had the slightest effect, however, upon the intractable Hillyard, and finally the court was cleared. Suzanne took the court again, a ghost, her black eyes red-rimmed in an ashen face. She staggered slightly while putting her equipment back upon her chair and, giving Hillyard a burning glance, she walked slowly to her end.

Helen took up her position briskly for she had thought her last stroke well in. Here was a second chance and she intended to take it, for quixotic turnarounds were part of the west coast way of life.

Suzanne tossed up one ball from a shaking hand. Fault. She hit another service out to lose her second match point and a moan of dire pessimism arose as she lost the game. Helen responded in true American style, going straight for the kill.

Suzanne, who several times had been close to losing the initiative in the set before the call debacle, could easily have been forgiven for losing not only the set but the match. Instead, she showed why many critics still believe she was the greatest player of all, and in the absence of her beloved papa too. Reaching deep into the reserves which had enabled her, when but a girl, to overcome the redoubtable Mrs Chambers, she surged into action.

Forsaking her favourite baseline position, she took the ball much earlier and moved quickly in behind it. Attack, the best form of defence, can swing any issue. Her first two volleys flew for winners, shaking the resolve of Helen who faltered beneath this unexpected onslaught. Within a few minutes it was all over.

Suzanne was again the winner, this time not by 6–3, 7–5 but by 6–3, 8–6. The players shook hands once more, this time almost as an afterthought. Suzanne smiled gaily as before while Helen was spirited away by a consoling mother who later gave her a lecture on the perils of letting opponents off the hook. In the next ten years she was hardly ever to do so again and, with Suzanne dying of leukemia at 39 after a brief professional career, Helen established herself as the supreme exponent of the women's game.

Suzanne came as near to a total physical and mental breakdown as any player ever has. Coco Gentien, another French champion and one of the few present who had the knowledge and experience to appreciate fully just what she had been through, quickly thrust her into a wooden kiosk near the gate which had been used to store takings.

Alone and in semi-darkness, the exhausted Suzanne gave vent to her deepest feelings. She had just defeated the toughest opponent she had faced since Mrs Mallory, not once but twice in the same match. For several minutes, she sobbed passionately, tears washing the mascara down her cheeks. In a state of semi-hysteria, she picked up handfuls of paper money and scattered francs over herself.

Five minutes later, apparently totally calm and wearing an expression of pure joy, she walked out in the daylight and the adulation of her supporters.

Later, dining with friends in the town, she overheard a snatch of conversation: 'There is Suzanne. She is still the queen.'

'Yes,' said Suzanne, half to herself, 'but for how long?'

Vijay's Special Person

Tom Koch

Vijay Amritraj is where East meets West and both give and take a little.

It would have been easy to predict that once America had taken over his brain, India would be crowded from his thoughts. He came from Madras, India, and fell in love with America. He Americanized the family name, feasted shamelessly on McDonald's french fries and jetted freely about the world with his headquarters in the US.

And surely, surely, when it came time for him to end his bachelor days he would pair himself with an American woman.

Vijay's actual name is Amritharaj. That's what his parents, Robert and Magdeline (Bob and Maggie – sounds American doesn't it?) go by. Vijay and his brothers – Anand and Ashok – decided that was too tough on the American tongue, so they dropped the 'h' and 'a' from the middle. 'Bud Collins had difficulty with it on television,' Vijay said. '*Armitage* is an American word and it sort of worked in with that.'

According to Indian custom the sons and daughters marry in sequential order by age. When the first-born son, Anand, married on 12 October 1980, the attention focused on Vijay, the most famous of the Amritraj clan.

Indian custom also calls for the parents to select a bride for their son. Because of his worldly travels and love of the West, Bob and Maggie told Vijay he could do it by whatever method he wanted. But Vijay had not forgotten his roots. He wanted this to be traditional. Hang the french fries, bring on the curry.

'The oldest son generally gets married first but there is no law,' Vijay said. 'If there is a girl in the family, depending on her age, she will go first even though she might be the second child in the family. After Anand got married only then did they think of me getting married. It is very unlikely in India that the guy stays a bachelor so long that he does not allow the second child to get married. Usually by 30 the guy is married. Then the second one and so on.'

The basic ingredient of the institution of American marriage is love. By having his parents arrange his marriage, Vijay is not marrying someone he really loves.

'There is no love at first,' Vijay admitted. 'In real, real orthodox families marriages are arranged just by the parents. They decide the girl is good for the boy and the boy is good for the girl and most of it is done and the children agree. In my particular case, considering the fact that I travel so much they wanted me to have the first say in the matter, but I turned round and put it back in their shoes. I had no pressure to do it that way. It was something I wanted to do. I was keen on marrying a Catholic Indian girl. If I was spending a lot of time in India and I got to meet a lot of Indian girls it might have been possible to make my own choice right away. But that would have been difficult for the simple reason that I am fairly well known in my country and it becomes difficult for an individual to go out with me on a date and dating is not very common at home, especially in the south where we come from.' Vijay retained a veto power. So Bob and Maggie began to pass the word – 'their friends, friends of their friends . . . it pretty much goes around the country and India is a very big country.' Bob and Maggie interviewed some 100 prospects. Of that group Vijay personally met and turned down three. Then the parents approached the Sri Lanka High Commission to recommend some people. They came up with the family of noted industrialist M. G. Wenceslaus from the capital city of Colombo. Wenceslaus is from India, but has spent most of his life in Sri Lanka, an Indian Ocean island nation of 14 million which was known as Ceylon until 22 May 1972. Wenceslaus has a daughter named Shyamala. 'My parents thought she was an absolute doll,' Vijay said.

'After I played WCT-Richmond [February 9–14] I had a strained sciatic nerve so I went home and she just happened to be there with her family. During six days at home I saw her every morning – very, very formal. I met her one-on-one with my parents in the next room with her parents. When I got to the airport I told my parents not to look any further.'

What did Vijay like about her? 'She was Catholic – my

parents would not have recommended anyone else – she was fairly tall [five foot six] for an Indian girl. Nice looking, but the most important thing, I think, was that she had a tremendous personality, very straightforward. Bright. Looks to me is not everything. I'm somebody who talks to everybody and I wanted someone I could easily converse with and share everything I do.'

Shyamala like movies, books, cooking and can perform Indian classical dancing called *bharabhanadayam*. 'That is very difficult to do,' says Vijay. 'You have to go to school or something like that.'

The engagement ceremony was set for 2 June in Colombo. After checking with jewellers in New York and Los Angeles Vijay went to Adelstein's in Dallas during the WCT finals.

'After WCT-Strasbourg [March 21] I visited her in Colombo and asked her what kind of ring she would like,' Vijay said. 'I really didn't know what I was looking for. She said, "Whatever you like, I like." She was, like, so nice it was a joke.'

Shyamala sent over her ring size with Maggie. 'My mother is very good with jewellery. All the things she wears she designs. It's a hobby for her. She saw some things she really liked at Adelstein's. Shyamala's fingers are very, very thin – slender and long. We wanted something delicate, not big and flashy. I don't go for stuff like that. It's really like a wedding ring but we exchange rings at the engagement ceremony.'

Maggie liked the looks of two rings with 16 diamonds in each. She wanted them put together and, thus, it was done. The ring was picked up on a Friday. In fact, in this entire process everything will be done on Wednesday or Friday. 'According to Indian mythology Friday is the best day to do anything major,' Vijay said. 'The practice has been there for generations. So I picked up the ring on a Friday. The engagement ceremony was set for Wednesday. We [he and younger brother Ashok] bought our house in Los Angeles on Friday.'

About 300 people and a priest attended the 2 June ceremony. 'The whole rigmarole was done in a traditional way. You pick the best time of day according to Indian mythology which is between 4 and 6 p.m.' Part of the ceremony involved Shyamala being seated on the floor. Eleven *happily* married women bring gifts on trays one-by-one and sit them before the bride-to-be – jewellery, coconuts, bananas, etc. Then the bridegroom-to-be is received at the house of the bride by the future in-laws. Shyamala is seated in a love seat. When the blessing is over she goes upstairs to change into the *saree* the bridgegroom's parents have given her.

Vijay made his entrance to help cut the cake. 'I wore a double-breasted suit,' he said. 'You can wear what you want. She absolutely adored the ring I gave her. The one she gave me wasn't exactly all bad either – it was fabulous.'

What awaits is the wedding – 17 January 1983, in Madras. It will involve a Catholic church ceremony and four days of celebrating at a large hotel. Then the honeymoon. 'She always wanted to go to Maui [Hawaii] and I wanted to go to Bali in Indonesia, so I thought we might do both – four or five days in each place.'

Though he admits love does not immediately enter the picture, Vijay is anxious to have Shyamala at his side. 'My feelings for her are very strong at this point,' he said recently. 'But not love . . . it's not exactly like falling in love, then thinking about marriage. When the engagement came around it was amzing how much we wanted to be together. I'm just waiting to go back. I'm anxious to see her again. I'm looking forward to 1983. She'll be travelling with me. It's making me as anxious as I was in 1973 when I came over and started travelling around. It will be fun travelling with somebody and being able to show her things she's never seen. We bought the house in LA with the idea of me getting married – Ashok, my wife and I living together – so we set it up just so the girl can walk into the house.'

So Ashok is next in line. Vijay will be 29 when he marries on 17 January. That is also Maggie's birthday. Shyamala's birthday is 18 January. Ashok was born in February, but Vijay says he has a few years of bachelorhood remaining. Ashok has been involved heavily in Amritraj Productions.

'He has my 50 per cent vote to run it the way he sees fit,' Vijay said. 'But he consults me on all major issues. He has learned so much the past year. The movie business is such a close-knit circle in Hollywood and to even break into that is like breaking a computer code. It's very tough. What Ashok has done in the 16–17 months that we've been in business is absolutely incredible. It should take ten years to do that. Trust is something they don't have over there and he has brought it in. We have a lot of projects in the making and Hollywood in the next few years is going to hear a lot about Amritraj Productions. We are doing the WCT highlight films for Dallas and Forest Hills. That is a good start for our first behind the camera scenes. WCT has never been in all the countries we're going to take those 30-minute films.'

Vijay was excited about the making of the WCT finals because it meant that Amritraj Productions would be filming *him* in action at a major championship event. But the year was hard on his ranking. He decided he could not serve two leaders in 1982. Because he chose to play only WCT events and not the Grand Prix circuit, it meant he had to qualify for Wimbledon, a tournament he loves dearly.

'It came down to making Dallas or the Masters in New York,' he said. 'I figured it would be easier for me to make Dallas. WCT tournaments are so professionally run, so well spaced out that to me it seemed illogical to try to do both and not make either one. But the only tournament I wanted to play on the Grand Prix that meant a lot to me was Wimbledon. So I said I'd play all the WCTs and hope I make Dallas and then qualify for Wimbledon. Which is exactly what I did. I made Dallas and did fairly well. Won a match, defeated Jose-Luis Clerc. At Wimbledon I won three qualifying matches and two in the regular round.'

'I have to admire Vijay Amritraj,' said another gentleman of tennis, Fred Perry. 'He had to qualify for Wimbledon and he did. That's the kind of spirit the game needs.'

Vijay has stopped concentrating fully on tennis. He once hoped to launch an acting career as some sort of cowboy but that fell through. Now he has landed a role in the new James Bond flick, *Octopussy*, due for release during next year's Wimbledon. 'I'm not typecast,' Vijay said. 'I don't play tennis. I play a secret agent – James Bond's counterpart in India. It's a very good role and the movie portrays India in the right light. I'm a good guy and when Bond (played by Roger Moore) comes to India I help him in all his adventures.'

His brother Anand has long been his best friend. 'Best in the world,' Vijay said. 'The most intelligent person I know. He was sort of a genius in school. We're very different but that might be why we like each other so much.'

Players

In late July Vijay's lymph nodes and salivatory glands became so inflamed he couldn't eat or talk. Even his shoulder was swollen. He spent five days in a hospital and had to be fed intravenously. Anand's wife, Helen, flew in from New York just to take care of him. It was similar to the early sacrifices by his parents when he was so ill.

Vijay was a sickly child and at times when he was laid up in the hospital Maggie would attend his classes and take notes so he wouldn't fall too far behind. He wasn't crazy about tennis but the doctors ordered plenty of outdoor exercise and Bob and Maggie liked the game. They were strict about practices and never let up on Vijay.

'My parents never thought of themselves first,' Vijay said. 'Never, ever. Never went on a holiday. Never went to the movies. Everything they did was for one of the three of us. I appreciate the way of life in the United States, but because of my parents and education it is important to stay Indian. I always hoped I could pick the best of both sides. Obviously, I've been exposed to a lot around the world – you just hope you can pick it right.' Very diplomatic. He has blended East and West better than Henry Kissinger ever dreamed.

Points

The Most Memorable Wimbledon

Roy McKelvie

The English summer of 1949 was hot. Not quite so torrid as 1976 but it spawned a far more distinguished Wimbledon. In the minds of many, including myself, 1949 was the greatest Wimbledon ever played. It was Ted Schroeder's year and the meeting produced a host of most memorable matches including four involving the man who described himself as 'a Los Angeles refrigerator salesman'.

Ted had not previously played at Wimbledon. Indeed his appearances in major championships were extremely rare after winning the US title seven years previously, in 1942. Ted was just short of 28 when he rolled, like the Navy man he had been during the war, into London puffing an old corn-cob pipe and calling for a pint of English beer.

Without bombast Ted announced that he had come to win Wimbledon and such was the man's charisma that nobody really disbelieved him. On the strength of his Davis Cup record – he was unbeaten in the 1946, 1947 and 1948 challenge rounds – Ted was seeded No. 1 over the holder Bob Falkenburg, the US champion Pancho Gonzales, the Australian champion, Frank Sedgman, the French champion Frank Parker – his US Davis Cup colleague – the South African champion Eric Sturgess and other top stars.

Even Schroeder's most ardent supporters received a shock when he drew another US Davis Cup player, Gardnar Mulloy, a semi-finalist the previous year, in the first round. It was an obvious Centre Court match and that famous arena holds terrors for those who have never played on it. Mulloy knew it well but for Ted it was bound to be a forbidding experience. The fact that Ted had beaten Mulloy in the Queen's Club final two days before Wimbledon began had little bearing on their meeting.

The Centre Court gates were closed to further spectators

when Schroeder and Mulloy began what turned out to be the most exciting and dramatic first round match ever played there. Mulloy won the first two sets. The first time Schroeder led was at 3–1 in the fifth set but he was caught at 4–4, lost a match point at 5–4 before squeezing home 3–6, 9–11, 6–1, 6–0, 7–5 after two and a quarter hours of gruelling and high tension play.

The long second set was Mulloy's downfall. He had a chance to win it 6–4 but took another ten games before doing so. This gave Schroeder, who had much difficulty in timing the ball on what was virtually a virgin grass court (the Centre Court is never played on other than during the Championships), the chance to 'learn' the court. It also took a lot out of Mulloy whose stamina and speed at 34 were not the equal of his opponent's. Mulloy's effort in recovering to 5–5 in the final set after a game of seven deuces was a brave one. But it finished him physically.

For the next six days Ted's journey through Wimbledon was relatively peaceful, though he had a couple of close sets against the Czech, Vladimir Cernik. But elsewhere in this celebrated field of class players there were some memorable matches.

Falkenburg, the defending champion, had a curious contest agaINT the Hungarian Josef Asboth, a semi-finalist the previous year and 1947 French champion, before winning 6–4, 7–5, 2–6, 0–6, 6–4. The lanky American, whose habit of kneeling on the court earned him the nickname of 'the Praying Mantis', tanked the third and fourth sets and, after winning a break in service early in the fifth, made no effort on Asboth's serve for the rest of the match.

Jaroslav Drobny, a great Wimbledon favourite, outlasted Budge Patty 6–4, 6–8, 7–9, 6–0, 6–2 in one of the many marathons these two future champions played during their colourful careers. Then Gonzales, the No. 2 seeded player, went down in four sets to Geoff Brown, a double-handed Australian and 1946 runner-up who, despite his small stature, had a serve as fast as Roscoe Tanner's and some mighty strokes. Gonzales suffered Centre Court nerves and Brown, with four winning service returns at 4–3 in the second set (Gonzales won the first), turned the match in his favour.

By the end of the first week the last eight men lined up as follows: Drobny v. Brown; John Bromwich v. Falkenburg (the 1948 finalists); Sturgess v. Parker; Schroeder v. Sedgman. Has there ever been a last eight like that one?

Each of these matches went to five sets and so absorbed had the British public become by this Wimbledon that the serious-minded *Manchester Guardian*, for whom I was then writing, put the reports on the front page instead of the sports. To add to the relish four British women players reached their last eight, along with four Americans.

Schroeder's win over Sedgman 3–6, 6–8, 6–3, 6–2, 9–7 was a classic. Not only did Ted come back from being two sets down, as he had done against Mulloy, but he looked well beaten at 0–3 in the final set and, to crown it all, survived match points at 4–5 and 5–6.

The match point at 4–5 has a special niche in the game's history. Schroeder was foot-faulted on his first service but with the boldness of a born gambler (or buccaneer) thumped in a second as hard as his first and volleyed Sedgman's reply into the far corner of the court. No one who saw that moment can ever forget it.

The second match point was almost as cheeky. Schroeder made his winning volley off the wood! And in that game Sedgman failed to kill a mid-court lob that would have given him 40–15. This had to be Ted's Wimbledon.

Meantime, Bromwich achieved some consolation for his defeat in the 1948 final by beating his tormentor, Falkenburg, 3–6, 9–11, 6–0, 6–0, 6–4. Falkenburg's tanking of the third set was understandable. He had survived two set points at 4–5 in the second set and the winning of it ten games later taxed him severely. But throwing away the fourth set was inexplicable. It gave the Australian the momentum and will to win.

Drobny outstayed Brown 2–6, 7–5, 1–6, 6–2, 6–4 and Sturgess won a classic groundstroke duel against Parker 3–6, 6–4, 3–6, 6–1, 6–3 being the younger man, a much better and quicker mover, and of equally imperturbable temperament.

Schroeder's semi-final win over Sturgess 3–6, 7–5, 5–7, 6–1, 6–2 was another example of the astonishing manner the American got himself out of trouble by his determination, audacity, ability to scramble, brilliant shots at important moments, his adventurousness, luck and anything else you can think of. Sturgess had chances of being two sets up. But one may well ask if that would have made any difference. Schroeder's star was high in the sky and remained there in the final against Drobny who had easily beaten Bromwich in the other semi-final.

The last two sunbaked days of that Wimbledon saw Schroeder become one of the very few players to have won the singles title at his first attempt (he did not return for 20 years, and then only as a veteran), and Louise Brough achieve a very remarkable feat of endurance.

Schroeder's win over Drobny 3–6, 6–0, 6–3, 4–6, 6–4 was unlike his previous close contests in that he led by two sets to one instead of being led. In the final set Drobny had the advantage of serving first but was broken at 3–3 with two of those match-winning backhands that Schroeder scattered throughout the fortnight at crucial moments. In that last set Schroeder's service was so dominant that Drobny hardly won a point off it. Schroeder's daring, his unremitting pace and skill as a match player triumphed, deservedly.

Louise Brough went onto court to play Margaret Dupont at two o'clock on the last day of the meeting. Somewhere around eight o'clock that evening she dragged herself to the women's dressing room having played three finals and 117 games. She beat Margaret 10–8, 1–6, 10–8, partnered her to victory in the women's doubles, but, with Bromwich, lost the mixed final to the South Africans Sturgess and Sheila Summers 9–7, 9–11, 7–5. And hardly a soul left the Centre Court until it was all over.

Later that evening at London's Grosvenor House Hotel Schroeder made his champion's speech – 'When I came here I read about a man named "Lucky Schroeder". It couldn't be me, I thought. After beating Mulloy I again read about "Lucky Schroeder". When I won that second match point against Sedgman I began to think the Press might have something. When I hit the last shot past Drobny I realized how absolutely right they were."

The following day a friend drove Schroeder to London Airport. Ted sucked his corn-cob and ruminated, 'I still can't make out how anyone could foot-fault me when match point down.' Then he lapsed into thoughts of his own. Ted had left an indelible mark on the story of Wimbledon.

The Final Seal of Approval

David Irvine

No one who saw it, either in the breathless hush of the Centre Court or by proxy, goggle-eyed by the goggle-box, will ever forget the lacerating intensity of that extraordinary tie-break played by John McEnroe and Bjorn Borg in the Wimbledon men's final of 1980. For 22 minutes these two young gladiators held an audience of millions spellbound with the theatrical ingenuity of their performance. Yet their play-within-a-play was no scripted drama. Like all great sporting occassions the fascination for the watcher lay in the spontaneity of their reactions and the total uncertainty of the outcome.

The record books will forever remind us, of course, that though McEnroe finally won the tie-break battle, he ultimately lost the war. Borg remained the King. He was the stronger, at least mentally, and went on to recover and win 1–6, 7–5, 6–3, 6–7, 8–6 and take his fifth consecutive singles title; a unique achievement in modern times.

What no record book reveals, however, is the effect those 22 magical minutes had in earning the tie-break the acceptability many thought it could never achieve; not at Wimbledon certainly. For after a contest of such strength and will, who can argue with conviction against an innovation capable of producing such passion, drama and emotion?

It was in 1971, and following the US Open's lead, that Wimbledon decided to try Jimmy Van Alen's revolutionary system; even though the reaction to what many people saw as a betrayal of tradition – a further Americanization of the most English of sporting festivals, or, as some put it, 'a gambler's charter' – did not exactly endear the committee of the day to those opposed on principle to change.

Two variations of the tie-break were then operating in America – the 'sudden death' method, sometimes referred to as a

101

shoot-out, with a nine-point maximum and the winner being the first player to reach five; the other, known as 'lingering death', was introduced at 6–6 with the victor being the first player to reach seven points with a two-point margin.

The committee, rightly conscious of the historical significance of the two-point margin and unmoved by the US Open's use of the first, had little hesitation in opting for the second. And, as if further to underline its independence in such matters, it decided that the tie-break should apply at 8–8 instead of 6–6 and not operate at all in deciding sets. Not until 1979 was the thirteenth game accepted as the tie-break game.

In the first Championships under the new rule some 70 sets – 32 in the men's singles, 24 in the men's doubles, five in the ladies' singles, three in the ladies' doubles and six in the mixed – were decided by the tie-break but nothing occurred to support the view of some diehards that the tournament would degenerate into a three-ring circus.

By 1973 the tie-break issue, though still liable to send some folk into a rage, had become a matter of little consequence compared with the much more damaging players' boycott that was to keep so many leading contenders away that year. And yet, by a curious quirk of fate, it was a tie-break in a Centre Court match that captured most of the newspaper headlines following the tournament's opening session.

Because so many of the leading stars, notably the Americans, were absent, the favourites included a number of young, relatively unknown players and it was one of these, the then 17-year-old Borg, who not only found himself seeded in sixth position but playing his very first Wimbledon match, against the Indian Premjit Lall, on the Centre Court.

Though Borg won in straight sets, and served devastatingly in the first two, the third produced what is still the longest tie-break in the history of the Championships: 38 points in all with the Swede winning 20–18 on his eighth match point after saving five set points.

By 1980, and his other great tie-break with McEnroe, the Wimbledon Centre Court had effectively become Borg's second home. Although he lost to Roger Taylor in 1973; to Ismael El Shafei, another left-hander, in 1974; and to Arthur Ashe, the eventual champion, in 1975, Borg began a winning streak in the

Championships of 1976 that was to run for more than five years – an unsurpassed sequence of 41 victories – before McEnroe finally stopped him in 1981.

That, though, is another story. By general consent, there has been no more memorable final in the last decade than Borg's five-set win over McEnroe in the 1980 decider.

The mix was perfect. Right-hander v. left-hander; introvert v. extrovert; the good guy against the villain; the King against the Pretender. Younger spectators, many of whose older brothers and sisters had mobbed Borg as 'teenyboppers' a few years earlier, gave their wholehearted allegiance to the American. But those over 25, or so it seemed, couldn't wait to see the cool Swede put the hothead down.

Yet the match transcended such violently opposed stances, for the place both these tennis advanturers won in the hearts of those fortunate enough to be present must forever be assured. In terms of sustained quality there may have been better finals but none, dare one suggest, of such nerve-jangling compulsion and fought at a pace so hot that the combatants' rackets were in danger of catching fire.

Some of the rallies could not have been choreographed with greater care for detail. Chip, chop, dink. Clatter, bang, wallop. Drop, lob, smash. The applause broke like thunder accompanying summer lightning, then died as suddenly as 15,000 awaited the next thrust, leaving only the chirping of sparrows to disturb the players' concentration.

While the final score reflected the length, intensity and sway of the battle, a contest that embodied the very essence of sporting challenge, the finer details are necessary to provide the key to the drama. For what the score omits to reveal is that McEnroe captured the fourth set after saving no less than seven match points.

'I think losing that tie break would have broken the spirit of most players,' said McEnroe wryly after it was all over. 'You would have thought that with four titles already, he'd have let up and said "forget it" you know.' But that would not have been Borg. He had saved his best for the home straight, serving with such fierce pace and accuracy in the final set that McEnroe captured only three points off it – including the first two of the opening game.

That Borg should finally overcome McEnroe by out-serving him was probably the most cruel irony of all, for the American had almost blasted him off the court in the first 70 minutes when the Swede's back was permanently to the wall. 'It was the best set I have ever played on my service game,' admitted Borg later. 'On almost every ball [25 out of 31 to be exact] I had my first serve in and John was missing the return. I kept thinking "don't get tight" because I had been in the first set and lost it.'

It was a match McEnroe might so easily have won in three sets instead of losing in five, for at 4–4 in the second Borg had to save three break points. Yet he did so each time with a service winner. At 6–5 McEnroe's confidence was suddenly eroded when Borg hit two incredible returns to reach set point and the younger player, perhaps overcome by nerves and tension, surrendered the initiative when he stabbed a backhand volley into the net.

The next hour was Borg's. McEnroe kept slugging away, hoping that something would turn up, but all seemed lost when he was broken in the ninth game of the fourth set after losing the third. It was 4.54 by the Centre Court clock. Wimbledon prepared to salute its hero again. Who would have believed at that moment that the fight was only beginning?

A forehand winner gave Borg two match points at 40–15. McEnroe rallied, looping his returns with no pace whatever, and then let fly a backhand pass. Borg never saw it. Still match point, though. Again McEnroe rallied before stunning the holder with a forehand volley. The first crisis had passed.

So to that tie-break. It was even to begin with, the points going with serve, but on the ninth McEnroe was broken, only to level again on the tenth. At 5.07 Borg engineered his third match point. Again he failed to make it and, within a matter of moments, a fourth had come . . . and gone.

At 7–7 the McEnroe camp noisily revived as a cross-court backhand winner gave him his first set point. Borg's riposte was a return of serve which had the American scrabbling on his knees in a vain attempt to volley. And so it went on. Match points to Borg, set points to McEnroe. Agony, ecstasy; enough drama to induce a heart attack.

The scoreboard and the clock ticked silently on. 10–9 to McEnroe, 11–10 to Borg. This way, that way, and on to 16–16.

Would it ever end? An attempt at a forehand winner by Borg was unsuccessful, giving McEnroe set point number seven, and quite suddenly it was over as Borg almost lazily chopped a McEnroe return into the net. The time was 5.22. The squeals and roars were deafening. Even Wimbledon had never seen anything quite like it before.

'I knew', said Borg later 'that if I made one stupid mistake it would be two sets all. I think I was not too clever to attempt that drop, but I tried it anyway. There was more spin on the ball than I had expected and it came down too quickly for me.'

And yet, remarkably, Borg was never threatened thereafter. His crosscourt backhand returns grew in authority, along with his serve, and McEnroe – always a game behind – could never escape the pressure. He did save a break point in the eighth game but at 15–40 in the 14th he was caught at the net by the Swede's rifling two-hander and after three hours and 53 minutes – 94 minutes after his first match point – Borg's fifth championship was completed.

Not since 1906, when Lawrence Doherty won his fifth successive title, had Wimbledon been ruled over for so long by one man. But Doherty had only to defend in a single match each year after winning in 1902, for those were still the days of the challenge round. Borg's win was his 35th in succession.

As for McEnroe, it was probably the turning point in his career. 'It matters not how a man dies but how he lives,' said Samuel Johnson. McEnroe, so often the game's chief rebel, disputed the final like a man. It really mattered little that he found a pot of lead at the end of that particular rainbow. Both finalists in their separate ways were champions.

A Totally Mixed Affair

Curry Kirkpatrick

At the World Mixed Doubles, which outsoaped the soaps, the reunion of Chris and Jimmy stole the show.

Soap update. In last week's episode of *Estranged Couples As the Search Turns*, Chris told John she wanted to play with Jimmy, so Patti took Brett and they all went to see Bjorn hit himself in the face. Bettina, who recently recovered from losing half her hearing, joined Bjorn, and Butch, who recently recovered from testicular cancer, joined Betsy, who has a clothing line in Japan, from where Jimmy just returned. Meanwhile, John returned to his other partner, Wendy, and Andrea put down her Walkman long enough to join Roscoe, who played too rough for Wendy. Then Ilie hit Andrea, Roscoe got mad at Ilie and tried to hit him, Roscoe hit Hana, Andrea hit Ilie, and Ilie gave everyone the finger. So the questions remain. Will success spoil Aaron and Lisa? Can Adriano find a diet doc before it's too late? Is it over already between Sherwood and JoAnne? Do Vinnie and Carling do it – colour their hair – or don't they? Who's Hu? What? And if Chris and John and Jimmy and Patti and all the rest keep playing around like this, how will Bret get enough chicken McNuggets?

So it was that the game of tennis merged with the battle of the sexes once again to produce the fascinating sport of mixed doubles, right there in Houston's Astroarena. You remember the Astroarena. Originally constructed to house the annual horse show. Now a boxing palace. Son of Astrodome, next door, where ten years ago Riggs-King introduced modern-day show biz to tennis. Well, the second annual World Mixed Doubles championship was flavoured with all these elements, not to mention a whole lot of money – 100 grand to the winning team, 15 just for showing up. 400,000 smackers total purse.

Of course, moola had nothing to do with this year's star-spangled field. Oh no. You think Bjorn Borg, the famous television announcer, would leave his elocution lessons in the golden hills of Monte Carlo to come to the Astroarena, get aced by a *girl* and split open his forehead with his own forehand just for the big bucks? You think Jimmy Connors would skip a tournament in Stockholm, risking a $10,000 fine, or that Chris Evert Lloyd would hazard wedded bliss to team with her former . . . what – beau, fiance, paramour? – simply for the cold cash? Guarantees? Come on. We're talking dedication here, gang, love of the game.

Sherwood Stewart to Roscoe Tanner: 'What are you doing winning that match? Now we'll miss our tea time tomorrow.'

Chris to Jimbo: 'How about practice at two?'

Jimbo: 'Naw, I got to go shopping.'

Actually, by the time the glamour-puss pairing of Connors-Evert Lloyd had whipped Tanner and Andrea Jaeger 6–4, 6–2, 6–4 in the finals on Sunday night, some serious tennis had been played, a tribute to several of the tour's best and brightest, who had dared to get into a situation that most couples of reasonable sanity have always attempted to avoid. The final confrontation, matching two, shall we say, pick-up teams, would tend to put to rest the canard that doubles is a maze of intrigue demanding long hours of working together, intimate knowledge of each other's capabilities, an overwhelming sense of *team*. Over the long haul, maybe. But for a one-shot tournament – nope.

With the defending champions, Peter McNamara and Martina Navratilova, retired – McNamara from the game, Navratilova, as many have observed, from serious competition – the only established teams in the draw were the Nos. 1 and 2 seeds, John Lloyd and Wendy Turnbull and Stewart and JoAnne Russell. Lloyd-Turnbull won Wimbledon this year, and Stewart-Russell were runners-up at the World Mixed in 1982. Both teams exited whimpering in last week's quarter-finals, Turnbull wanting to depart after seeing perhaps three Tanner service missiles.

These upsets were hardly noticed because the allure of this event is the gimmicky pairing the player agents contrive: teen-scream, groupie-dream combos like Vince Van Patten-Carling Bassett, or the Motown tots, Aaron Krickstein – Lisa Bonder, or the Northwestern – Far Eastern connection, Marty Riessen-Hu Na, or Power 'n' Puff, Tanner-Jaeger. Also on hand were Fish 'n' Chips, Chip Hooper and Kathy Horvath, who's still trolling for the secret that enabled her to beat Navratilova in Paris, and Sweet 'n' Low, Beth Herr and Eliot Teltscher. ET's last venture in mixed ended with his barrage of vulgar and sexist insults aimed at Leslie Allen, a beaten opponent in the French Open finals. Finally, there was the ever-marvellous combination of Bonnie Gadusek and Adriano Panatta. Though cute and athletic, Gadusek has the air of a gun moll, and Panatta has obviously been hitting the fettuccine at full throttle. Call this team Bonnie and Wide.

Call Connors-Evert Lloyd sexual electricity. Even against such a strong repertory cast, and with Borg co-starring in approximately his 13th return from exile, Connors-Evert Lloyd was top bill. Then both their marriages were floundering last year, tour rumours flew hot and heavy: Jimmy and Chris were sending notes to each other in sneaker boxes. Chris and Jimmy were phoning up. J and C were *back*.

Chris at joint press conference: 'It can be very difficult to play doubles with your spouse. Emotional. Since there are no feelings, emotions, between Jimmy and I . . .' – smirk, glance at Connors – '. . . I'm sure we'll make a great team.'

Chris at cocktail party: 'I know I gave you the room key, John. Either you . . .' – smirk, laugh – 'or I gave it to Jimmy.'

Jimmy at team practice, laughing, joking, playing right-handed, shooting a few quick moons. To Chris: 'You know, I'd pay you to practise with me every day.'

The Lloyds and Connorses both stayed in suites at the Inn on the Park. The first afternoon the couples visited in the Connorses' suite for a couple of hours. They mixed at a party at Sonny Bono's restaurant. Jimmy and Chris practised every day, sometimes with John. Patti invited Chris up to have her nails done by a manicurist. Chris couldn't make it. Jimbo took 4-year-old Brett to the amusement park and the Putt-Putt. 'We asked Jimmy and Patti to come to dinner one night,' said Chris, 'but Brett's favourite is chicken McNuggets, and we couldn't handle that. He loves that kid.'

Jimbo used the tournament to unveil a midsize prototype racket made by Wilson, and Chris was breaking in her new frizzy hair cut. Nevertheless, they both performed as if nothing had changed in the nine years since they won the singles and played mixed doubles at Wimbledon and, oh yes, broke their engagement as well. Last week Connors was brash, crude, tough: Evert Lloyd was consistent, elegant, tough.

Good humoured fun infiltrated their matches up to the finals, straight-set jobs over Jimmy Brown-Zina Garrison, Van Patten-Bassett and Butch Walts-Betsy Nagelsen, at once the spunkiest and most obscure of all the duos. Walts having licked cancer, Nagelsen a household word only if your house is in Tokyo. C would put away a crisp volley, and J would stride off as if to say 'excuuuuse me'. The two would get crossed up, leaving the court open, whereupon J would point a finger at C, crying 'your fault'. J did much strutting. C much giggling. Both said it was 'easy', that it wasn't as if they were 'strangers'.

'You had a great feel for the angles,' John Lloyd said to Connors after one match. A few minutes later Chris told the press she would not like to meet her husband in the finals. 'I would,' Connors roared, pounding the table.

While the Lloyds and Connorses appeared ecstatic about being together in Houston, Borg was lucky to get out of the city alive. Paired with Bettina Bunge, who has been off the circuit since undergoing an ear operation in August, Borg looked fit, happy, content – and about Top 30 calibre. 'He's not coming back,' Riessen said firmly after his partner, Hu Na (no relation to Sha Na), fooled Borg a couple of times and Riessen-Na lost a third-set tiebreaker. Later, against Enigma, Inc., the team of Ilie Nastase and Hana Mandlikova, Bunge played as if it were her *eyes* that had been impaired. Then Borg was rudely aced by Mandlikova. 'That's not the first time,' Borg said. Sure, Bjorn. 'No, I don't remember who the other woman was.'

Early in the second set a Nastase serve took a bad bounce and Borg unloaded one of his roundhouse low-to-high discus-thrower swipes, slashing the ball off the wood high into the rafters. While everybody watched the ball's flight, murmuring 'same old Bjorny, he can miss 'em just like me', Borg strolled off the court, blood streaming from above his left eye. 'I have been hitting myself quite a few times,' he said later. 'I am not really surprised.' After Borg had been patched up, the team of Hana K (for killer) and Nastase put BB-BB out of their misery, 6–3, 6–2.

Points

'I have missed the fans and the atmosphere,' Borg said, 'but I think I will survive.' Nobody asked if he meant the cut or the retirement, but on his next come-back Borg had best bring along Dr Ferdie Pacheco.

It wasn't only Swedish blood that was spilled in Houston, either. The semi-final pitting Tanner-Jaeger against Nastase-Mandlikova took on the charm of a tag-team wrestling bout after Nastase slugged two overheads in the general direction of Jaeger's tender gams. The second one connected – hard. At the time, Nasty-Mandy were ahead 6–2, 3–3. When Tanner figured out that Nastase was trying to add injury to insult, he quickly retaliated with one of his laser deliveries, which nearly parted Nastase's sneer on the fly. 'Was I trying to hit Ilie?' said Tanner. 'Aww, that was just my long, flat one. If I can nail him from 80 feet, he's not as quick as he used to be.'

Target practice continued with Tanner drilling Mandlikova – accidentally, of course. Eventually, Jaeger, daughter of a former boxer, remember, took aim and sledgehammered an overhead of her own obviously intended to render Nastase a cripple for life. The ball crashed into the tape. Nastase turned and pointed out his rear end to Jaeger. This time Andrea grabbed another ball and threw it at her tormentor. Bulls-eye. 'Nasty's good for the game and bad,' Jaeger said after she and Tanner rallied to win 2–6, 7–5, 7–5. 'But if he had hit me in the face I would have been really mad.' Not to mention, in surgery.

Ah well, all's fair in love and mixed. While Borg will remember his self-mutilation and the women players may recall Tanner's terrifying service with night-screaming, it's the sparks from Connors-Evert Lloyd that will endure from this tournament.

'It was weird,' said Jaeger, 18. 'I mean I watched that press conference on TV, and the camera kept shooting back and forth between John and Jimmy, John, Jimmy, and all you heard was Chris's voice making cracks. Wow, weird. I don't know *what* the public thinks.'

When she grows up, Andrea will find out.

The Old 'Uns Alive-O!

Bud Collins

A lost tennis civilization called Australia was rediscovered momentarily when Fred Stolle, 43, took a fatherly interest in John Newcombe, 37, and dragged him from a Manhattan saloon long enough for the two of these relics to crash the semi-finals of the US Open men's doubles at Flushing Meadow.

While archaeologists assiduously sift the dust of Sydney for remains of the world conquerors and clues to the decline and fall of the world-conquering Aussie Dynasty, a couple of missing links, Stolle and Newcombe, were playing improbably fine tennis and upstaging numerous full-time pros at Flushing Meadow.

That should have been enough memory lane stuff. Wasn't this the US Open? And weren't the Old Hacker, Stolle, and the Moustache Man of TV and magazine commercials, Newcombe, over too many hills by this time?

'Even when we could play we didn't play together,' said Stolle, who went to the Open primarily to coach Vitas Gerulaitis and do TV commentary for Australia. 'I entered this time with Roy Emerson for old times' sake, and Newk entered with Owen Davidson. But those two decided not to come, so here are Newk and I together.'

'But', said Newcombe, between groans from a dressing room rubbing table, 'don't forget Boston '70. Two against five, at Harvard, remember? Fred and I took on the US five-man team, and won the World Cup for Australia. We won both doubles.'

Yeah, but that was 11 years ago, and Newcombe devotes himself now to business enterprises and TV work. Newcombe won the US singles title in 1967 and 1973. Stolle in 1966. Even though they've long since decided covering half a court was better than one, the thought of their scaling the doubles semi-finals seemed remote.

111

'They'll show up in wheelchairs,' scoffed Peter Fleming, the larger half of their semi-final opponents, Wimbledon and US Open champs Fleming and John McEnroe.

'Careful you don't get run over,' replied Stolle. 'I've been watching you, Flim Flam, and you couldn't hit a bull in the ass with a handful of buckshot.'

So it has always been with that vanished race of tennis supermen, the Aussies.

As soon as they completed the 7–6, 7–5, 3–6, 4–6, 6–3 quarter-final victory over Wisconsinites Tom Gullikson and Mike Cahill, Newcombe reverted to his role as a TV type. A microphone was thrust into his hand by a CBS stage manager, and he began to interview Stolle.

'Fred, how does it feel for such an old fellow to be in the semi-finals of the US Open?'

'It would feel a lot bloody better if I didn't have to carry you for five sets, Newk.'

'Well, how did you do it?'

'I drank enough beer last night and it was hardly any trouble at all.'

At first the quarter-final starting time, 11 a.m., seemed an impossible imposition for the 80-Year-Old Team.

Nine hours earlier Stolle and Newcombe were practising their continental grips on glasses at a bar room called Jim McMullen's. The occasion was a pre-match victory party, but Stolle was growing restive. 'Newk, you've got to get to bed,' he screeched in a fatherly tone. 'We're playing in a few hours.'

'You go, Fred, and sleep for both of us,' was the characteristically Australian reply.

Nevertheless Stolle got his partner out of there, although when they showed for the match, 10 minutes later, Newk's eyes looked like a reflection of Stolle's shorts – a red checkerboard pattern.

'Gawd, Fred, there's the sun. Where did that come from?' moaned Newk.

'It frequently appears at this time of day, Newk – but we don't,' Stolle explained later. 'We've been the entertainment for alcoholics out here – the late, late show. They've put us on last match at night every time until today. We started about 11.15 Monday night and finished at quarter to two the next morning.'

'Boy, was I stiff the next day. I mean my muscles,' laughed Newcombe, 'but I came up right today.' He was serving and volleying with almost the old force. Stolle in the left court returned brilliantly, always keeping the ball in play, the 80-Year-Old Team's steady and guiding light. Although his ginger-coloured hair is thinning and his waistline thickening, Stolle is still dangerous.

Tom Gullikson and Mike Cahill, the Americans, felt as though they were in a foreign country. The crowd of 4,000 treated the Aussies as though they'd brought a case of lager to a dry party. 'You have to love those guys,' said Linda Washington, a spectator who may have been in a crib when the Aussies were big-time at Wimbledon. 'They're so loose and pleasant.'

Newcombe smiled and bowed to the gallery, rolled his eyes, pulled out the show biz repertory that made him such a popular champ. 'It was annoying, all that playing to the crowd, distracting,' huffed Gullikson. However, it was nothing new in gamesmanship. The Americans just hadn't been around when it was a regular part of Newk's spectator-charming routine.

The week that Tom Gullikson was born, just 30 years ago, Stolle remembers, 'I was winning the Metropolitan 14-and-under title in Sydney. I was 12. Ninety-six pounds and 5–10, a bloody beanpole.'

'Imagine us being the only Aussies left in the tournament,' Stolle said. The supermen of the Southern Hemisphere with names such as Hoad, Rosewall, Laver, Emerson, Roche, Fraser are no more in his precinct, but the 80—Year-Old Team has given a few seminars at the Meadow on the nearly lost art of doubles. 'We make sure of our returns, keep the ball in play,' Stolle said. 'The kids now want to rip every return, and only sometimes the ball goes over.'

But, save your Australian money – the South Pacific gang may rise again. Newcombe said, 'We've been working on a good junior development programme at home and the results are showing. The Aussies will be back in three, four years, and keep an eye on 16-year-old Patrick Cash, our best in some time.'

But will he be able to live up to the Australian reputation as a beer drinker? 'Hard to say,' said Newcombe. 'He probably didn't start till he was ten.'

Minutes after Stolle showered and dressed a tournament

official came up to him and said, 'Fred, don't go away. Your doubles in the senior tournament is coming up.'

'Jeez, I forgot that,' said the semi-finalist, a big leaguer again for a couple of days. 'Hey Newk,' he called to his partner, 'get to bed early tonight.'

'What time, Fred?'

'Quarter past.'

'Quarter past what?'

'Just quarter past anything before we play again. That't the best I can do with Newk.'

Smith Achieves Greatness in Breathtaking Final

David Gray

Wimbledon's extra day brought a tremendous bonus. For the third successive year the men's singles final went to five sets – and this was the best of the three and the most exciting end to the Championships for years. After two hours and 41 minutes Stan Smith, who had held service from 0–30 at 4–4 in the final set and had missed two match points in the next game, beat Ilie Nas̄ ̄e, the first Rumanian to reach a singles final at ̄ ̄ ̄don, by 4–6, 6–3, 4–6, 7–5.

̄ ̄athtaking match last year's runner-up proved that he ̄t a heavy server and volleyer. In the crises he forced ̄ay flexible and imaginative shots of a kind which ̄ar beyond his range in the earlier rounds. On the ̄he became a great player. He produced the ̄strength and skill to defeat the most talented s ̄nodern lawn tennis.

̄ents when Nastase was erratic. But at the end ̄t he began to concentrate properly and moui ̄ounter-attack. The last few games were ablaze ̄ Smith won by the narrowest of margins. 'The enu ̄ guts and the rest of it just a little luck. Obviousl ̄one either way,' he said at his press conference ̄ bathed him in champagne and he was still wij ̄air.

Wimbledon ̄mood. Rain had washed out play on Saturday ai ̄rth time in 50 years the tournament had been stretc ̄to a third week. Admission was free and the crowd, having waited, were determined to enjoy themselves. Finals usually begin quietly. Even the opening rallies were applauded loudly yesterday. The Centre Court affections were divided equally. For once, in a final, the crowd were not absurdly partisan. Smith, with his straight back and quick marching between points (is that all that he has learnt from the US Army?), is a popular figure at Wimbledon. They like his calmness and absence of fuss, the way he obviously enjoys his tennis.

Sometimes, of course, his tennis has been too plain for them and he has been disciplined to the point of dullness. No one has ever been able to say that about Nastase. The Rumanian is the circuit's great entertainer, its spoilt and talented child, who uses his racket as a weapon of wit, and its favourite actor. If steadiness is one of Smith's greatest virtues, the ability to climb to sudden peaks of inspiration is one of Nastase's strengths.

But there has to be drama, if his game is to work properly, if the magic lamp is to be rubbed . . . just as there has to be someone or something to blame – a line judge, an umpire, a doubles partner, a bad bounce or, as happened yesterday, the stringing of his rackets when things go wrong. Apparently, his rackets had been newly strung and when he began to play, he found them too tight. He kept looking desperately at his friend, Michele Brunetti, a lawyer from Ancona, who was sitting in the players' box and talking vigorously in Italian. Once Brunetti and an official of the Rumanian Tennis Federation left their seats in response to urgent glances. It was not until the middle of the third set that he began to settle down and concentrate.

'I thought it was a good sign that he kept changing rackets,' commented Smith. 'If you keep changing your racket back and forth, you obviously haven't found one that feels good. When you get into a tight situation like that, it is very easy to look for excuses.'

Smith thought that Nastase's concentration had been too brittle: 'When he got a little upset over net-cords and line calls, it really hurt his concentration, I think. Overall, he has improved quite a bit as far as temperament is concerned. Today under the extreme pressures of the final it might have bothered him a bit.'

Nastase won the first set while Smith was slowly gathering power and accuracy. By the fifth game battle had been properly joined. He had presented the American with a series of sharp-reflexed challenges and Smith, who had lumbered through many of his earlier matches, surprised the Rumanian's supporters by the speed with which he moved to the ball. His backhand, which had been his major problem against players like Ken Fletcher and Alex Metreveli, suddenly regained a good deal of its old force. The spur of playing in the most important tournament in tennis improved his strokes wonderfully. He began to look sharper and more resilient, getting to low volleys with surprising ease for such a big man and sometimes launching himself across the net to stretch for shots that scarcely anyone else in the game could have reached.

But it took him a little time to set the machinery in motion. In the early stages Nastase was serving with more accuracy and fluency and the American was groping for his returns of service. Nastase broke him in the ninth game to win the first set, but then started to hesitate and to fret about his rackets and Smith was given the chance to take the initiative. He captured the second set and all the time Nastase was looking dismally at the strings of one racket after another. His gestures to Brunetti became more and more dramatic. The Italian sat, looking slightly embarrassed, with a cigarette drooping from his lips.

And the more anxious Nastase became, the more confident Smith looked. The Rumanian buzzed about the court. Smith was content to graze on it, profiting from the errors that Nastase made. In this part of the match he was relaxed and unemotionally efficient. Nastase was hurrying too much, missing the kind of shots that he uses to torment his opponent and doing less with the ball than he does on his confident days.

The start of the fourth set was notable for a long baseline rally which Smith won. Equally surprisingly, he was winning the greater share of points from the delicate exchanges at the net. Which of the prophets would have thought that about a final like this? But just when Smith seemed to be advancing comfortably, Nastase's mood changed. He swept in, broke him once and captured the set. Two sets all – suddenly, what had seemed to be an easy American victory became a battle again.

Now it was clear that Nastase thought he could win and confidence came flowing back to him. It was Smith's turn to hang on desperately. The sunlit Californian smile with which he had greeted all the chances and changes of the match began to droop a little. 'In the fifth set it was just a matter for me to get my first serve in. If I could do that, then I could hit a more forceful volley,' he said. 'I began to think that he might pull it off and that I would be a bridesmaid again.'

His first crisis came in the fifth game, which he called 'exacting and crucial'. That went to deuce seven times. Nastase held two points for it and Smith won it with his seventh point. He breathed again there. But in the ninth game he was in danger again. Nastase passed him on the first point and then beat him with a low lob. Love–30 and very little room for salvation! He served. Nastase hit a return and Smith volleyed off the wood. The ball dropped over the net and Nastase ran into it.

The whole of the fifth set was crucial, but that was the most critical point of all. Smith won the next three points – taking the last for 5–4 by diving for a backhand volley, which was almost the most spectacular shot of the afternoon. He held up his arms after that in a gesture of triumph. Suddenly he looked full of confidence again.

Nastase saved a couple of match points at 5–4. Smith should have got the first, but did not have much chance with the second. 'It flashed across my mind then that my chance might have gone,' he said. He served his way safely through the next game and then saw another match point disappear. He needed only one more. Nastase had a chance for an easy high volley, misjudged it and put the ball into the bottom of the net. It was a sad end to a great battle.

The scene then was tumultuous. Smith received the cup with the broadest of grins and waved it at the crowd. He was the first American winner since Chuck McKinley in 1963. 'When we Americans win, we certainly make the most of it,' said an American player in the competitors' stand. Nastase sat slumped on a seat behind the umpire's chair. When he received the runners-up medal he showed that to the crowd too, imitating Smith's gesture of jubilation. There had been so little difference between them – but the difference in the rewards was enormous.

A Cup for the Cabhorses

Fred Perry

A short winter tour of South Africa, in which a British team made up of Betty Nuthall, Eileen Whittingstall, Mary Heeley, Pat Hughes, Harold Lee and myself lost all three 'Test matches', did not exactly help to dispel the gloom over our Davis Cup defeat by the Germans in 1932, and as we prepared for the 1933 Davis Cup with the same team – Bunny Austin, Hughes, Lee and myself – the moaners surfaced again.

Some sections of the media advised the LTA not to send 'the same old cabhorses' to Barcelona for the first-round tie with Spain. By now we found the whole thing amusing and referred to each other as 'cabhorse'. When I won the US National title later that year Austin sent me a cable which read, 'Well done, old cabhorse', and to this day when he writes to me he refers to me as 'Dear cabhorse' and signs his letters 'The other cabhorse'.

But we were annoyed when it was suggested that the LTA might have saved face – together with half the fares – by sending a junior team to represent Britain instead of those who had supposedly let the nation down in Berlin.

We shut up the critics by beating Spain and then Finland, while I won the Hard Courts title for the second year by defeating Austin. Next we thrashed Italy at Eastbourne, after which I took a week's break (spent with Jack Hylton's band in Brighton), before going back to Eastbourne to help beat Czechoslovakia in the fourth round.

I went into the 1933 Wimbledon quite fancying my chances – only to be knocked out in the second round by Norman Farquharson, a South African and Cambridge blue. He was a pretty good player and an excellent volleyer, though he was better known for his doubles expertise. He decided to attack me at the net and had one of those days at Wimbledon when everything comes off. The new super-fit Perry, I'm sorry to say, was beaten in five sets.

Wimbledon was also the setting for our next Davis Cup tie in the 1933 competition, against Australia, and it promised to be a toughie, since their number one, Jack Crawford, had just won the singles title at the championships.

Sure enough, Crawford beat Austin in the opening rubber, but I levelled it by defeating Vivian McGrath. Contrary to popular opinion that the double-handed backhand was invented by Jimmy Connors and Chris Evert Lloyd, the first player to use the shot was McGrath in the early thirties. He hit his forehand with his right hand and had a two-hand backhand on the other wing. In fact, he had a quite heavily top-spun forehand drive – not as exaggerated as Borg's, but top-spun nevertheless. Well, then Hughes and I won the doubles. Austin clinched our success on the third day by outplaying McGrath, which was just as well because I had injured my shoulder and Harold Lee took my place for the final 'dead' match with Crawford.

I stayed behind in London for treatment at the skilled hands of a wonderful osteopath, W. F. Hugh Dempster, while the rest of the team set off for Paris, where they were to meet the United States for the right to challenge the champions – France. It was agreed that I should arrive by the boat train on the following Wednesday evening for a work-out with our coach, Dan Maskell, at Roland Garros Stadium before the team was announced the next day.

When I met Dan he told me we could practise as long as we liked because we were not necessarily required, as was usually the case, to join the rest of the team for dinner. The practice revealed no problems, so Dan phoned the captain, H. Roper Barrett, to tell him I would be able to play, and then we made our own way to dinner.

We passed a rather posh restaurant called the Café Royal in the Bois de Boulogne, a lovely place near the lake, so I suggested we eat there. Why not? Maskall considered it a bit expensive for the likes of us, but I pointed out that the rest of our team, not to mention the LTA officials, would very likely be in a similar place with wonderful food; I proposed to dine equally well.

So in we walked. The maître d'hôtel, who was one of the owners, welcomed us personally by name, and as the orchestra struck up 'God Save the King' Dan said, 'Do you know these people?' I never even knew the band.

We had a memorable meal and asked for the bill, wondering whether we would be the first Davis Cup players ever to have to wash the dishes. But the owner insisted on taking care of it himself. 'It is my pleasure,' he oiled.

Dan and I got back to the Hotel Crillon at about 10.30 p.m. to all sorts of flak. Nobody would believe we had had a free meal at such a fabulous place, but the fact that we had was yet another indication of the level of interest in the Davis Cup at that time, with France doing so well.

Dan Maskell was a valued member of that Davis Cup squad and went everywhere with us. He was also coach to the All England Club and the LTA, based at Wimbledon. Other non-playing members of the group were the captain Roper Barrett, our trainer Tom Whittaker, of Arsenal fame, and the secretary of the LTA, the likeable Anthony Sabelli, who came along to pay the bills. A lovely story comes to mind about Anthony Sabelli. Some years later we were all at the Grosvenor House in London at one of the LTA balls. It was a rather sumptuous affair with a toastmaster and MC in a red coat, and the LTA President and his wife standing at the top of the stairs to greet the incoming guests. As you came in, you gave your name to a fellow with a loud voice who announced you to the throng below, and then you would be presented to the President and make your way down the staircase with as much dignity as possible. Sabelli entered with his wife in due style and whispered his name to the announcer, who turned towards the ballroom and bellowed, 'Sir and Lady Belly!'

I guess Dan Maskell's role on the squad was 'troubleshooter'. I don't think it was a question of actually teaching us anything because Austin, Lee and I all had our own personal way of playing by now. But if I wanted to practise something Dan would work with me for hours and hours, even days. He helped put the finishing touches to our preparations.

We worked hard on those preparations and studied the opposition a little more carefully than most of the other teams did. In addition to our on-court captain and trainer, we stationed a man at each corner of the court amongst the crowd so that if anything happened – and in Europe it could happen all the time because the Europeans are so nationalistic – we could head for the corner to let off steam without getting into trouble and could find a friendly face instead of someone who was booing us.

The key to our success over the Americans that year was the wonderful form of Bunny Austin. He routed Ellsworth Vines, who had just reached the Wimbledon final and who had beaten him in the previous year's final, in straight sets with some thrilling tennis, and I beat Wilmer Allison almost as easily.

Although we lost the doubles to that redoubtable combination of George Lott and Johnny Van Ryn, Austin clinched our place in the challenge round with a four-set win over Allison. The tie might have been decided, but the drama was by no means over. Vines and I got embroiled in an exhausting five-set battle until eventually I stood at 7–6 in the 'fifth set and 40–15 on his service.

He threw up the first ball to serve. Fault. As he prepared to throw up the second, I moved over to run around the serve on my forehand, as if to tell him, 'Here it comes, my friend.' As he leaned into the ball to hit it, Vines collapsed face forward on to the court. He had injured an ankle in the fourth set, and the combination of pain, a hot Sunday afternoon in Paris and the stress of being match point down, even in a 'dead' rubber, had been too much. Vines was carried off court and that was the end of the match. I knew then that, despite that second-round setback at Wimbledon against Farquharson, I was now good and ready.

So we moved on to what's known these days as 'the big one'. With the comforting presence of Roper Barrett at our side, whispering sharply to us at every moment of crisis 'HYBT' (Hold Your Bat Tight), we swept the two singles matches on the opening day of the final against France.

Austin brushed aside the French nineteen-year-old André Merlin at a cost of only seven games, but I had the devil of a battle to subdue Henri Cochet 8–10, 6–4, 8–6, 3–6, 6–1. It wasn't until Cochet began to tire noticeably in the fifth set that I knew my superior fitness would again be the crucial factor.

One of my methods of injecting a little gamesmanship into a big match was to vault the net if I had won and congratulate my opponent, thereby giving the crowd the impression that this Perry fellow was fit enough to play another five sets. It's rather like a boxer who has been clobbered senseless dancing around to make people think he didn't feel a thing.

I had another trick up my sleeve if I was involved in matches with a ten-minute break at the end of the third set. I'd start by wearing off-white gaberdine trousers and an off-white shirt, then, after the rest period, I would re-emerge in dazzling white duck trousers and a fresh white cotton shirt, my hair neatly parted. The crowd always thought I looked twice as fresh as the other man, but of course it was just window dressing.

Well, there I was in my dazzling white gear at match point against the redoubtable Cochet. In desperation he came to the net and I threw him a lob over his backhand side. He took off after it, but it was obvious he wasn't going to make it. I went to the net and was preparing to spring when Roper Barrett shook his stick at me and shouted, 'Stay where you are; don't you dare move!' The moment the ball hit the ground on Cochet's side of the net he said, 'Now you can go.'

Vaulting the net after such a gruelling match definitely *was* the boxer's shuffle on my part. In the privacy of the dressing room I passed out completely, then came round to find myself on the massage table with Roper Barrett and Maskell fanning me. My condition, due as much to the mental strain as physical exertion, was hushed up for tactical reasons, and as a precaution I was rested from the doubles, in which Pat Hughes, now partnered by Harold Lee, lost to Jean Borotra and Toto Brugnon.

It's hard for anyone who wasn't there at the time to understand the particular strain of playing the challenge round of the Davis Cup in Paris. We were trying to take the Cup away from the French on their own territory and Paris was like a seething cauldron. You never knew what was going to happen and everything you did was like another step along a tightrope. The court was purpose-built to suit them, so the French had every advantage to start with, and the 15,000 people who were jammed into Roland Garros Stadium that day were all frenzied Frenchmen, whistling and jeering. If there was a bad call, it took four or five minutes to silence the eruption. It's a very nerve-racking thing to play tennis in that kind of charged atmosphere. And to try to beat Cochet, who, let's face it, was my idol, on his own territory, in the Davis Cup Challenge Round and in such a decisive match, was a staggering responsibility. I think, when I beat him, the bottom dropped out of my act. I think it was the sheer joy and relief of thinking, 'My God, we made it!'

I had still not fully recovered twenty-four hours later. When the doubles match was over Roper Barrett ordered Austin and I out for a quiet practice session as a loosener for the next day, but within five minutes the captain had decided I was not even up to that and packed me off to bed. After a good night's sleep I felt decidedly better, though still far from 100 per cent.

The final day's play, with the Davis Cup on prominent display, was again hard on the nerves. Cochet, twice a set behind, outlasted Austin in a match that went the distance, and once more it was up to me to win for Britain and deny France a record-equalling seventh consecutive year of Davis Cup possession.

Showing remarkable maturity and coolness, young Merlin passed me time and again at the net in the early stages. I lost the first set and had to save two set points in the second before things began to go my way. On one of the set points I cracked the ball down Merlin's backhand side as he came in and it hit the line, making a clearly discernible mark because in those days the lines were of porcelain. The ball skidded and was called good.

Pandemonium followed, however, as it usually did (and still does) on this sort of occasion involving a Frenchman. Boos, catcalls, whistles. But the point stayed good. Yet as I prepared to receive the next serve, I noticed a fresh official on the line. The poor devil who had called my ball in was *out*.

Eventually I broke serve in the fourth set to lead 5–4 and needed only to hold my service for the match – and the tie and the Cup. I remember some pompous idea I had in mind of showing the French nation how to finish off a tennis match, but I promptly lost the game and needed to work very hard to break Merlin again for a 6–5 lead.

As we were changing ends, with no time allowed for a sit-down in those days, of course, Roper Barrett got up from his chair and said to me, 'Let's go for a walk.' While I was taking a drink, he looked around us and said, 'Nice day . . . big crowd . . . Look over there in that corner: now, there's a good-looking girl. I'll tell you what, win this game and I'll get you a date with her.' (I think he was just talking to take my mind off the race. It certainly did the trick.)

That changed the whole picture. I wasn't straining any more. I held serve, won the match 4–6, 8–6, 6–2, 7–5, and Britain had possession of the Davis Cup for the first time since 1912. The Associated Press reported that when the Cup was formally presented to Roper Barrett 'he hugged it tightly as though it were a baby, while the fans, with lumps in their throats, bade it godspeed'.

After standing motionless for the national anthems I missed the rest of the post-match ceremonies and celebrations. I was flat on my back in the dressing room again, having passed out for the second time in three days, drained as before.

On the way back to the hotel in our open-topped bus we tastelessly flourished the trophy we had taken away from the French after six years, much to the disgust of the passers-by.

That evening, after the official dinner for both teams, Cochet, swallowing his national sorrow, said to me, 'Let's go out for a night on the town and take the Cup with us.' 'We can't do that,' I said. 'Oh, yes we can,' he insisted, and we did. With a few friends of his we got the trophy out of the hotel and set off on a tour of the Paris night clubs. Everywhere we went the band would strike up the 'Marseillaise', followed by 'God Save the King'. We would fill up the Cup with champagne, everybody would take a drink, and then we'd go off to the next club. Well, the others were drinking: I was sipping.

The celebrations went on all night and it wasn't until about 7 a.m. that we made our way back to the hotel across the Place de la Concorde, carrying the Davis Cup and followed by an orchestra we had picked up along the way and a decidedly mixed gathering of hangers-on.

I don't suppose the tennis authorities would have approved had they known that their precious trophy had been on a grand tour of Parisian night spots, but despite this the LTA found the Cup where it was supposed to be when the time came for them to take it back to London that morning.

On arrival in Dover, where a telegram of congratulation from King George V awaited us, we all looked a bit green because the Channel crossing had been rough. But we soon pulled round. The whole length of the journey up to London on the train people were standing in their back gardens waving to us as we held up the Davis Cup, and at Victoria Station it was chaos. About ten thousand people swamped the police cordon, grabbed Austin and myself, and marched us off on their shoulders. The ring-leaders were a few people from my part of Ealing, though I didn't know that at the time. I lost all my baggage and rackets in the turmoil and thought they had disappeared for ever, until two days later my coach Pops Summers called up and told me they were safe in his car.

When the Wind Blew in 1883

Lance Tingay

Let me introduce my hero, Herbert F. Lawford, a big, burly man aged 33. Let me introduce my other hero, James Ernest Renshaw, aged 23, and rather slight. The date is 1883 and the occasion is the first round of the Wimbledon Championships.

It was not perhaps the greatest of Wimbledon Championships. This was the seventh year of the tournament. There was just the one event, the men's singles. The entry was 23.

One was William Renshaw, also aged 23 since he was the twin brother of the other Renshaw that I have called James Ernest. I will call him Ernest from now on since no contemporary ever dreamed of identifying him in any other way.

If you have not heard of the Renshaw twins you should have done. They began to play tennis when it was a game. They turned it into a sport. William won Wimbledon first in 1881, and defended his title successfully against his brother Ernest in 1882.

So William was defending his title again in 1883. In those days the defending champion did not enter into the hurly burly of the tournament. It was up to his challengers to find the best among themselves before he put his title at risk.

As for those challengers in 1883 there were two outstanding above all others. One was Ernest. The other was Herbert Lawford. Had there been seeding for the event Ernest would have been seeded one and Lawford two.

But that was years before seeding was even thought of. It would have been regarded as a legalized form of cheating. I am not so sure that it isn't, but that is by the way.

You can, of course, guess what happened. Ernest Renshaw and Lawford were drawn against each other in the first round.

It was, though, rather more than a clash between the two best players other than the title holder. There was at that time a controversy raging about the merits of two styles of play.

The baseliners were at war with the volleyers. The baseliners, I must stress, had been given ammunition the year before. In May 1882 the height of the net at the posts was lowered from 4 feet to 3 feet 6 inches, its present dimension. That was done by the then joint administrators of the game, the Marylebone Cricket Club and the All England Club.

The avowed purpose of lowering the net was to help the baseliners against the increasing onslaughts of the volleyer. Let me quote from the current indignation. 'Was lawn tennis to be reduced to the interchange of three or four sharp repartees from the service-line, followed by a smash from the vicinity of the net?'

A lower net meant effective passing shots. None the less the volleyers continued to have the best of it. And none more so than the Renshaws. The 'Renshaw smash' was a by-word for all that was terrible and destructive.

But among the first-class players on the day just one man stood out against what was described as 'the contagion of the volley'. That man was the burly Lawford.

Ernest Renshaw and Lawford both had strong personal views on the question. Wrote Renshaw: 'Before many years taking the ball off the ground will be quite the exception; and in its place there will be far finer and more exciting rallies in the volley than have ever been up to the present.'

Lawford dissented: 'Perfect back play will beat perfect volleying. It is always possible to pass a volleyer with the court as it is at present; and I know that when I lose a stroke by being volleyed it is my own fault.'

Years later the Frenchman René Lacoste held much the same views. He won Wimbledon twice and the US Championship twice. He retired from the game around 1929 and was the last of a line.

But in 1883 the issue was hardly so clear cut as it has become in recent years. Nor would I pretend that their famous clash at Wimbledon resolved the dispute. But their clash of theories about the game added piquancy to their clash as first-class players.

They played one of the most extraordinary affairs in the history of the first class game.

Monte Fresco's memorable, award-winning picture for the *Daily Mirror* of a ball-boy offering a quick prayer for the well-being of Bjorn Borg at Wimbledon

The many moods of John McEnroe, from mean to magnificent, with an excellent interpretation of the dreaded 'choke' on a key point

The balletic elegance of Virginia Wade, the darling of the Centre Court and 1977 Wimbledon champion

Another award-winning picture, this time by Jack Kay of the *Daily Express*, of Jimmy Connors defusing a potentially explosive confrontation with Ivan Lendl at Wimbledon

The style, determination and elegance that made Billie Jean King the outstanding postwar woman, with a crop of twenty Wimbledon titles to her credit

Power and determination, too, from the world's number one, Martina Navratilova, in pursuit of a low return at Wimbledon

The inimitable Bjorn Borg, in action on his favourite surface – clay – at Roland Garros stadium, Paris, where he won the title six times

A wind, something approaching the strength of half a gale, was blowing down the court. I would mention that in those days there was no precisely laid down method for changing ends. In that particular match the players changed ends at the end of each set.

Renshaw led 5–1 in the first set. Lawford took the next five in succession to take the set. He was playing down wind.

As for taking the set with five games, that made the score, of course 6–5. Such was the method then. Only in the final round were advantage sets then played.

Lawford, a set in front, did not prosper playing against the wind. Renshaw won the second set 6–1. He went on from the other end to take three more games.

Then Lawford, 0–3 behind, took six games in succession for the set at 6–3 and the lead by two sets to one. He took the first two games of the fourth set.

But Renshaw, from 0–2, won the fourth set 6–2, another sequence of six games in a row. And so to the final set. Lawford now playing down wind again as in the first. Lawford led 5–love.

The triumph of the baseliner against the volleyer was imminent. It did not work out like that. 'In despair', as a current account puts it, Renshaw delivered an underarm twisting service. Helped by the strong wind it drove Lawford right out of court. Instead of taking it on the backhand Lawford tried to kill the ball on the other wing. The tactic, it seems, failed. Renshaw won the match with six games running, his score being 5–6, 6–1, 3–6, 6–2, 6–5.

Whether or not Lawford had match points does not seem to have got recorded. Nor would the incredible sequence of games on either side seem to add much fuel to the argument about the baseliner versus the volleyer.

None the less the statisticians were hard at work. Some hard note-taking person, even if inconclusive about match points, has left it for posterity that, excluding the service and return of service, there was a total of 626 strokes played.

Of those, 502 were taken off the ground. 124 were taken on the volley.

It seems, also, that Lawford, when it came to the crunch of playing a tough match, was a more practical man that his high-sounding theories indicated. 'Perfect back play' indeed! Of those 124 volleys 97 were played by Renshaw and 27 were played by Lawford.

What was the baseliner doing, playing 27 volleys? For that matter what was he doing to let slip a final set lead of 5–0?

Lawford did win Wimbledon once. That was in 1887. Ernest Renshaw only won the singles once also. That was the following year, 1888. Lawford and Renshaw played many times. The affair in 1883 was the most astonishing.

Nothing, it seems, was quite the same again. At any rate in 1884 they let in the women. That was the beginning of the end. Or maybe the end of the beginning.

Nastase v. Ashe

Richard Evans

Arthur Ashe was left pondering the enigma that is Nastase after the Commercial Union Masters in Stockholm at the end of 1975 – a year that for Ilie had become a series of running battles with officialdom all over the world. The night before their memorable encounter at the Kunglihallen, Nastase had staged a little scene-setter for Ashe's benefit in the bar of the Grand Hotel. That the preview turned out to be a lot funnier than the main act was unintentional but perhaps predictable. Off court few people mind if Nastase gets a little outrageous. On court, especially against a man like Ashe, it is different. At any rate when Arthur strode into the bar for a nightcap, Ilie was already holding forth. Perched on a bar stool he was chattering away with a whole group of people from the tennis world.

'Ah, Negroni,' exclaimed Ilie, addressing Arthur in his customary manner. 'How you feeling? Good, I hope. Tomorrow night you will need to feel good.'

Ashe, who genuinely enjoys Nastase in this kind of mood, smiled and sat down next to the Romanian. Without saying much, but laughing heartily at times, Arthur sipped a drink and let Ilie rattle on.

'Such a good serve you have, Negroni. Such a pity for you they put Supreme Court over the tiles. The tiles they are so much better for your serve, no? But it does not matter because I beat you anyway. Tomorrow night I do things to you that will make you turn white. Then you will be a white Negroni.'

Although most of the people in the bar were falling about by this stage, it was nothing new for Ashe. He had heard it all before. He also knew how to handle it. Pushing his drink tab towards Nastase, he leaned across and with an air of quiet authority, said to the barman, 'That'll be on Mr Nastase's check.' With that he slipped gently off his stool; tapped Ilie on the shoulder by way of recognition and, with a satisfied grin on his face, walked out. It was the kind of exit only Arthur Ashe could have pulled off with quite so much dignity and timing.

Twenty-four hours later the contrast was total. From the serene, understated, imperturbable human being I had always known, Ashe had been reduced to a screaming, nerve-ruined wreck. I have never seen him like it before or since. And the cause of it was, of course, Nastase.

It had started in a drearily familiar way. Ashe was leading 1–6, 7–5, 4–1 and seemed set for victory. Then Ilie started arguing over a line call and a heckler in the crowd began baiting him. Almost invariably that triggers a response in Ilie which I do believe is instinctive and compulsive. He shouts back. A lifetime's training might have made him able to ignore the lone loud-mouth but it is too late for that now. He just has to answer back. And so it started. Every time Nastase would bounce the ball and begin his service action, the man would call out. Each time Ilie stopped, turned and shouted back. This happened four or five times. The umpire repeatedly warned Ilie that play must be continuous but Ashe suddenly decided there would be no play at all.

Striding up to the umpire's chair, simultaneously shaking his head and waving his arms in front of him to signal termination, Ashe's high-pitched voice cut through the sudden buzz of the crowd. 'That's it,' he said. 'I'm not putting up with it any longer. He's contravening the rules and I'm not taking it any more.'

With that Ashe picked up his rackets and was off the court before the West German referee, Horst Klosterkemper, could reach the court-side and activate the decision he had taken seconds before the American's dramatic exit – namely to disqualify Nastase.

When I got down to the locker-room a few minutes later, confusion reigned. Klosterkemper, the umpire, John Beddington of the sponsors Commercial Union and Hans-Ake Sturen of the Stockholm Open were milling round trying to decide what should be done. All that would have been normal under the less than normal circumstances had it not been for the condition of Arthur Ashe. I have known Arthur a long time. I have seen him in dire situations on court and even tougher situations off it, as when he faced a militant group of black students in South Africa. I have seen him angry, sometimes very angry. But never before had I seen him lose control of himself.

'I'm not taking any more of that crap,' he screamed, his voice a whole octave higher than normal. 'There's no goddamn way you're getting me back on that court. He's broken the rules, goddamm it. I helped write them. I ought to know.'

Ripping off his damp shirt he flung it down on the bench, his whole lithe body trembling with emotion. 'That son of a bitch isn't going to get away with it any more. I'll damn well see him run out of the game before he tries that kind of stunt with me again.'

The subject of this tirade was sitting somewhat sheepishly behind a row of clothes and towels that almost completely hid him from Ashe's view. It was not difficult to see that he had been shocked by Ashe's sudden flare-up. 'What you go so crazy for?' he asked plaintively a couple of times in between long bouts of brooding silence. 'Shit, what you want me to do, say I'm sorry? I'm sorry. But that guy kept yelling at me, what could I do?'

But Ashe was not about to get drawn into a verbal slanging match with his antagonist. He knew his emotions were running wild in a manner that was quite foreign to him and he thought he had better try and channel his anger as best he could. So he ignored Nastase and confined his attention to the various officials who were trying desperately to come up with a solution. The problem was that Ashe, by walking off court, had committed an offence just as grave as Nastase's. The fact that Klosterkemper was on the point of defaulting Ilie when Ashe made his move was, technically, of no consequence. Instead of remaining on the court and demanding that the referee implement the rules, he had taken the law into his own hands and left the arena. And, even some 15 minutes later, as the argument raged on, it was still Ashe, not Nastase, who was refusing to continue the match.

But no one wanted to default Ashe and give the match to the Romanian. The fact that Arthur had been provoked also had to be taken into consideration. It was also impossible to overlook the fact that he was not merely president of the ATP but one of the most orderly and respected players ever to grace a tennis court. Orderly, however, did not quite describe him at this point.

Half-naked, dripping with sweat and still taut with rage, he caught the gist of several half-whispered discussions between Klosterkemper, Beddington, Sturen, myself and others and quickly interjected, 'Don't think you're getting me back on that court – there's no way. I've quit and it's his fault. You guys work it out any way you like but I'll tell you this – if you penalize me I'm walking straight out of this tournament right this minute.'

We all stared at him like men hit with a sudden attack of migraine. He was not making it any easier. As the Masters is partially played under a round-robin format – two groups of four play round robin to produce two semi-finals that are then played off on a knock-out basis – any player walking out on the first day would leave a nasty hole in the scheduling. But the round-robin format also offered Klosterkemper the possibility of a compromise solution. I don't know whether I was the first to suggest it to him or whether he had already thought of it himself but I remember whispering the suggestion to him as he talked on the locker-room phone with the ILTF President, Derek Hardwick, who was back at the Grand Hotel, having left the Kunglihallen half an hour before the incident occurred.

The solution was to default them both. In a knock-out format this would, I agree, have been too hard on Ashe. But in round-robin play, it is quite possible for someone who loses his first match to go on and win the whole tournament. Nastase himself had done it in Boston two years before and, as it turned out, was destined to repeat the feat that week in Stockholm.

By simply depriving both men of the point one of them would normally have gained for a victory, they would be left joint bottom of the White group after the first round of matches – a handicap certainly but not an insurmountable one. Klosterkemper liked the idea and initially Hardwick agreed. 'It's your decision, Horst,' the ILTF president told him on the phone. And so indeed it was. One of the younger and more progressive members of the European tennis hierarchy, Klosterkemper had made his reputation in the game by organizing the Grand prix event in Düsseldorf each year – a tournament considered by most of the players to be one of the best-run in the world.

But nothing he had had to face in Düsseldorf had posed as many delicate problems as the situation facing him now. Emotionally he wanted to overlook Ashe's indiscretion because he knew how genuine Arthur was in wanting to make a stand against the kind of behaviour he felt was intolerable. But his teutonic respect for rules could not allow him totally to ignore the fact that Ashe had committed a serious offence by leaving the court. So Klosterkemper finally decided on the double default solution and, rather bravely, considering the American's frame of mind, walked over to Arthur to tell him.

'I'll appeal against that,' Ashe retorted. 'You won't get away with it.'

Incredibly, he was right. In one of the stranger decisions professional tennis has witnessed over the past decade, a tournament committee consisting of Hardwick, Klosterkemper, Beddington and his Commercial Union boss, Geoff Mullis, voted to overturn Klosterkemper's original decision and award the match to Ashe.

It was an enourmous compliment to Ashe's standing and reputation in the game that he was able to convince the committee that this was the correct course of action. I understand how important it was to him to be officially exonerated from blame. And to an extent I sympathize. But I cannot honestly say that I consider it to have been a good thing for the game. For an ATP president to use his position and his influence to have an official decision overturned on his own behalf throws up too many ethical question marks. But he got away with it and if one views it as a somewhat unorthodox bonus for all the esteem he has brought to his sport over the years, then one should not complain too loudly. During the particular match in question he had, if not technically, then in essence, been more sinned against than sinning and, to his credit, Nastase was the first to admit as much. Even now he looks back on the incident and says, 'That time I think I go too far. It was not intentional. Arthur had such a big lead I think he would have won the match anyway but this guy keep talking to me as I try to serve and what could I do?' He still does not have the answer.

He did, however, find an immediate method of soothing the last remnants of Ashe's anger. Having practised after the committee meeting in the morning, Arthur was having a late lunch by himself in the Grand Hotel dining-room, gazing out at the panoramic view of the steamers and fishing-boats riding at anchor in front of the Royal Palace. There weren't many other people in the room but even those unconnected with tennis could not have missed the significance of the little scene that was about to be enacted. Appearing at the door-way half hidden by a huge bunch of flowers, Nastase almost tiptoed his way across the room and then, with the half-scared look of a child who is trying to make it up with his father, laid the flowers across Ashe's table.

'Please forgive me,' he said with a smile.

Of course everyone laughed but in many ways it was an action, as Oscar Wilde once said, 'so sweet and simple as to hush us to silence'. Certainly he knew how and in what spirit he should approach his rival and as he flitted away as silently as he had come, Arthur lifted his hands in a gesture of despair and smilingly shook his head. 'That was so typical of Nastase,' he said when we talked about it later. 'You can't be mad at the guy for long.' Ashe also maintained that he was angrier at the officials than he was at Ilie. 'Nastase was just being Nastase,' Arthur said. 'I was just furious that everyone was letting him get away with it.'

Santana v. Osuna

Geoffrey Green

A great wave of good feeling flowed through Wimbledon yesterday. It was nothing to do with the overdue entry of sunshine – it was closer to the heart than that – but to an exhibition of lawn tennis the like of which we shall be fortunate indeed to see again for the rest of these Championships.

For an hour and a half M. Santana and R. H. Osuna regaled us with true artistry before Santana won by 2–6, 0–6, 6–1, 6–3, 6–4. At the end a voice from the thick crowed who were standing on their toes cried out 'Encore!' It was a cry from the heart echoed on all sides.

Here was Spain against Mexico, Latin sons full of expression. They were almost too full of riches. Each was replete with grace and beauty, and the line 'He nothing common did or mean' might especially have been dreamed up for the two of them. Though Santana won beautifully, Osuna also lost beautifully, for here was a match that produced two victors.

The abiding misfortune, as it proved, was that they should meet so soon. Osuna, who felt that he could snatch the title from an unfeeling, inconsiderate seeding committee, should have been protected within the draw. But that is the way the cards fell. Yet what a rich, coherent, and dramatic final this would have proved.

To try to find words for it all now seems to strip it of dignity. To try to analyse it, too, seems a detraction. It was a match one would have watched again and again, day after day, until tomorrow week.

Not that it would necessarily produce the same esoteric pleasure each time. Yet the odds would be on the side of the poetic instruction, for the racket in each man's hand seemed to know what he was feeling and so gave him its support and confirmation. When it was over Osuna said that he had seldom enjoyed losing a match more and that in the final set both had reached a stage when every stroke played was played for a winner. 'What can you do', he remarked, 'when you raise the chalk with what you think is a winner and it comes back to spatter the white line at your own end?' What to do, indeed.

After this it was almost a sacrilege to see anything else on the day. Significant, too, that the players' gallery was full to the concrete steps. If there was friendship, respect and a smile on court as each man applauded the other's winning reply, there was no ghost of a smile from the other attentive competitors. They might have been taking notes at a lecture. The margins must have been full of annotations.

Perhaps it was not a epic, but it was certainly lyrical. And at the close the eyes of both were surrounded with circles of fatigue after many a feverish minute.

Here was an intelligent hedonism in which each man basked. Osuna, ebony and feline, was as quick as thought as he moved into his volleys, cutting off the lines of attack. He flowed as he ran. Santana, unable to staunch the flood over the first two surprising sets, in due course revealed the subtle strength of his own hand.

If one were to translate – or try to – the strange, unbalanced language of the score it would be this. Santana emerged from a dark position because his first service duly began to find its mark before all was lost; and beyond that he unfurled a stroke which one had not seen in his repertoire before. It was a top-spun backhand lob which finally proved to be the executioner.

A dozen times and more he must have used it – sometimes defensively, sometimes in attack. Sometimes Osuna, darkly climbing some invisible ladder, found an answering smash.

But almost always it was then that the Mexican found the initiative wrested away. The delicacy and timing of this stroke by Santana was superb and more than once he hit the baseline. What Osuna must have felt at these moments is his own secret. Not by word or deed did he reveal his feelings.

When Santana, gaining touch, broke to 1–0 at the start of the fourth set, the future began to reveal itself. And when, after seven deuces, the Spaniard came to two sets all as Osuna ended with a double fault at 6–3, that future became predictable and probable. Another break at 2–0 put Santana into the clear and though Osuna once pulled back to 4–5 with flowing volleys and passes, deep down it was over.

Santana broke back for the match in the tenth game and did so with a backhand pass off service. It was a glorious shot to seal a match that deserves a small corner in some anthology, not least for the spirit in which it was played. More than once each applauded the other's winners, and when, at the end, Santana, with a whoop and a cry, bounded up to the net almost like a flamenco dancer, there he was met by a man with a smile as wide as a slice of melon. Arm in arm they went into our dreams.

At the end of it an All England member, leaving the Centre Court stand, remarked sarcastically: 'To think that we had to be taught manners by a couple of wogs.' For his own ill-starred comment he was almost shoved down the stairs.

Places

Wimbledon

Arthur Ashe

Monday, 24 June

At last, the first day of Wimbledon. I haven't played here since '71 – last year there was the Pilic dispute, and the year before Wimbledon banned WCT players. As terrible as everything is in my life, the start of Wimbledon is some kind of rejuvenation, a confirmation.

I was scheduled as the fourth match on my court, but after months of drought, it came up mean and drizzly today – not bad enough to cancel play, but enough to drag it out. Not until 7.30 did the referee, Mike Gibson, finally call play off, so that I hung around all day, like a cocked gun, waiting for someone to pull the trigger.

Notwithstanding the weather, the grounds were jammed today. Most tennis tournaments wither on the vine early in the week, but at Wimbledon, the early days always attract the largest crowds. The courts here are well separated, so that the fans can walk around and select any number of good matches to watch; it's a tennis smorgasbord. In fact, since there is a tendency to play the British players on Centre Court and Number One in the early rounds, some of the best matches can be found on the outside courts.

Part of the reason that Wimbledon attracts such great attention is that it is a bona fide, certified British tradition, and British traditions are just a bit more traditional than anybody else's – just as British royalty is a bit more royal. Given a head start, the British can always make their things seem more important than anybody else's. Wimbledon, for instance, is known here as 'The Championships', which is one of the great pre-emptive titles in the world. How do you top that?

Besides tradition, Wimbledon also possesses that companion

trait of continuity. Forest Hills, for example, is almost as vulnerable as Wimbledon, but it is difficult to accept it with the same reverence when you have college kids serving as locker-room attendants. Wimbledon, by comparison, has one fellow named Peter who has been here for years, possibly generations, and all he does is escort players to the Centre Court or Number One. The only fresh face I've seen around the locker room this year belongs to an elderly newcomer who serves the Robinson's Barley Water – orange, lemon or lime. There is still no guy to serve ice with the Robinson's Barley Water, largely because there is not enough ice to bother with.

The locker room has been done over in recent years and Newcombe convinced them three or four years ago to give players five minutes to warm up instead of three. The more important thing, however, is not what the particular rules may be, but that they are abided by. Five minutes to warm up does not mean fives minutes and ten seconds.

There is one other major change this year. Previously, the players have been transported to and from the grounds in large black limousines, flying the distinctive purple and green flag, piloted by chauffeurs; but this year our transportation consists of a fleet of Leylands, medium-sized British station wagons. Now that may sound like a loss of prestige, but the British very cleverly compensated by obtaining pretty young drivers. I don't know about the girl players, but none of the men is bemoaning the demise of the limousines – we're all too busy asking the drivers out.

The British sound so good, you don't even mind when they say *no* to you. What Shaw said about the Americans and the British being two peoples separated by a common language must be all the more true. Because Americans just use the language, without really caring for it, I doubt if we could have made English the pre-eminent tongue in the world the way the British did. We seem capable only of spreading marketable items, from Coca-Cola on up, while the British really do carry more lasting things, like culture or language.

Before we leave the subject of language, I would like to speak briefly on behalf of *bloody*. In America, we don't have an all-purpose mild curse word like *bloody*. If we had had a *bloody* in our vocabulary, President Nixon wouldn't have had all those expletives deleted and would probably have the Judiciary Committee on the run right now.

I would also like to submit some other new British words that I have just learned for adoption into the American language. I especially like *niggled*, which, I understand, is to be mildly annoyed. I was niggled, for instance, that I had to hang around the locker room all afternoon without ever getting on the courts. And *twee*: adjective, meaning sort of cutesy-poo sweet. What I like especially about *twee* is that it sounds just how it means. You wouldn't call anyone twee unless they really were. The same can be said for *gnomey*, which means sort of super tacky. It is derived from those people who dress up their lawns with little plastic animals or dwarfs – flamingos and deer and elves and gnomes. Thus if you are the type of person who prefers that sort of decoration, you are *gnomey*.

For the British, Wimbledon is identified as 'The Fortnight'. It is an event. Americans have the impression that England is tennis mad, but no, it is merely Wimbledon mad. Other tournaments draw poorly. But tennis does, however, always remain in the British subconscious throughout the year. The British tennis press travels all over the world, filing stories back to London. While only a handful of other journalists – Judith Elian of France, Rino Tommasi of Italy, Bud Collins of the US – see big-time tennis regularly, as many as half-a-dozen London writers cover us throughout the year. The *New York Times* won't send a man to Montreal for the WCT doubles championships, but Fleet Street will have a squadron cross the Atlantic.

As a result, tennis players become part of the everyday landscape in Britain, and when Wimbledon comes our names are very familiar to the readers. And, since the BBC puts Wimbledon on one or the other or both of its networks for most of the day (plus the reprise, 'Match of the Day', later in the evening) you can't escape tennis. There is a play showing over in Piccadilly starring Maggie Smith, and in establishing the characters and the setting early on, one of the principles says to another, 'Oh, I understand Ginny is doing well at Wimbledon.' Immediately, everybody in the audience knows very well that the small talk is about Virginia Wade. So Wimbledon is a real dent in the whole public consciousness, and it is not just an athletic show overlaid with social attributes, in the way that

Ascot or Henley tend to be.

Of course, I'm hardly suggesting that Wimbledon is without social pretensions. The Fortnight is a prime social focus, and the ladies dress for the occasion. None the less, Wimbledon is foremost a national phenomenon. In fact, I think it can be argued that Wimbledon captures the imagination of a complete country more so than any other athletic event, simply because it attracts the interest of both sexes in a way that other great competitions do not.

Virtually every British schoolgirl is taught to play tennis, so that the whole female population is conversant with the game in a way large numbers of women are not with soccer or baseball or whatever. The base of Wimbledon is female; I'm sure there's no sporting event in the world that attracts women in such numbers. (They all must be issued autographs books along with their first bras too; British women lead the world in autographs books per capita).

The matches at Wimbledon don't start until two in the afternoon, because The Championships are held right after the summer solstice, and at this high latitude, the matches can be played in natural light until nine-thirty or so. In the afternoon, for the first few hours, the grounds are like a large ladies' lounge. You don't begin to see a few friendly male faces until five or six or so when the husbands begin to get out of work. Not until well after tea does Wimbledon begin to obtain the coarser sounds and jostling of the masculine area that we are all more used to.

In the afternoon, a guy like Roger Taylor was a matinee idol here before he was a tennis player. Glossy photos of the players do a brisk business, like bubble-gum cards for our American boys. This year the security forces are already girding to handle the additional hordes of schoolgirls who will be pouring out here tomorrow to see Borg, as if he were David Cassidy. But this kind of teenage swooning aside, the women here are knowledgeable fans.

Last February, when we were playing a WCT tournament at Albert Hall, the promoters figured they could squeeze in another pay-day if they scheduled a matinee between the two losing semi-finalists for third place. They got some tour groups of suburban matrons to pile onto buses and come into London to see the match. Well, it ended up a complete disaster – something like 6–1, 6–1 in half an hour of bad tennis, and those ladies were storming the ticket windows afterward trying to get their money back.

In most places in the world, you'll go to some party, and if a beautiful woman comes up to you, she'll ask you why that cute Nastase wears powder blue shorts and carries on that awful way he does; at Wimbledon, she'll come up and ask you why Nasty isn't getting as much effectiveness off his cross-court underspin backhand when he's returning second serve against left-handers.

The people of every nation are unique, but I especially love the British. How can you not love any people who adore flowers so and, on the other hand, devised the London taxi, which is the most efficiently designed mechanism ever created by man? I've often thought very seriously – as I am again right now – about taking a flat and living over here for a year or two. It doesn't really make a helluva lot of difference where I live in the world, and so I might as well stay in the most civilized place for a time.

Tuesday, 25 June

I was up at nine-thirty. My daily cycle works best if I go to bed around one and get up around nine-thirty. It was another dreary day, but I was the second match on Court Four, and we were able to start around three. I played an Austrian named Hans Kary, whom I'd never met before, and I beat him rather easily – four, two and four – but even though I won without ever losing my serve, I wasn't pleased with it and had no confidence in the damn thing.

I'll tell you, at times like these, I really feel empathy for the weekend player when he has service problems and can't figure out where he's gone wrong. Here I am, supposedly one of the best three or four servers in the whole bloody world, and I don't know what the hell I'm doing wrong.

After the match I came into the locker room, and Nastase chose this time to make one of his periodic assessments of my colour. He also had Kodes in tow with him. 'Hey, Negroni,' he called. I kind of wrinkled my brow in reply. 'Well, what am I going to call you, Negroni? You're black. But don't worry,' he added then, quite solicitously, patting me on the shoulder, 'you're not too black.'

'Not so black as Amritraj,' Kodes said with a big smile, getting his two cents in.

'No, no, no,' Nastase said. 'Not that black. You're just like candy. Candy Man, we'll call you.'

'Candy Man,' said Kodes.

If the whole world were collapsing, I think Nastase would still be sponsoring interludes like this one.

Late in the afternoon, Roscoe and I beat Crealy and Parun, the French champions, two, three, and four. We really played quite well, and I'm gratified, if nothing else, to have gotten through the first round in the minimum of six sets. Sometimes you can get worn down in the first rounds of a long tournament, like a bull being worked over by picadors, and then you are no match when the real competition comes along. Rosewall has gotten a great break – the only player to have played two rounds already. I'm supposed to meet him in the round of sixteen. Usually I don't like to look at my draw in a tournament, because it distracts you by making you think ahead, but Wimbledon is such a fishbowl that there can be no secrets. Barring upsets, I know exactly whom I'm supposed to play, all the way to the finals. And what a draw I've got. I must beat Roscoe in the third round just to get to Muscles so I can play Newcombe so I can play Smith. And then I get to the finals. If, if . . .

Wednesday, 26 June

It was one o'clock before our ATP board meeting ended last night and so I had this strange sensation of being relieved when I woke up and looked out the window this morning and saw that it was pouring down rain. Of those players on the board, I figure that three of us – Newcombe, Smith and myself – have a good chance to win this tournament, and Newc was scheduled to play the first match today against a tough opponent – Geoff Masters. Newc is staying at a house way out in the suburbs, and so I'm sure it was past two o'clock before he got to bed last night. It would have been on my conscience if he'd gotten up tired, gone to the courts and been upset by Geoff.

As it was, the rain held up his match until late in the afternoon, and then Newc beat him. I sat around most of the afternoon waiting for my court to dry, before Mike Gibson finally called everything off at seven-thirty.

All this dampness has kept my cough going wonderfully. The one good thing is that I'm so caught up in the excitement and the turmoil that I haven't had time to think about my broken romance.

Thursday, 27 June

I'm playing Kakulija, the number two Russian. We were the first match on Court Number One, and I ran through him 5–1 before the rain came. We waited for an hour and a half (with the court covered). Then we came back and tried again. I broke him again to run out the set at 6–1 and we played to four-all in the second before it really started pouring and Mike Gibson gave up the ghost and called off the rest of the day's programme.

So, I spent most of another day in the locker room. Borg has the locker next to mine. The lockers here are arranged horizontally, like drawers, so that it somewhat resembles a morgue, and to continue the analogy, Bjorn is like a cadaver. He finished beating Snake Case today and was mumbling 'I'm so lucky' afterward – which I've heard often enough not to pay any more attention to – but now he really does appear whipped and drawn. He seems to have no heart for the game now, and he has to be smuggled around and in and out of secret entrances less the teeny-boppers reach him and do whatever teeny-boppers do if they ever should reach one of their idols. The other day, when I was playing Kary, Borg started his match on another outside court, and the place started going bananas all around me and generally disrupting the tournament, so now they must schedule every Borg match on the Centre Court or Court One, where the bobbies can keep the chaos to a minimum.

Actually, I don't think Bjorn minds all the fuss, but he is simply exhausted from playing all year and from the publicity pressures that have accrued since he reached the WCT finals and then won in Rome and Paris. I think, subconsciously, he would find defeat here to be a satisfying escape. Holecek beat him last week at Nottingham, and Bjorn came off smiling. There was no way he should have played that tournament; it convinced me that every player should be allowed one pre-emptive withdrawal a year.

Friday, 28 June

I finally beat Kakulija, one, four and three. We played on One again, which is the fastest court at Wimbledon, but it has dried out so from the spring drought that it was bumpier than I ever recall. Right after we finished, the showers came again, and now the whole schedule has gone haywire. Like it or not, Gibson is going to have to hang tradition and start matches at noon or earlier. Roscoe hasn't even gotten his second-round match in, so that the soonest we can play will be Monday. We can't play any doubles before then either. Hell, some of the girls haven't played a single match yet, and we're already five days into the tournament.

Saturday, 29 June

This afternoon I went out to Queen's with Dennis Ralston and he worked on my serve. As I had suspected, my toss was off. Charlie Pasarell and Stan Smith and I all have a pause near the top of our serve, so that if our toss is not just right, we are inclined to rush the action of the stroke, or hold it back too long. When my toss goes off, it throws my whole rhythm haywire, and when you lose that groove, you start to struggle and expend a great deal more energy.

I hit volleys for a half-hour too. I'm really not dissatisfied with the rest of my game, so I might still come around if I can just get my serve back.

I won £43 at the Playboy Club at roulette tonight.

Sunday, 30 June

It's amazing how people can talk themselves into something and then reinforce a false opinion. Everybody is saying that the rain delays will help Newcombe because it will condense the last rounds into a few days' play, and that since Newc is such a big, strong guy, this will profit him. Virtually every newspaper has played this same angle – and everybody you talk to is repeating the theme. The facts are completely opposite. Newc is big and strong, sure, but there's no correlation between strength and the kind of sustained energy that everbody's talking about. He might yet win, but if he does, it will be in spite of the rain schedule, not because of it.

El Shafei and I worked out this afternoon at Queen's. He had a good win the other day over Jurgen Fassbender, a tall, good-looking German who tells German jokes and who is the best up-and-coming ladies' man on the circuit. Also a very good grass player. Izzy always somehow beats players better than he is and then gets upset himself by nobodies. He plays Borg tomorrow, and he has a good chance because he does play his best against the best and also because Bjorn is so down.

I hit with Izzy because I needed some practice against a left-hander in preparation for Roscoe tomorrow. I've had time to think about playing him, and I know what I have to do. First, I've got to be consistent with my serve. Roscoe doesn't have a great return, so that he want to go for blazing winners off your second serve. Don't give him the chance. And don't get shell-shocked at how hard he hits it. He's going to bust a few past me, and the best way to combat that is to expect it, and then, when it happens, just to take it in stride. If people think I am expressionless, they ain't seen nothing yet. Tomorrow, I am going to be the ultimate poker face.

Roscoe beat me in Denver for the first time the last time we played, and while that hasn't any real relation to our match tomorrow – he was just blazing balls in the altitude – it was psychologically crucial because now he knows that he can beat me. I've got to get him doubting again.

Monday, 1 July

I'm sorry it all has to end like this. I mean Wimbledon, of course, but this book too. There isn't even much reason to talk about the match, except that it will be the last one in the book. It was planned to cover through Wimbledon, 1974.

We were out on Court Seven. It was windy at times and the sun was wicked serving on the one side – but what the hell, that just says that Roscoe adapted better than I did, and that's what this whole thing is all about. He served much better than I, on both sides of the court. I went right back to throwing the ball up all wrong. I don't know what the hell's the matter with my toss. I swear, I haven't served well since that match against Ray Moore in the quarter-finals at Denver in April.

But look, I had my chances. At two-all in the first set, I had five break points on him – five of the bloody things – but he served out. And then at 5–6, my serve, I had him 30–15, then 30-all, then I hit a goddamn forehand volley long and a backhand volley into the net, and there's the set. I only hit about a thousand volleys over the weekend.

He won the second set 6–3 with one break, and not long after that I could see the press begin to gather, one by one, like vultures, assembling up on a little balcony that overlooks court seven. Until today, not a single seeded player had been eliminated, but Izzy was also whipping Borg up on Number One.

To start the third set, I double-faulted on the very first point and lost my serve at fifteen, and he held and was serving for the match at 5–4 when I finally broke him. I did it with a backhand crosscourt that hit the chalk. He held serve to eight-all, then, and I clubbed him seven points to two in the tie-breaker for the set.

Now, suddenly, I was confident. I felt good, sure I could win. Roscoe had to be doubting. He was still playing a match he had won, and my serve was coming back. So, what do I do? I lose my first service game at love, my next at fifteen, and like that, I'm down 0–5. Izzy had mopped up Borg by now, so the press had returned in force to catalogue my defeat. And at this point, damn if I don't straighten up, break him and come back to 3–5, thirty-all on his serve. But it was too far for me to go. He held: 6–3 in the fourth. I was out of Wimbledon in the round of thirty-two.

It's tougher losing when you don't expect to. I feel embarrassed that I lost to Roscoe because I feel I'm a better player than Roscoe. He hasn't done what I have. But I don't

mean that, after the match, I was embarrassed to face other
players in the locker room, anything like that. The embarrassment is all within.

Everything in this game is within. There's never anyone to
console you, because nobody cares that I lost today, not really.
Oh sure, I want Charlie to win, and Stan, and I'm sure they root
for me too, because we've known each other for so long and been
so especially close, but I can't afford to get involved in their wins
and losses. You can't do that. I practised with El Shafei over the
weekend, so sure, I'm glad he got a big win today, but I wouldn't
have really cared if he lost. And Izzy doesn't really care what I
did. We must be dispassionate. Hell, believe this or not, but I'm
glad for Roscoe. As soon as it's over, it's incidental that it was me
he beat. It's just: El Shafei got a big win and Tanner got a big
win. Good, they're my friends. And Ashe and Borg got beat.
Tough, and so what: you've got to remember that half of us get
beat every day.

But my losing hurts me. I take defeat harder all the time. I
just wanted to be left alone after the match. The girls kept
jamming their autographs books at me, and I turned them
away. 'I'm sorry, I really don't feel like signing now,' I said. I
rarely do a thing like that. I saw the press, but I didn't want to.
After a defeat, they make me feel as if I'm on trial.

Sympathy for myself comes next. I methodically took off my
clothes and showered and sat there and felt sorry for myself.
Just you, all alone. That's why it's even more wonderful when
you win, when out of 128 players, you are the one who adapted
better than anyone else. But nobody in the locker room cares
then either. You win alone, just as you lose alone.

Only after the embarrassment and self-pity does the disappointment begin to set in, and then, at last, when I'm removed
by time, when I've finally gotten out of the locker room, I can
begin to see the defeat in cold technical terms. This evening, as
always after a hard loss, I waver between two extremes,
between the emotional and pragmatic solutions. First, I decide
that I must break my game down and go out like a tiger and
practise every component part three hours a day. I will
overcome my weaknesses, *defeat* them. And then, on the other
hand, I say to hell with it. Why don't I just give it up and take a
job at Philip Morris and collect my gold watch 35 years from

now?

That's the way I lose, and everybody must learn to lose, because you can't play the game if you can't take the losing. Most guys lose in character. Nikki might throw a racket just to get it out of his system. Nastase will jabber compulsively in defeat, talking incessantly about why he lost. Rosewall and Roche never say a word.

As far as I can tell with Okker, he has forgotten about the defeat before he reaches the locker room. Lutz and Pasarell lose as hard as anyone. Sometimes you'll see the tears in Charlie's eyes, and he'll say things like, 'I'll never play Wimbledon again.' Drysdale is perhaps the most philosophical. He just wants to sort it out in his mind why he lost, where he failed technically, and once he has that filed away for future reference, it is all forgotten. Newcombe, when he hit his bad patch last year, was a great loser. He was losing to guys like Gerken and Holecek, but he would come back to the locker room, unemotionally, and would sit down and analyse his defeat, much like Drysdale. Hewitt, the loser, is of all the players most at variance with the person that the public sees on court. He leaves everything out between the chalk lines and is a subdued, even gracious, loser.

It's tougher for the single guys – I think anyway, maybe because I'm single. My chief focal point is tennis. I have a lot of other interests, but no one single counterbalance, like a family. Defeat is always hardest for me the next day, because it stays with me and swells. The married guys seem to have more of a safety valve. How many times have I seen a guy come off the court, really way down after a hard loss, and he walks out of the locker room, and his pretty little daughter runs up to him, and it's all forgotten.

And I can't drink it away either. I'm not a guy for chemical crutches. I'll have dinner and gamble a little.

I'm sorry the book had to end like this.

Paris – The Pathos and the Pleasure

Rex Bellamy

In the next world, as a reward for distinguished service, we may sometimes be given a day off from stoking duties, or dusting the harps, and issued with the equivalent of Army 'leave warrants'. Perhaps they will insist, when handing over the travel vouchers (one-day return) that we resume our former, mundane labours. If they do, I shall spend that day at the French championships – first ensuring that the programme includes matches in which the likes of Pietrangeli, Santana, or Panatta will tease the likes of Laver, Rosewall, and Emerson. If he behaves himself, Nastase can play too. All the matches will last five sets and four hours, even the winners will collapse on the massage table like houses of cards, and I shall miss a few deadlines. But the birds will be singing and the wine will be waiting.

A day at the French championships can mirror a lifetime's hope and frustration, beauty and pathos, pleasure and pain. In the few past years the emphasis has shifted slightly away from finesse. But that is probably no more than a passing phase, based on the prevalent dominance of the slickly tailored attritional methods embodied by Bjorn Borg and Chris Lloyd. Did you know that, on the slow clay of the Stade Roland Garros, each has been beaten by only one player? Adriano Panatta beat Borg in 1973 and 1976. Margaret Court came back from 6–7 and 3–5 down to win her 1973 final with Miss Evert, as she was then. Borg has been champion fives times, twice without losing a set, and Mrs Lloyd has been champion four times. Last year a record total of 222, 316 paying customers saw them in action. In five years, the crowds have trebled.

The French championships became an international event in 1925 and the Stade Roland Garros was built in 1928. Nowhere else is the grandeur of tennis displayed in such rich variety – and nowhere else is the physical and mental cost of creating that grandeur so cruelly high. In short, Paris is the best place to play it. Ask John McEnroe and Jimmy Connors, who are still learning the trade on slow clay, or Arthur Ashe, who never quite managed it (though he came close, and always found those famous courts an irresistible intellectual challenge). The women's game thrives only on faster surfaces: but in Paris, even women's tennis has often been painstakingly painted in colours of gold.

All this has been true for a long time. But as a public promotion the championships have bloomed only since the national federation acquired the inspiring leadership of the boldly imaginative Philippe Chatrier, a vain, prejudiced, charming romantic who likes to be known as 'The Poet'. He made things happen. Like shifting the offices of the French Federation to Roland Garros and raising the money to rebuild the place. Like expanding the centre court accommodation to 15,000 (maybe 17,000 at a squeeze) and incorporating in the redesigned premises an intimate new 'show' court with room for 4,500. Like introducing a faster ball to compensate for the slow surface. Like improving the food for both body and soul (retaining leafy, grassy islands of shade while adding a fountain, more flowers, and extended promenades). Like 'live' television coverage – and a comprehensive range of associated facilities for public, players and press.

The French have made mistakes. The new 'show' court is a little short on run-back (especially at the sides) and the doubles game has been demeaned in terms of prize money and sche-duling prominence. But people who never make mistakes never make anything.

Every year, something changes at Roland Garros – but the essentially sensuous pleasures of the tournament remain untarnished. Sensuous? Yes. Because the mind's appreciation of the game is locked in with the sight and sound of tennis at Roland Garros, with the taste and smell of it. With the smell of French cigarettes; garlic; and sun-warmed flowers. With the taste of wine; coffee; crisp French bread; and the inescapable steak frites or sandwich jambon. With the sound of birds singing; umpires nasally intoning *quinze, trente, quarante, égalité, avantage*; and the inimitably soothing slither of shoes shuffling on shale. With the sight of russet-coloured courts amid the grey of concrete and the green of trees; swirling clouds of dust at the mercy of some passing breeze; shirt sleeves and summer dresses in the bright heat of May and June; brilliantly hued crowds on the soaring centre court terraces (like giant rockeries built round a stretch of beach); and line judges dressed in green and grey – among them a chic blonde who flashes just enough leg to remind us that there is more to life than tennis.

Roland Garros has many separate areas of interest, each with its own character and charm. But the centre court sums it all up. It is here that the close rapport between players and public is most exciting. The specatators are cultivated, perceptive. They respond to the mood of drama and players with a passionate, caring, yet discriminating urbanity. At times their noisy enthusiasm threatens to dominate a match by affecting the composure of players and court officials. And in the evenings the echoes of combat rumble on as matches are replayed over dinner – perhaps along the Champs-Elysees, perhaps at some candlelit restaurant in Montmartre, Montparnasse, or the Latin Quarter.

What makes the French the supreme, all-round test of tennis, the most arduous tournament to win, is the combination of heat with a loose, gritty surface that, by means of friction, takes the pace off the ball. The quick-footed, violent cut-and-thrust that prospers at Wimbledon and Flushing Meadow is not good enough for Paris. The ball hovers – rather like the kind of rain that seems to hang about, as distinct from merely falling. Players use slacker stringing in Paris, because ball control matters more than mere power. Rallies last longer. The ball cannot be put away easily. So matches become a prolonged series of tactical manoeuvres containing every trick in the book; every variation of pace and length, spin, angle, and trajectory.

These sweating, straining endeavours demand both physical and mental stamina. They demand a discreet, concentrated patience on the one hand, and, on the other, a constructive alertness to a sudden threat or opportunity. They demand a delicate balance between sparring and a commitment to attack. Openings have to be shrewdly and carefully created – often three or four times in the course of a single rally. Even the superficially simple business of sliding into a shot – so that positioning and balance are perfect – can be desperately difficult unless you have been brought up to do it. And the longer a match lasts, the greater the threat of cramp, shrieking agony, even tears.

A glib analogy between Paris and Wimbledon might be that between a carefully composed classical score and improvized jazz. But the analogy falls down, for me anyway, because I prefer Paris and New Orleans to Wimbledon and Beethoven. When watching tennis in Paris, all kinds of images leap to mind: music, geometry, chess, poetry, fencing. Nothing much seems to be happening. Then, suddenly, everything is happening – a flurry of punches, perhaps, or the whisper of a drop and the buzz of a top-spin lob. Alarm bells tend to ring in the midst of the most soporific, hypnotic exchanges. Thus the need for mental stamina – the ability to stay alert when everything in you cries out for mental and physical repose.

Watching a match go on court can be like popping a joint in the oven. It can safely be left for a while. You can pop back in an hour or so to see how it's cooking. That was how it was in 1961, when Manuel Santana went to Paris and won his first major championship. He beat Nicola Pietrangeli in a five-set final and was so overcome by the cessation of emotional stress that he burst into tears – and Pietrangeli went round the net, took Santana in his arms, and comforted him like a father calming a child who had woken from a nightmare. That was how it was when, the same year, an Australian teenager called Margaret Smith played in Paris for the first time – and was beaten 7–5, 12–10 by Ann Haydon, as she was then. Cramp hit Miss Smith in the second set and the Australian manager, Nell Hopman, dashed on court to help her (in those days, compassion was sometimes allowed to override the rules).

That was how it was, too, in 1969, when John Newcombe somehow produced two aces to beat Jan Kodes 11–9 in the fifth set after more than four hours of an exhausting slugfest. That was how it was in 1972 when Kerry Melville took three hours and 55 minutes to beat Pam Teeguarden (who served for the match four times, had two match points, ultimately ended the ordeal with a double-fault – and sat down and cried). Finally, that was how it was in 1980 when Paul McNamee took four hours and 18 minutes to beat John McEnroe in a match of four tie-breaks: and Jimmy Connors came back from 3–6, 2–6, 2–5 and 30–40 down to beat Jean-François Caujolle. There had been nothing quite like that since 1958 when Robert Haillet recovered from 0–5 and love–40 down in the fifth set to beat Budge Patty.

It would be an exaggeration to suggest that matches like these are the norm in Paris. But their content was a totally authentic guide to the character of the French championships. How the memories do crowd in – the best of them featuring a subtle clay-court specialist countering the hammer blows of some mighty exponent of the 'big' game.

So I'll stoke the fires, or dust the harps. Just get the 'leave warrant' ready, and leave the rest to me.

Hrry Crpntr

Clive James

The first week of *Wimbledon* (BBC 1 and 2 recurring) starred Harry Carpenter and his famous Rain Commentary. During the opening days there was hardly any tennis, but there was more than enough rain for Harry to perfect his commentary, if perfecting was what it needed.

It has been years now since Harry began calling Wimbledon Wmbldn. Later on he contracted Wmbldn to Wmln. This year it is back to being Wmbldn, possibly because Harry's lockjaw has been loosened by the amount of rain demanding commentary. 'Covers still on the outside courts. Thousands of people waiting, hoping against hope . . . Not a pretty sight is it?' The cameras zoomed in elegiacally on the canvas covers as the raindrops bounced. 'Still, we're pretty cosy here in the BBC commentary box under the Centre Court, and what's more I've got Ann Jones with me.' Obviously it was a Beatrix Potter scene down there in the burrow.

The downpour lifted long enough for Borg to demolish El Shafei and his own racket, which exploded. To be more accurate, it imploded, since it is strung to a tension of 80 lb. As we saw in *Borg* on London Weekend Television, the young champion strings his rackets so tightly that they go 'ping' in the night, thereby waking up his manager. Borg runs a taut ship. He likes his headband tight, too, to bring his eyes closer together. He likes them touching. 'Do you think it's going to make any difference to Borg's play, when he gets married?' somebody asked Gerulaitis. 'I hope so,' was the sad reply.

Like a Volvo, Borg is rugged, has good after-sales service, and is very dull. There is no reason to begrudge him his claim to the title of greatest of all time, although it is not only Australians who believe that Rod Laver would have won Wimbledon ten times in a row if the absurd rules against professionalism had not kept him out during the best years of his career. But Borg's role as chief mourner in a Bergman movie becomes positively treasurable if you compare him with Nastase, as it was possible to do when the rain briefly stopped on a later day.

I turned on the set hoping to see more rain, but instead found Nastase on his hands and knees banging his head against the turf. Then he got up and pretended to skate. Then he got back down on his hands and knees and had a lengthy conversation with the electronic eye, a machine which threatens to crab his act, since he will be able to dispute no more line calls. Imagine how exhausting it must be being Nastase, especially during those terrible few minutes in the morning when there is nobody to show off to except his own face in the shaving mirror. You can imagine him drawing moustaches on himself with the foam, sticking the brush in his ear, etc.

'There's a drain down both sides of the court where the water can escape,' Harry explained. 'Brighter weather is apparently on the way. But it's going to be some time . . .' More rain next week.

Borg's Little Bit Extra

Clive James

The second week of *Wimbledon* (BBC 1 and 2) was largely occupied with yet more rain. Between downpours Borg dealt rapidly with Glickstein. 'The reason Borg is the champion that he is', explained Mark Cox, 'is that he has that little bit extra to pull out, and he certainly has pulled it out in these last four games.'

Thus Borg progressed majestically into the closing rounds, continually pulling out that little bit extra. When McEnroe pulled out his little bit extra, you rather wished that he would tuck it back in. For a long time he did his best to contain his awful personality, tying his shoelaces between games instead of during and merely scowling at the linesmen instead of swearing. When sulking he kicked the ground but raised no divots, nor did his service take more than a quarter of an hour each time. You have to realize that McEnroe is serving around the corner of an imaginary building and that his wind-up must perforce be extra careful. He has a sniper's caution.

Finally the rain got to him. By Thursday he was behaving as badly as ever, thereby confirming the rule that Wimbledon, like alcohol, brings out the essential character. Virginia Wade tried losing to Betsy Nagelsen but couldn't make it, even when she resumed her old habit of throwing the ball out of reach when attempting to serve. 'I must say, Ann,' said Peter West, 'that Virginia's living dangerously.' 'That's self-evident, Peter,' said Ann Jones. In the last set Virginia managed to convert her 5–1 lead into a 5–3 lead by making even more unforced errors than her opponent, but it was too late: defeat had eluded her.

What she needed was an opponent even younger and more inexperienced than Nagelsen. Andrea Jaeger was the ideal candidate. With a smile that looked like a car-crash, Jaeger practically had to be wheeled on in a pram. Her range of gesture was no more prepossessing than McEnroe's, plus the additional feature that she expressed annoyance by driving the edge of her racket into the court, the next best thing to attacking the turf with a mattock. This was just the kind of opposition that Virginia knew how to lose to. Having duly sacrificed herself, our girl was last seen talking to David Vine.

The rain went on. Eventually is got to Harry Carpenter himself. Harry's Rain Commentary continued triumphantly into the second week, but the mark of a true champion is not to be made nervous by success. Like Borg or Nicklaus in their separate fields, a great rain commentator must be single-minded. Above all he must not be rattled by criticism.

As the cameras once again surveyed the system of lakes forming on the court covers, Harry showed signs of cracking. 'These shots will please one or two of our critics in the national press,' he gritted. 'Seem to prefer the rain shots to the tennis, some of them. It's not raining. It's drizzling. The forecast earlier wasn't too optimistic . . . it gave the impression that once the rain started it might hang around for some time . . .' He still had style, but his confidence was gone.

Dan Maskell, on the other hand, never falters. He might say break point when he means set point, or either when he means match point, but his authority only increases with the years, or yers. 'Ooh I *say*! That's as brave a coup as I've seen on the Centre Court in *yers*.' It takes more than a flood to stop Dan, who would wear Scuba gear if he had to, and often sounds as if he is wearing it already. Self-control is everything, as Martina Navratilova proved by losing to Chris Lloyd. Navvy has the talent, but Lloyd has the temperament. A bad call lost Navvy the second set, but the way she brooded on it lost her the match as well. Dan convicted her of 'somewhat wayward temperament'.

Navvy was lucky to last that long. Only failing energy stopped Billie Jean King from putting her out a round earlier. 'Well, this is an up and downer, Ann, isn't it?' 'You can say that again, Dan.' For a moment I thought Dan might, but he decided not to. It was a thrilling match, but still had nothing on the Olympian struggle between Connors and Tanner, during which the ball was only occasionally visible.

Tanner won the first set in a few minutes. Connors would have done better to take a seat in the stands. Right up until the sixth game in the fifth set they sounded like frantic woodchoppers in a frozen forest. Then Tanner slowed down and Connors broke through. Jimbo is not a particularly attractive personality – although compared with McEnroe he has the charm of Arthur Rubinstein – but we should enjoy him while we can.

Grunts, Bikes and Brats

Julie Welch

It's all over for another year. Put the dust covers over the ivy, sweep the bonbon wrappers off the concourse, check the Royal Box to see if anyone's dropped an engagement ring and take John McEnroe's uneaten Champion's Dinner home to the dog.

For a long time to come, Wimbledon '81 will stick in the memory, and probably in a few throats as well. Right from the first Monday when McEnroe declared war on the umpiring system till the final Saturday when he gave the finger to his hosts at the Champion's Dinner, the scene was set for the biggest culture clash since King Kong paid a trip to New York. Disruptive, noisy, unrepentant, twitchy and yet magnetically likeable, Wimbledon's new champion polarized the feelings of the world as it turned its eyes and ears towards a tiny path of real estate in one of London's most exclusive suburbs.

He was a spoiled brat or a misunderstood genius, depending on where you stood. And where that was depended on whether you were young or old, a Brit or a Yank, a blimp or a lout. For every umpire who sympathized with McEnroe's braying anguish over incompetent line judging, you could find another who, in the words of one, 'would like to grind my heel in his mush'.

Even the world's journalists, a matey crew whose shared problems and pressures and deadlines normally transcend all linguistic and cultural barriers, got shirty with each other at a McEnroe press conference. Insults were slung. Harsh words. Punches. Only one thing united us all, and that was that when it came to playing tennis John McEnroe was a gifted and brilliant champion.

It was also the Wimbledon of the Grunt. 'Hargh!' bellowed Jimmy Connors as he slammed his way to that epic semi-final against Bjorn Borg. 'Yurgh! Erch!' Connors is the world's first tennis player who you can follow on the wireless. These days, people don't come to see him play. They come to hear him play. 'I'm grunting well this year,' he declared to us in one of the tournament's lighter moments. He is the leading exponent of the all-snort game.

Grunting, we were informed, is a way of getting rid of all that tension that would otherwise have you forming ulcers or carping at the linesmen. It is also a reflex action at the end of a tiring match. McEnroe does it. Brian Gottried does it, even the lovely, elegant, graceful Mrs Evert Lloyd does it. 'I've heard kids in the parks back home doing two-handed backhands and going "Ugh!" ' said Connors. In the United States, coaches are telling their pupils how to do it. I am absolutely serious.

It was also the Wimbledon of Jeff Borowiak's bike. Let me set the scene. Gawping spectators stand ten-deep outside the lofty entrance to the All England Club. British Leyland limmos chauffeured by sun-tanned girls wait in a purring line to whisk the superstars from club to hotel. Suddenly, there's a ripple of shock from an outside court. Jeff Borowiak unsung, unseeded, has just put out Brian Gottfried, number seven in the pecking order. The crowd strains to get a glimpse, a touch, of this latest hero. Borowiak walks off court, goes past the limousines and takes the padlock off a very old rusty bike that has been chained to the railings outside the South-West hall. He gets on to it and pedals off into town.

Later, Borowiak explains. A modest soul, he's not billeted at one of the flashy hotels where the courtesy cars collect. Nor do his funds run to hiring one of his own. So he went to the bike shop down the road and lashed out five quid on this terrible old bone-shaker.

Weather-wise, the first week was the bad one. A woman wearing a ski-jersey, woolly tights and sou'wester told me she blamed it on the space shuttle. 'Since the Americans sent that thing up,' she said, 'we haven't had two decent days together.' The ballboys had purple knees to match their purple and green uniforms. When it wasn't cold it was very rainy. Perhaps the All England Club should have got Dannimac to sponsor the tournament.

Even a monsoon wouldn't have deterred those single-minded souls who queued outside the gates to the men's final. And when

I say queue, I don't mean your average 20-minute work-out down at the Post Office. This was a mega-queue which had begun to form on the first Saturday. Led by Mike, a banker wearing the costume of a jester, and his mate Nigel, a stockbroker who had come dressed as Andy Pandy, a good 500 stalwarts had pitched camp on the pavement in order to bag the prime standing positions round the edge of Centre Court.

They brought tents, TVs, radios and portable stoves. They slept on airbeds and deckchairs and covered themselves in anything from sleeping bags to bin liners. There was no pushing in. Each new arrival had to sign the waiting list. On the night of the final Friday, they even held a street party. 'I suppose,' said one of them, 'you could call this Alternative Wimbledon.'

Inside the grounds, though, Wimbledon's more traditional delights were being enjoyed. Pimms and champagne flowed in the commercial hospitality tents, beer and Yugoslav Riesling in the public sector.

For the millions of people who didn't have tickets, there was the consolation of the familiar voice of Dan Maskell, evoking an English midsummer as they sat by their television sets. While John McEnroe was dragging an indignant Wimbledon into a troubled new era, one Ribena-cheeked old colonel summed up its past. 'I got as tight as a newt last night,' he hrumphed, 'and when I got home I found I'd sat on a strawberry.'

The British Way to Court Disaster

Ronald Atkin

Williamsburg, deep in the heart of that part of America we once cherished as a colony until George Washington got a bit uppity, attracts 2,500,000 visitors a year – testimony to its popularity as a permanent monument to British defeat.

So it was with a neat sense of history that Britain's tennis ladies were invited to Williamsburg to have the portcullis dropped on them by their United States sisters in the annual embarrassment of the Wightman Cup.

Colonial Williamsburg is a thinking person's Disneyland in which the costumed locals strut the pavements in bonnets and three-cornered hats. Though its charm is a trifle plastic, the bit players perform their role conscientiously, an example which has been followed for the past three days by the Americans on the tennis courts at the impressive stadium of William and Mary College as they moved irresistibly towards their 45th Wightman Cup in 55 attempts.

There are plans to offer the Wightman Cup a permanent American home in Williamsburg, which may be good for the tourist business, but will not do much for anyone in the area looking for a closely contested tennis match.

As even the British admit, we need to make more of a contest of it. There is regular talk of turning the event into the United States v Europe along the lines of golf's Ryder Cup, but this is just as regularly poo-poohed by the British and even the American tennis officials anxious to preserve tradition and to hell with the final score.

The social scene surrounding the match is pleasant indeed, with receptions aplenty, though it is doubtful whether the after-dinner comment of the exotically-named President of the US Tennis Association, Hunter L. Delatour Junior, that 'whatever happens on court I know we will all be happy about it' is necessarily shared by the British team.

It is not stretching the analogy to say that for Britain's tennis women to challenge the United States in serious competition annually is like Wycombe Wanderers being invited to play Liverpool.

The Americans offer a different squad the chance to beat us every year, and they could turn out three or four teams capable of doing it. The current United States side contains one girl, Pam Shriver, who has played in the Wightman Cup previously (five years ago) and four newcomers, while Britain needed to invite Virginia Wade, at the regal age of 38, to appear in the competition for a 19th time.

The dismay when Miss Wade lost to the 16-year-old Kathy Rinaldi on the opening night was profound. Here was a match Britain had publicly banked on winning, and Miss Wade was, with good reason, a little nettled that she is still expected to shoulder the burden of our hopes after all these years.

She pointed out, 'It is difficult for me at this stage of my career to have the sort of dependence placed on me because that's not the way I'm playing any more. I like to go on court now knowing it's not the end of the world if I lose.'

Whether Britain should consider selecting someone who cheerfully admits she plays nowadays for fun rather then glory is debatable, and it was tempting to suggest she should be nudged nearer the exit after the dismal way she lost to Miss Rinaldi.

But on Friday evening, contrary as ever, she was catapulting about the court tugging an erratic Sue Barker in her slipstream and playing with all her old zest and skill to beat Paula Smith and Candy Reynolds 7–5, 3–6, 6–1.

That British victory, the first in America for eight years, cut our deficit to 3–1 and did the box office a good turn by prolonging the contest into the final day on Saturday.

The win, welcome if unexpected, literally lifted the rest of the British camp to their feet in fevered congratulation after the shock of seeing another trump card, Jo Durie, overturned by Miss Shriver, with distressing ease 6–3, 6–2, to put the Americans 3–0 ahead.

Miss Durie's surge up the rankings this year has been spectacular, and included two wins, one an injury default, over the American girl. But on Friday night Miss Shriver was a different proposition from the player who lost in straight sets to Miss Durie in the semi-finals at Brighton a fortnight ago. On that occasion, she claims, she was travel-weary and 'at the end of my rope'. This time, after a 10-day break from the game, her tennis was newly minted.

She served impeccably, applied the pressure relentlessly, and never permitted the British number one to dominate from the net as she likes to do. Miss Durie, still learning her trade, allowed herself to be rushed and become a little flustered. One of her biggest weapons, the first serve, worked only intermittently and, worst of all, she failed to seize several opportunities to take control of the second set.

Little wonder that she said afterwards: 'I'm annoyed and frustrated. I just wanted to go out there and play it again. She took her chances to break me and I missed mine.'

As the top-rated player in Britain Miss Durie bears a heavy weight of responsibility. That pressure will increase when Miss Wade decides to call it a day, and will not lessen until we are able to bring talented young newcomers to her assistance.

In the depths of her post-match misery at Brighton, Miss Shriver had knocked the Wightman Cup, saying it would have no relevance until Britain produced a team capable of beating the best the United States has to offer.

Now, in the warm afterglow of victory in front of her home folk she admitted: 'One you come here and see all the ceremony and play for your country, you realise what a wonderful event it is. I hope it never changes.'

Friday's win over Jo Durie meant a lot more than revenge to the tall girl from Baltimore. Here only other appearance in the Wightman Cup was in 1978 at the Albert Hall, the last time Britain won the trophy, and it was a miserable experience.

She took time off from school to play, and lost both her singles – 'to Michelle Tyler, a girl who now works in Harrod's, or somewhere' – and the deciding doubles and she was in tears at the end.

When Pam got back to school she was ordered to write an essay on what had happened to her. 'My essay was a letter to God asking why I had been put in the position I was. I got an A.' In Williamsburg she earned an A-plus, first for beating Jo Durie and then for routing Sue Barker 6–0, 6–1 in 38 minutes to complete the formality of victory for the Americans.

Bath Buns, Ivy and Strawberries

Patrick Collins

'Mark my words,' said Max Roberston, staring down from the commentary box at the figure of John McEnroe, 'That young man's going to have a weight problem when he's a few years older.'

Christine Truman glanced up from her microphone and considered the belligerent New Yorker, muttering, glaring and stamping around Centre Court. 'Hmmm,' she said. 'He is getting a little chubby. Too many bath buns, I expect.'

Bath buns! I have long since forgotten the match, but the mental picture of McEnroe rampaging around the tea shops of south-west London will remain forever.

In a couple of sentences, the delightful Miss Truman had captured precisely the way in which Wimbledon sees itself: not so much a place but rather an attitude; marooned forever in the late twenties, when young chaps grew chubby on bath buns and fell for great big mountainous sports girls called Pam and played strenuous singles before prep and blushed modestly when they won and were jolly quick to pump the hand of their opponent in defeat.

It is a seductive illusion, and Wimbledon does its best to propagate it: grave, ivy-clad walls, strawberries upon the lawn, self-conscious curtsies to the Royal Box and the venerable Maskell gasping: 'Oooh, I say!' whenever the words will not come.

Everywhere there are echoes of an age which had abolished doubt, which dealt only in certainty. The tournament itself is known as 'The Lawn Tennis Championships', as if no other existed. 'Crazy', says Arthur Ashe, 'but you have to admire their conceit.'

And the men's event is, officially at least, 'The Gentlemen's

Singles Championship', carrying the prize of two Challenge Cups, one presented by King George V, the other presented by the All England Lawn Tennis and Croquet Club. The winner also receives quite a lot of money these days, but the official programme – with impeccable taste – rather glosses over that unsavoury fact.

Suggest that the place is somewhat less than perfect and you are made to feel a distinct outsider, rather as if one had criticized the Queen Mother's dress sense.

I remember offering a few mild remarks about spectator facilities a year or two back, and being taken aside by the eminent tennis correspondent of a national newspaper, 'I think,' he said 'that you were rather . . . naughty.'

It was the kind of nursery rebuke which one could receive only at Wimbledon. 'Naughty . . . super . . . chubby', such is the currency of conversation, and its all serves to strengthen the illusion that all is as it was, that Britannia is still ruling the waves, even if Miss Lenglen is doing rather too well out on court.

The truth, of course, is far less beguiling. The illusion may require us to believe that 'The Ladies Singles Championship' is contested solely by Betjeman's sports girls. But in these ambivalent times, a line like: 'See the strength of her arm, as firm and hairy as Hendren's,' would bring a writ in the morning post.

The sounds of Wimbledon have also suffered a dramatic change. No longer: 'Ed-vahn-tage, Mrs Wills-Moody', or 'Game and second set to Tilden.' Oh, no. The sound of Wimbledon '81 will be: 'You really called that ball out? You blind, for Chrissake?'

Or, even worse, as you hand over the ransom for the golf-course car park and churn the hub caps through the fairway mud: 'Who wants two together? Who's got tickets for Ladies Day?' The timeless cry of ye olde Wimbledon tout, recycling his Cup Final profits.

Tradition, as generations of American tourists have discovered, is an expensive commodity. Wimbledon tickets are expensive, a large round of Wimbledon drinks requires a cheque book. And to afford the strawberries and cream ritual, it is necessary to win the championship.

Even the cost would be acceptable if spectators were well treated. They are not. In order to survive a modern Wimbledon, it is advisable to train for a week at Harrods summer sale. There you will learn about crowds; you will learn to queue and occasionally to push; to suffer frustration and exhaustion and treat those two imposters just the same. A week in the cutlery department and you will be ready to take on both the Wimbledon fortnight and the London Marathon.

For Wimbledon is largely about queuing. Everyone who makes the journey to the Championships knows that far too many others are making that same journey. They will be admitted, but not all will see a ball struck.

Yet the aura of the place renders them curiously passive. Like the infantrymen at the Somme, they will stand around sullen and silent, and if you touch upon the subject of the organising committee with them, they will say: 'Oh, well, I suppose they know what they're doing. It *is* Wimbledon.'

And therein lies both its power and its attraction. It *is* Wimbledon and, as such, invulnerable.

It is, above all, the tournament which the players want to win, which is why the best in the world turn up year after year. They are the people who make it worthwhile, yet one suspects that even they are slightly overawed by the place.

In 1973, they screwed up sufficient courage to stay away. The men's championship was instantly reduced to a farce, with a final involving Kodes and Metreveli. Yet back they came the following year, and one felt that they were slightly shame-faced. Even they seemed to subscribe to the ludicrous myth that the tournament is bigger than its players.

Yet, in a way, one can understand the attraction. When one has played the US Open at Flushing, with the stench of hot dogs wafting through the polluted air and the big jets screaming over from La Guardia every couple of minutes; when one has toiled through the superbly presented but essentially artificial American indoor circuit, Wimbledon must seem a desirable, inspiring stage on which to play your tennis.

So the great ones will be back again this year: Borg and McEnroe, Connors and Evert. And they will excite us with their skill and their cunning, and when it is over we shall, hopefully conclude that '81 was one of the great Wimbledons.

The staid old lady, clad in ivy, will accept the credit. And if you listen carefully, you may just hear her murmur, in cultured and complacent tones: 'Yes, it *did* go rather well, didn't it? But then . . . it usually does.'

The Ace of Clubs

Reginald Brace

One writer in the 1930s described Ilkley tennis tournament as the Nimbledon of the North. A cute phrase scarcely reflected the quality of performance, but it did capture the mobility of the scene when play is in progress.

There are 15 grass courts, three hard and two covered. Seen from a vantage point on the hills overlooking the ground the club seems to have been taken over by a colony of white-clad worker ants.

Back and forward, side to side they scurry as the air rings to the plonk of ball on racket and the occasional heartfelt curse. Only the nimblest survive at Ilkley tournament which begins today with a gargantuan programme of 31 events embracing every age group from under 12s to veterans.

This year there are 516 entrants. By the end of the week the referee, Geoffrey Cutter, intends to complete 1,030 matches whatever the weather might have in store. It is Yorkshire's biggest tournament and numerically one of the largest in the country.

As this is the club's centenary year there will be a message of goodwill from the Lawn Tennis Association who are understandably delighted that at time when senior tournaments in Britain are dwindling – the figure dropped from 76 in 1970 to 56 last year – the Ilkley event continues to flourish.

'It is very important to retain tournaments like Ilkley,' said Peter Johns, the LTA's secretary. 'Life is not easy for the tournaments in the middle – the events which fall between the purely local and the big money promotions. Ilkley is one of those middling tournaments designed for people who want to play tennis but have no ambitions to be globe-trotters, playing the game for a livelihood. Tournaments like Ilkley are part of the backbone of the British game.'

The Ilkley club was formed in February 1880 at a meeting chaired by a local cleric, the Rev. A. B. Ottley. Membership was restricted to 60 families, the minimum age was 14, and to launch the venture 20 rackets were bought at 12s. 6d. each along with six dozen balls.

This first tournament was held five years later. There were 61 entries in five events and the winner of the men's singles was appropriately an Ilkley man, Edward Fletcher, who had been the first winner of the Yorkshire title a year earlier. Mr Fletcher, a solicitor in Leeds, carried on playing until he was over 70 and when he died an obituary mourned the passing of 'the best type of English Christian gentleman'.

With intervals for the two wars the tournament has been held every year since Fletcher's triumph in 1885. The rival attractions of golf and cycling were fended off at the beginning of the century and although the club decided to dispense with croquet in 1914, the game of lawn tennis, and the Ilkley tournament, prospered.

Between the wars the men's singles was dominated by Yorkshire's Colin Gregory, Jack Chamberlain, Jack Harrison and Henry Burrows. In the period after the Second World War the tournament adopted a new role as a stepping stone in the development of young British players.

Roger Taylor, Mark Cox, Mike Davies, David Lloyd, Graham Stilwell, John Feaver, Gerald Battrick, John Paish, John Clifton, Stanley Mattews, Peter Curtis and Paul Hutchins are among the Davis Cup men who have paraded their skills on the Ilkley club's riverside courts. Mike Hann, the Leeds player who would have played in the Davis Cup if he had reached his peak in a different era, won the title three years in a row in 1956-7-8.

Elizabeth Starkie, Rita Bentley, Nell Truman and Winnie Shaw are leading women who have played at Ilkley. And in their later years there were glimpses of the mellow artistry of Jaroslav Drobny, Bobby Wilson and the indestructible Dane, Torben Ulrich.

The reason for Ilkley's survival, however, does not rest in its stars, welcome though they are to spectators and opponents alike. It is to be found in the loyal support of county players, club members, juniors and happy hackers who comprise the bulk of its mammoth entry.

Places

These are the uncrushable competitors who sign in every year – many of them living under canvas or in caravans in the makeshift village which sprouts on the adjacent cricket field, and all of them ready to endure the notorious vicissitudes of the weather. Some years are better than others, but it is an unusual Ilkley tournament which is not bedevilled by rain.

Such are the demands made by the weather on the referee's patience and ingenuity it would appear to be a job guaranteed to slice years off that long-suffering official's life, but curiously there have been only five Ilkley referees in living memory.

Clement Pflaum, a stern but respected disciplinarian, did the job from 1902 until his death in 1939; Arthur Kay filled the post for several years after the Second World War; Bernard (Bunny) Austin for 20 years until 1974, Eric Wild for four years, and finally the present holder of the office, Geoffrey Cutter.

Bunny Austin, now nudging 70, ran the tournament like the commander of a Panzer battalion, and woe betide anyone who disobeyed orders. 'People *may* leave court if they wish' was his time-honoured announcement as rain started to pour. Then 'Players *will* come off court' when it became worse.

His microphone manner was sometimes reminiscent of a Nuremberg rally, but he did a difficult job well, and never lost sight of his target of finishing the tournament on time. One year he completed more than 1,100 matches in five days, including an interruption for rain.

'Sometimes I had to be firm and crack the whip,' he recalled 'People had to be reminded that the referee had power to scratch. But through the years it has always been a friendly, matey tournament particularly devoted to helping young players to improve. We flirted with sponsorhip, latterly with Green Shield, but when that ended six years ago the tournament reverted to its old style. I believe it is better like this. Unless you are getting major stars, lavish sponsorship can often be a waste. The present format is much more enjoyable for all concerned.'

Mr Austin remembers the time when he had to use a little discretion in pronoucing the name of a Portuguese player called Soras. With the agreement of the player, he mispronounced it throughout the week.

On another occasion he had to reprimand a young player for

some indiscretion. The youngster went on to lose and when asked why he looked so miserable replied: 'Well, I only had one ball.' Told that he should have reported the fact to the referee he said: 'No point. It was him who chewed the other off.'

Bunny Austin was a benevolent martinet whose name is firmly implanted in the folklore of a tournament which seems to have been around as long as Ilkley Moor itself, and attracts characters like Bjorn Borg collects Wimbledon titles.

This week sees the 84th instalment of Ilkley's long-running story of tennis folk. Wet or fine. And only the nimblest will succeed.

Discourtesies on the Court

Julian Barnes

Doris Hart, one of the 17 women champions on parade at Monday's *Wimbledon* (BBC 1 and 2), doesn't watch much tennis nowadays. Interviewed the other week on a warm-up show, she admitted that she didn't much care for the manner in which the game is currently played. Louise Brough concurred: 'I think the way we handled ourselves in those days was something special. We never sounded off at linesmen.'

Has anyone else found this Wimbledon one of the least enjoyable in recent years? The weather has been excellent, the standard of play high; Buster Mottram has been absent, and (unless I've struck particularly lucky) there hasn't been a single shot so far of Larry Adler sitting in the crowd. But despite these bonuses the event has been more of an agreeable duty than a fierce pleasure. Partly it's the lack of new players coming through; all those Borglets were eliminated early on, and some of the matches have exuded a wearying sense of *déjà joué*. Who cares whether the lanky, fretful Miss Shriver beats the lanky, fretful Miss Jordan this time or not?

But it's also something wider. A tournament can survive predictability of personnel, regular dominance by the same champions, and even a diminution of skill at the highest level. What it survives less well – and you don't have to come from Blimpsville and wear cavalry twill underpants to believe this – is the loss of the sporting ethos. McEnroe's behaviour has rightly attracted the attention of tennis moralists; but it's part of a wider decay. Nowadays we find ourselves sheepishly praising players not for behaving well, but for not behaving badly.

Examine them as they shake hands at the end of a match: from the expressions on their faces you would think the opponent was a VAT-man with herpes. Scott Davis played extremely well when losing to Lendl, as did 15-year-old Steffi Graf when falling to Jo Durie; but from the way they reacted at the end, you would have thought they had just had their mortgages foreclosed. Nobody smiles in defeat any more; and winners give no more than a wry pout.

Other minor but essential courtesies are also disappearing. Few players congratulate their opponent on a good shot (the maximum offered is a sort of snarled 'Yup' which really conceals a self-lacerating 'Christ, how come I didn't see *that* a mile off?). Nobody apologizes any more for gaining a point from a net-cord. Few bother to inquire after the health of an opponent who falls over. It's perhaps surprising that the habit of holding up new balls is still retained; though I suppose the gesture is now less of civility than a butch warning: 'Listen, sucker,' it says, 'with the help of these I'm *really* gonna bust your ass.'

But if the game has now become more crudely defined in terms of victory, money and ego – in interview the top players are almost psychopathic with solipsism – the tone of the accompanying TV commentary has also shifted down market. there have been times over the years when Dan Maskell's little mannerisms (like doggedly calling a player by his opponent's name, or the ten-year struggle to articulate the surname 'Navratilova') have got on the viewing wick; but Maskell is a sage, wit and master of the English tongue when set beside his colleagues, most of whom seem to believe that the microphone will conk out unless you constantly huff banalities into it. One of the troubles, perhaps, is that there simply isn't all that much to say about tennis. This column would normally kill in defence of Virginia Wade; but even she can fall into the rut of waffle: those 60 seconds during changeover don't *have* to be filled with words.

As for having a Great Champion guesting at the mike: well, last year's experiment with Bjorn Borg made us all realize that the true spelling of his Christian name is Byawn; and the performance this year of Billie Jean King has certainly lacked the sharpness she used to impart to her volleys. She even commits that basic commentatorial double-fault of confidently reading a player's mind during the changeover, as if she were Madame Sosostris. 'There you see Chris', Mrs King informed us as an expressionless Mrs Lloyd rested on her chair, 'thinking about her concentration.' Or maybe she was just concentrating on her thinking.

So all viewers who hold Wimbledon dear should send hampers of royal jelly to Dan Maskell and pray for his eternal sprightliness. Trying to guess who might succeed him from out of the present kerfuffle of commentators makes the work of Kremlinologists seem a doddle; but if anyone is nosing ahead in the struggle to follow Dan Chernenko, then it must presumably be Gerald Williams. Barely a couple of years ago, Williams was restricted to his unctuous-elf interviews with the players; then he was elevated to studio sage for the evening highlights; now he has been further raised to Centre Court commentator.

That Williams presents a verbal contrast to the Maskell era was made clear during the Durie–Graf game. His strategic summary of the English girl's failings went like this: 'I still think she's got the abdabs on the forehand volley.' His real forte, though, is as a purveyor of cute background colour. Of Carina Karlsson: 'She tells me that some of the money she earns here she will give to hungry people – she has a great sense of hunger in the world.' Well, jolly good; but it was such a Miss World moment that you expected Williams to add, 'A blonde with hazel eyes, Carina is five foot six and studying beauty science at Uppsala University.' A moment later, after a brightish rally from Miss Karlsson, Gerry was back as it again: 'She's clever girl, on court and off it. She's reading Solzhenitsyn at the moment.'

The rival styles of Dan and Gerry were given dramatic form during Monday's march-past of champions. Dan was down on the turf doing the public address, while Gerry was sitting on the Maskell woolsack up in the commentary box. After Dan had introduced each champion in terms of her tennis pedigree, Williams would chip in like Crawfie with his own homelier touches. Margaret Court, we were pleased to discover, is married to Barry, owns four children and has just been going to Bible college. Angela Mortimer 'lives in happy domesticity with her husband John Barrett'; who would deny her that?

Second from the end came a nut-brown Alice Marble. Maskell filled us in on her Wimbledon record, younger viewers tried to remember if they had ever seen her on film, the lady herself walked forward to collect her glass daffodil jug from the Duke of Kent, and Williams intoned: 'It's wonderful to see her here because she's undergone surgery five times in recent years.'

Idols of Clay

Laurie Pignon

Sadly there are those who will only remember the British Hard Court Championships as the turning point in lawn tennis history. They will recall that on the sometimes dusty, sometimes windswept red clay courts of the West Hants Club on the leafy fringe of Bournemouth in April 1968 the game became honest.

This was the first time anywhere in the world that a few genuine and some phoney amateurs faced professionals in open competition, and we reporters, like the rest of the game, applauded the dawn of a brave new world. In our ideological innocence, or was it ignorance, we celebrated the end of an era in which strife was rife, and welcomed the new one in which those who controlled the tournaments and those who played in them were at last on the same side. Or so we thought.

It was an English spring and our hopes were Bournemouth blossom bright, and thoughts of future bans and boycotts and lumbering lawsuits did not invade even our worst nightmares. Every day brought its new excitement. At the start Mark Cox beat Pancho Gonzales and so wrote his own small page for posterity by becoming the first amateur to beat a professional; and it ended with Ken Rosewall defeating Rod Laver in a final which won him £1,000.

Such was Bournemouth's date with destiny, but there are those of us who remember the tournament for different reasons, nostalgic reasons, when our world was daffodil young and the Bournemouth Belle steamed her way out of Waterloo Station.

Twenty-two years earlier – in 1946 – the British Hard Court Championships had been my first Fleet Street by-line. I discovered our press room to be a small tent next door to the referee's hut where Col. John Legg used to conduct affairs with military magniloquence, and such was his command that in spite of interruptions for rain and the men's singles and doubles being decided over five sets he completed the events in six days.

It was in this same tent, put up especially for us and taken down each year, that one of our most respected lady reporters, whilst taking a rest on a rather warm afternoon, went to sleep with a lighted cigarette in her hand and set her hair alight. The commotion that followed was equalled only some time later when another unsuspecting reporter discovered a grass snake in his bag of luncheon sandwiches. His curious reaction would not be taken amiss today in a modern disco.

Nor were we without music in those days, for Torben Ulrich, the Dane with a face of a prophet, and the touch of an angel with his racket, did not go anywhere without his clarinet.

Some of the older hotel guests, obviously not disciples of Benny Goodman, did not fully appreciate his nocturnal serenades, and more than once he could be found practising in a nearby telephone box.

In the pre-prize money days those who did not receive guarantees could at least afford their idiosyncrasies, and not only did these add to the amusement of the spectators, but they made a reporter's job easier. I remember going into the old dressing room at the West Hants where the rather testy attendant spent much of his time counting the bath towels or cleaning the richer competitors' shoes, and seeing something that even in those days was unusual. There was George Godsell and beside him two bags, one full of lemons, the other carrots. He was cutting the fruit in halves and rubbing them all over his body, and eating the carrots. George was a very polite chap and instead of taking umbrage answered my question as if he were stating the obvious: the lemons were to stimulate his body and make it more lithe and the carrots were to help him see the ball better. Of course, how silly of me to suppose otherwise. He reached the semi-finals that year.

The draw abounded with characters, and those of us old enough, like Lance Tingay and myself, to be weaned on Laurel and Hardy, Harry Roy and free tea tickets (for players as long as they remained in the mixed doubles) remember with great affection the adventures and misadventures of Howard Walton, especially at Bournemouth. It was his Valhalla, and for those seeking copy with an unusual slant Howard was the answer to a sub-editor's prayer.

He first arrived with two old rackets, as loosely strung as G-strings on a double bass, and claimed that he had learned the game from a six-penny secondhand book. He was a retriever whose cunning placements exasperated opponents and made them feel as if they were trying to hammer in six inch nails with a wet sponge. So successful was he that within two years he made the British Davis Cup team, but new rackets, pristine playing kit and the amenities of a dining room in a five-star hotel, which came with selection, had a drastic effect on his game.

His *pièce de résistance* took place on the Club House court at the West Hants where, finding it difficult to keep his feet, he sent for a washing-up bowl of water, and at each change of ends stood in it with his shoes and socks on. I never knew what effect it had on his feet, but it certainly did not help his opponent's concentration.

Bournemouth was not only a lot of fun but a stage on which we saw much courage, and none more so than from Eric Sturgess. In 1948 this elegant South African, who was one of the few great players not to win a Wimbledon singles, retained all his three titles at Bournemouth, but to do so he was on court all day, playing five matches, fifteen sets and 126 games.

Ironically, professionalism which provided the British Hard Courts Championships with its page of history was partly responsible for its demise, for in the crowded calendar it proved difficult to attract the right entry which would encourage sponsors and television alike.

If I had one wish to bequeath to the game it would be a successful BHC with men and women competing as they used to in those golden yesterdays – when sometimes we had a little laughter on court.

People

The Voice of the Game

Julie Welch

If it were possible to bottle people's voices, some whizz-kid businessman would have made his fortune by corking up Dan Maskell's and marketing it worldwide as 'Essence of Wimbledon'.

Mr Maskell (it seems rather brash to call this august phenomenon just Maskell, let along something as disrespectfully matey as Dan) is Britain's best loved and most accomplished sports commentator. He would probably make a compelling job of describing a 6 a.m. army uniform inspection. He is scrupulously well informed, charmingly modest and enviably fluent and when he turned 73 in April was putting in the sort of day's work that would have a mule complaining of exploitation. What he doesn't know or instinctively understand about tennis could be written on Bjorn Borg's toenail.

Being the BBC's major voice on tennis is a year-round job, but Maskell comes into fullest bloom around the last week of June. To the millions of people whose closest link with the All England Club is provided by Radio Rentals, Dan Maskell *is* Wimbledon, encapsulating these British middle-class midsummer rites just as John Arlott embodied cricket. He is the Mr Big behind the sudden spate of urgent dental repairs and great aunts' burials that afflicts our working population for the same two weeks every year. Arthur Ashe once said, 'If I woke up at 4 a.m. in Timbuctoo in a fever and heard the inimitable voice of Dan Maskell I would know I was listening to Wimbledon. It just wouldn't sound right if I heard a different voice.'

Your Tennishood lives with his second wife Kay in an elegant bungalow on a hillside within lobbing distance of London. A most approachable and courteous chap, there are none the less several questions you don't ask him. The major one is 'Who the hell is Bill Tilden?'

Shortly before I spoke to him, he had completed another commentating marathon for the BBC. Britain had taken on Italy in the Davis Cup and won. Maskell, who as coach to the All England Club from 1929 to 1959 forged the most successful Davis Cup side in the history of British tennis – the all-conquering Perry and Austin team of '33 to '36 – was as drained as he was delighted.

'I spent seven hours in the commentary box on the first day, and having been associated with the competition for so many years, and being a team man in any case, my involvement was more personal than normal. I am generally regarded as a man of integrity, privately and publicly, and I like to think I have taught myself to be reasonably restrained. But we're flesh and blood and we are patriotic and we sometimes do get a rush of blood to the head, and I think it would be wrong to suppress too much. I don't think a Briton commentating on the Davis Cup *should* be neutral. It would be false.'

This informed sincerity explains a lot of Maskell's popularity. One or two commentators might match him for vocal equipment but it only takes a couple of minutes before you realize that what you're listening to is beautifully modulated twaddle. Maskell probably speaks Serbo-Croat better than he does twaddle. And the viewers respond. Several years ago when Clive James, the *Observer's* television critic, directed some gleeful malice at Maskell's infectiously courtly style, letters of outraged protest arrived in sackfuls. The maestro, like the Queen Mother, is a national institution.

'A commentator', he says, 'is very privileged. You have the opportunity, as Lord Reith put it when he was head of the BBC, to "inform, entertain and explain". I go in with the feeling that I'm sitting next to someone on Centre Court who knows a bit, but not that much – who might be asking, "Why did he do that?" "Why was that backhand a flop?" I try to give the viewer a deeper understanding and experience of what is going on.' At the same time, he has to avoid boring the plimsolls off people who really do know the sport.

He has a lot of experience on which to draw. Born in Fulham on 11 April 1908, he became a tennis buff at the tender age of 12, spending his school holidays ballboying at Queens Club round the corner from where he lived. His father was an engineer and

Maskell Junior was encouraged to follow suit when he left school. Instead he decided to combine business with passion and joined the full-time staff at Queens. The 15-year-old ballboy took home 12 shillings a week.

His appetite was not confined to tennis. In winter, he played rackets and at 16½ he was Britain's Junior Professional Rackets Champion – Albert Cooper, who he beat in straight sets in the final, went on four years later to become the world champion.

Football was another source of pleasure, and in later years he and Fred Perry used to train with the Arsenal side that contained Bastin, Hume and Jack. 'I saw the apprenticeship of Eddie Hapgood,' he says, 'and I'm still an Arsenal fan.' Of all sports, though, perhaps his favourite was ski-ing. 'At heart, I'm an amateur, although my life has been professional.'

As a professional, he forfeited his right to take part in the Wimbledon championships or represent Britain in the Davis Cup, and that is something he still regrets. Nevertheless, in 1927 he won the newly established title of World Professional Champion, and remained British Champion for 16 years, so there was ample compensation. His job as coach to the Davis Cup team was another satisfaction. 'I've always preferred doubles to singles. If I play golf, I like to play foursomes – I'm a gregarious animal, not a strong individualist, and I got so much pleasure coaching individuals to become team members. That is why I like working for the BBC – it is a most professional team in which everyone backs everyone else up. I feel so lucky and privileged, as anyone should do who is able to follow something they love and get paid for doing it. I could never have been a person going to and from the City every day. I like helping others. If I had my time over again, I would choose to be a doctor.'

Maskell worked with dotors during the war, helping to rehabilitate injured air crew, for which he was awarded the OBE in 1945. Again he feels he was privileged – 'I was working with one of the finest medical teams in the world. Some of the men were terribly badly injured, yet instead of being bitter they were desperate to get back into the air again. When I returned to Wimbledon and coaching, I knew much more about what made men tick. I could teach men to give more than they knew they could give. I was lucky – I had a creative war rather than a destructive one, and temperamentally I'm creative.'

This recurring fulfilment might tempt you to think that Maskell's life has been liberally spread with jam. It is a judgement that sticks in the throat when you learn that 11 years ago his son Jamie died in an air crash – that in 1979 his first wife, Con, drowned in a swimming accident.

'I think work was the only thing that saved me,' he says, 'and I had some wonderful friends.' Among these was Kay, who like Maskell was now alone. She had known Con well and he had seen her daughter grow up. 'I just saw her at Queens one day, helping Jack Moore to reorganize the Lawn Tennis Foundation.' They married last year.

A pile of daily newspapers in Maskell's living room testified to the amount of homework he does. He reads every report avidly, cuts it out and files it; although commentating is his main job, he also doubles as the LTA's consultant on junior tennis.

His busiest time is during Wimbledon, when he gets up at seven, has breakfast, then barricades himself in his study for two hours to make notes – 'I inspect the general programme for the Centre Court and I also look who's playing outside to see whether there's likely to be any surprises.'

Whether it is for Wimbledon or any other tournament, this meticulous preparation is his way of psyching himself up. 'One particular day, when there were five matches on the Centre Court, I didn't really do my homework on one player. By the time I got to the club, I already felt wrong subconsciously. I had a really bad day. I didn't quite go blank, but I was really uncomfortable, even inarticulate once or twice. There was no adrenalin. I didn't have that little windy feeling under the heart. Normally I go home at night and replay what I've said – just to see, for instance, if I've been using the same adjective too many times.' That evening, he could not face listening to himself.

By 11, Maskell will have arrived at the All England Club and made a visit to the press room – 'to see if Borg's broken his neck.' After that, he goes to the commentator's room, finalizes his notes and has 'a general natter' with the producer about the way they think the day ought to shape up. In his long career, he has had more producers than Zsa Zsa Gabor has been through husbands. 'Some have had an aesthetic feeling about

Wimbledon. Some have had a hard news approach. Some think that if humour is there is should not be missed. It's up to them. The whole show is under their control. We are just the front men.'

One of the few commentators who appreciates the value of the judicious silence, Maskell's golden rule is to clam up the moment the first shot of the rally has been struck. Not even a suspended hiss of admiration has been known to escape him. 'I've broken the rule twice; not through excitement, but because I didn't shut up in time from the previous rally.' Not so long ago, such a rally would end with an appreciative 'Ooh I say' from the master. It became a catchphrase. Wary of parody, perhaps, he has dignifiedly excised it from his repertoire.

Another unforgettable line was uttered when, some years back, a fresh-faced teenager appeared at Wimbledon to a reception that many pop stars would have envied. His name was Bjorn Borg, and as a party of autograph-hunting teenage girls pounded in pursuit of him across the Centre Court, Maskell was there to exclaim to the plugged-in millions, 'This is sacrilege. She's wearing high heels.'

Let us hope that such a voice will be floating through the airwaves for many years to come.

Fancy Pants

Ted Tinling

On a scorching August day in 1951, I was sweltering in the primitive customs shed of an airstrip on the Canadian border, when the customs inspector pulled out of my luggage some rather transparent nylon tennis panties I had promised to take to a friend in Toronto. In those days one could have unforeseen entry-permit problems: there had already been some difficulty over mine, and for a time it seemed doubtful I would be allowed to continue my journey. I felt cut off and miles from a friendly face. To add considerably to my bad temper, the inspector waved the flimsy garments around for all his colleagues to inspect.

'What, Mr Tinling, no lace this year?' he asked suddenly with a grin. The tension was immediately relaxed, and I was surprised he recognized my name. Such was the power of Gussy's panties. After that I knew my entry permit was going to work out all right.

The story of Gussy Moran and the lace-edged panties that I made for her in 1949 still remains one of the most unlikely happenings in the many legends of tennis. Gussy's panties caused shock waves that reverberated from Alaska to Antarctica. On the way they even led the English vicar of St Andrew's Church, Buenos Aires, to preach a sermon, the theme of which was the sinful implications of wearing this unsuspecting garment.

Years later it is still almost impossible to understand how a yard of lace, added to a player's normal undergarment and barely seen at five-minute intervals, could cause such a furore.

In 1977 the extraordinary Gussy story was still prominently quoted in almost every review of Wimbledon's 100 year history. To understand it one must also understand the unique news exposure of the Wimbledon championships and the out-of-proportion importance that can be attached to quite small happenings there. Major Wimbledon controversies have been related many times to items of women's tennis wear. In the past, these have been brought on by the chauvinism of a tennis establishment that did not appoint a woman to its committee until 1982. Whether the *cause célèbre* was showing one's wrists for the first time, as May Sutton did in 1905, or Suzanne Lenglen's frocks 'indecently' revealing a woman's natural silhouette in 1919, the resulting indignation stemmed each time from Wimbledon's erstwhile all-male philosophy at its worst.

Besides, before TV coverage, tennis was reported to the world exclusively by men. Today there are more and more women reporting the game. Had this been the case in 1949 Gussy's panties could not have caused the same shock reaction.

But very few things in life derive from a single cause, and like the roots of some ageing tree, the Gussy episode had its origins in a complex tangle of happenings that had gone before.

The era of masculinity in both the style and dress of women's tennis was spearheaded by Alice Marble in the late 1930s and was carried over to the post-war years by Louise Brough, Margaret Osborne, Pauline Betz and Pat Todd. One of the major factors in the explosive reaction to Gussy's panties was the conscious, and subconscious, revulsion against this masculinity that was still obvious in tennis even four years after the war had ended.

Christian Dior's Paris 'New Look' in 1947 created an international hunger for a return to femininity and sexual attraction in clothing. This was just beginning to find expression in the designer collections, but not yet in the sportswear of the late 1940s. In fact, Pauline Betz recalls that in 1946 sportswear hardly existed, and it was actually impossible to buy a tennis dress.

As I had been a pre-war designer of evening clothes and wedding gowns, and as I was also preconditioned to femininity by the glamour cult of Lenglen, I was the first to rebel against the uniform appearance of the post-war tennis players. In 1947 I conducted a strong campaign for femininity in tennis, demanding, to begin with, that the girls wear dresses rather than the severe shorts and culottes they all wore at that time. When I was released from the Army after seven years in uniform and picking up the threads of my dress-designing career, Mrs Hilda Gannon came to me with a welcome commission. 'I would like you to design something very special for my daughter Joy's first appearance at Wimbledon.'

By tradition, Wimbledon dresses had always been white. Although there were then no written rules, I had no thought of offending anyone. But I did suggest that a diminutive sky-blue or rose-pink hem could be added to an otherwise conventional white dress.

Joy Gannon, who was later to become the mother of Buster Mottram, Britain's top-ranking player, made her Wimbledon debut in my 'new look' in 1947. She looked adorable, and apart from one flattering paragraph in a London evening newspaper, nobody regarded the coloured hem as the least bit unusual. In the following year, Britain's No. 1 player, Betty Hilton, approached me before the Wightman Cup matches. She asked me to design her a tennis dress that also featured a coloured hem. The dress I made had a coloured hemline, but half an inch wider that Joy's and with a zig-zag top edge to the colour. Betty duly appeared in my design in the opening Cup match.

Hazel Wightman, who had donated the Cup, was still captain of the US team. She had a very dominating personality and had decided some years before that she was the ultimate arbiter of tennis etiquette around the world, and it so happened that she took great exception to Betty's dress. Moreover Betty lost to Louise Brough 6–1, 6–1. At the time this was the quickest Cup defeat on record, but I was still amazed when Hazel announced that Betty lost because she was self-conscious about the colour of her dress!

A short time afterwards the suntanned, shapely form of Gertrude Agusta Moran arrived in Europe from California. The press soon discovered the name 'Gussy' had been substituted as a more polite version of 'Goosy', the nickname one of her teenage boyfriends thought appropriate. 'Gorgeous' was added later.

Even at first sight, Gussy looked to me like a person who loved life, enjoyed being attractive, and enjoyed the excitement she gave to men. The late 1940s were the 'Lana Turner era' when curvaceous figures were emphasized. Gussy epitomized this with her provocative, sexy bodyline and a walk that had so much bounce she appeared to be treading on a succession of rubber balls. She had a beautifully modulated, laughing voice, and her skin had a lustrous California gleam. I thought of her as a person who actually shimmered.

This was also a time when American women's tennis probably enjoyed its greatest depth. When Gussy came into my life, she was, in fact, ranked fourth among the top ten women and was the US covered-courts national champion, which proves beyond argument that she was a first-class player.

For two years I wrote the first post-war tennis fashion column in a magazine called *British Lawn Tennis*, while Gussy did the same job in the counterpart magazine, *American Lawn Tennis*, so our names were well known to each other. Until 1949 we had never met, but Gussy wrote to me in the spring of that year telling me she was about to make her first trip to Wimbledon. She said she had Red Indian blood in her, and therefore was extremely fond of colour, always wearing bright ribbons in her hair, even around her wrists, and wanting as much colour as she could have in the clothes she hoped that I would design for her.

When she arrived in England and I took her some sketches the next day I had to explain that though there was no reference to 'all-white' in the Wimbledon entry form, I was convinced some stringent restrictions would be imposed. Gussy stared at me in disbelief.

Designing for a player as stimulating as Gussy, I first had to find a fabric that suited her ultra-feminine image. But in 1949 Britain we still had what were called 'Utility' restrictions on all fabrics and clothing: the government would not allow us more than five buttons on any dress; we were restricted to a limited yardage around the hem; the seams of every dress could not exceed a certain number. All this naturally posed a lot of problems for designers.

Looking for an appropriate fabric. I approached a number of my influential textile friends until Nance Ellis, then head of public relations at the Celanese Corporation, produced out of a secret drawer a highly prized, experimental sample of soft knitted rayon. More that a quarter of a century later this probably sounds very prosaic, but at the time it was an absolute curiosity and a pioneering miracle.

I thought of Gussy as a shimmering personality and, to capture this image, I decided to trim her dress with white satin.

People

She was absolutely delighted with the dress but, three hours later, back in my office, I received a call. Gussy was agitated, asking what she was going to wear underneath.

I had been completely unaware that Gussy had always worn shorts, that she truly had nothing to wear under a tennis dress because she had never owned one. 'What you wear underneath is up to you,' I told her with some scepticism. 'I do not think your underclothes are my responsibility.'

Gussy explained that she was playing Margaret duPont in the semis of the Queen's Club tournament the next day and would not have time to go shopping for anything at all. We both became rather irritable and finally she said, 'You'll have to make me something. You promised to take care of my tennis outfits.'

I had a French fitter at the time and told her, 'We have got to make Miss Moran some panties.' She frowned, but eventually produced some panties made from the left-overs of the dress fabric. 'They look heavy and dull,' I said, when she showed them to me. 'We cannot have any colour, so let's try some lace around on the legs!'

My fitter returned with some dainty 'handkerchief' lace, and again I thought we had missed out completely, remembering Gussy's startling mahogany-tanned limbs. Spectators never see championship tennis from close quarters, and I felt what we wanted was some lace with a bold design that would at least be visible from time to time in the stands when Gussy served. We finished up with coarse cotton lace my mother would have called 'kitchen' lace, because it was often used on household linen. So the notorious lace panties were born.

Wimbledon 'Ladies' Day' duly arrived with my prediction coming true. Notices were put up in all the women's dressing rooms, which read, 'Competitors are required to wear *all-white* clothing.'

The fireworks really began the day before Wimbledon at the annual Hurlingham garden party, arranged to give the players some carefree practice on grass when all the other clubs were closed under the no-Sunday-play rule. Gussy appeared in her new outfit, and before I knew what was happening, a friend came to me saying, laughingly, 'I think you've cost me my husband.' I was taken aback. 'What do you mean?' I asked. 'All the men are lying on their stomachs watching Gussy,' was her reply.

I went to the court to find some twenty photographers in this position. Out of the blue the *Life* magazine photographer appeared and asked for a court where he could take some exclusive pictures of Gussy smashing, guaranteeing a tantalizing peep of the panties. At the time *Life* was the world's most influential magazine. Overnight, Gussy was shown to the world not just as a tennis player but as a sex symbol. The next day, Gussy, locked in her hotel suite, was besieged by reporters wanting to know whether she was really going to wear the panties at her Wimbledom debut.

'Will she?' 'Won't she?' was the press room question of every hour. At Wimbledon the press boys even organized a bulletin board that reported Gussy's latest available answer from her hotel room. Every fifteen minutes a different forecast was posted.

Eventually Gussy felt, and I think quite rightly, that the publicity was too much for her. She had a singles to play against a competent competitor, Bea Seal, today a well-known referee. Gussy's first match at Wimbledon was going to be a difficult one, so she wore some old shorts and shirt. As soon as she appeared the crowd started a questioning chorus right around the stands whispering, 'Where's the lace?' The 's' sound reverberated across the courts, and Gussy at first thought she was being hissed.

Then the world asked the same question, 'Where's the lace?' and Gussy's indecision was interpreted as a masterstroke of showmanship and public relations.

Her next match was schedule for the No. 1 Court. By now even I was on tenterhooks wondering if, and when, Gussy would appear in the panties outfit. To this day I make a point of never asking a player what she is going to wear before a match. Her tennis must come first, and I purposely avoid embarrassing the players or myself by raising a question that could lead to a disagreement.

But I was still officially the call-boy for the two main courts, a summer holiday hobby I had enjoyed doing for many years, and my heart was in my mouth when I went to fetch Gussy. With the immense publicity surrounding her, I now had a vested interest in what she was going to wear. It was one of those moments in life when one feels one's whole future depends on the outcome.

However, for her second match, Gussy glided out of the dressing room, giving me a conspiratorial wink and wearing my dress with the much-discussed panties underneath! The huge crowd, feeling its curiosity at last rewarded, approved loudly and welcomed Gussy with its fullest roar of applause. In fact, walking behind the two girls, I felt rather sorry for Gussy's opponent, Betty Wilford.

Then we saw a rush of reporters scrambling to their telephones. The official count said there were nearly one hundred present. The match was unimportant. Gussy was wearing the lace panties! On court, the photographers machine-gunned Gussy merrily, led by Bob Ryder of Associated Press whose afternoon's work earned him the 'Photographer of the Year' award. The *Life* magazine picture was also the 'Picture of the Week' feature.

Then the situation began to snowball out of all proportion. Gussy was inundated with requests for personal appearances – everything from hospitals and garden fêtes to judging beauty contests. The Marx Brothers, in London at the time, invited her to join their act. A racehorse, an aircraft, and a restaurant's special sauce were named after her. The following week she was voted 'Best-Dressed Sports Woman' by the US Fashion Academy. The whole thing was staggering.

Meanwhile the Establishment resorted to the time-honoured tactic, 'If you don't like something, just disregard it.' Nothing was said to me at all. There was even a cold war from my colleagues in the inner sanctum of Wimbledon. Very determinedly they made no mention whatever of Gussy in my presence. I could only go about my job as if nothing unusual had occurred.

On Thursday Gussy, still shocked by the enormous amount of press exposure she had experienced, was scheduled to make her first Centre Court appearance. This was a third-round singles against the diminutive Chinese prodigy, Gem Hoahing, whose total height was less than twice the circumference of Gussy's most expressive dimensions. The combined emotions of the whole situation proved far too much for Gussy, and she was beaten.

The day after her singles loss, Gussy was surprised to be summoned personally by Sir Louis Greig the Wimbledon chairman. She told me afterwards she expected to be reprimanded about her panties. But he only told her that her mixed-doubles partner, Bob Falkenburg, had pulled out of the event.

The imparting of this type of information is strictly the job of the tournament referee and in no way the normal function of the chairman of the world's most famous tennis club. I have often thought, and so has Gussy, that in sending for her Greig intended, in fact, to upbraid her about her panties, but confronted with her personal charm, and hearing her lilting voice in his office, he backed down.

The cold war against me went on until my birthday on 23 June. With other members of the staff I was having our customary late dinner in the Royal Tea-Room after the rush and pressures of the day.

The caterers produced an imposing birthday cake for me when Jean Borotra appeared and asked if he might join us. Seeing the birthday cake on the table, he immediately ordered champagne for everyone. Then, with his usual infectious chuckle, he exploded the whole situation by saying, 'I don't know if we should drink to your birthday or your panties.'

There was deathly silence. Jean looked startled, and I felt I was being engulfed in a wave of open hostility. But I kept all my thoughts on the matter to myself until an incident at Queen's Club. Notwithstanding the championships, Wimbledon always closes for the middle Sunday.

During Sunday lunch at Queen's Club, which does not close, a member of the Wimbledon committee attacked me bitterly before all the members. 'How could you do something so tasteless having been with us for so long?' he asked. 'What do you mean?' I inquired. His reply was quick and caustic. 'You have put sin and vulgarity into tennis.'

This accusation really released my bottled-up feelings. In the previous week I had been asked innumerable times for interviews about Gussy's panties. I still hoped the ridiculous storm would blow over and refused all comment, although I never denied having made the panties. One of my feature-writer friends had already called me that morning and was annoyed by my silence. Now I was ready.

So on Wimbledon's second Monday morning a column appeared in London's biggest circulation daily that quoted me as saying I did not understand the Establishment's attitude because I had added at least an extra thousand spectators each day to the Wimbledon attendance. This set the stage for the eventual showdown with Sir Louis Greig.

Gussy had refrained from wearing her panties outfit after her second-round singles. But she and Pat Todd reached the doubles final against the title-holders, Margaret duPont and Louise Brough. In spite of all that had already been written, the question of whether or not Gussy would wear the panties in the presence of Queen Mary once again hit the headlines.

Throughout the history of Wimbledon controversies, pressure was frequently put on Centre Court players by telling them, 'Queen Mary might not approve'. In fact, she was a sporting old lady who smoked in public when this was still considered a questionable habit for ladies, and she always enjoyed a good joke.

On the final afternoon Gussy called every thirty minutes from her Dorchester suite to ask, in a frenzy of indecision, whether Queen Mary would be there to see her match.

Queen Mary was then eighty-four, and the intense heat of the day had already raised questions about her presence. She often arrived at Wimbledon about 3.00 p.m. but that day it was not until four o'clock that her equerry called to say she had decided not to venture out in the heat.

When Gussy was told Queen Mary was not coming she hurried straight to Wimbledon. Her emotional conflict was at least partly resolved, and if she could only pluck up the courage she was free to show off on the Centre Court her panties and the pretty dress that went over them.

With the enormous publicity, Gussy developed an over-sensitive self-consciousness. She began holding her racquet in front of her face when going on to court until the press photographers protested she was preventing them from earning their living.

In spite of a really sincere ovation from the huge crowd, Gussy, with her self-consciousness aroused to the full, hardly dared bend down during the preliminary knock-up. One ball-boy tossed her a low ball and she watched it, frozen, as it rolled by her feet. Other competitors in the stands roared with laughter, and Gussy signalled them to be quiet. It was only after she let two or three balls go by untouched that she plucked up enough courage to hit a few strokes.

Louise Brough and Margaret duPont, astonished, lost the first four games, but then asserted their superiority to win in straight sets. This was the end of two unbelievable, certainly unforgettable weeks for Gussy. She then left London, but for me the real drama was yet to come.

After the finals Greig held a private cocktail party in his committee room to which guests from the Royal Box were invited on their way home. Greig asked if I would recruit some of the stars for the party. Already among his guests was the current Prime Minister, Lord Attlee, who told me with a sly smile, 'You've done a great job for tennis this year.' During the party Louis Greig shook me (as I thought) spontaneously by the hand and said, 'My dear fellow, thank you so much for coming to Wimbledon this year. We could never do without you!'

Thirty-six hours later there was a ritual farewell cocktail party for the players, which I had attended for years past. Greig, as chairman of Wimbledon, was asked to say a few words. This time, the usual pleasantries completed, his whole appearance suddenly changed, even the muscles of his face seemed to go into spasm. 'Never,' he thundered, 'never shall we allow our Centre Court to become a stage for designers' stunts.' A hundred heads swivelled to see my reaction. Even knowing Greig's uncertainties, I could not forget the unnecessary congratulations so recently offered. I felt betrayed and offended in a situation in which I had no means of defence, so I took what I considered the only course open to my by severing my connections with Wimbledon.

The following year, as Gussy began once more to think of Wimbledon, she realized she would need some more tennis clothes, and I received a letter from her saying, 'Make me something even more feminine that last year. *Let's Dig Deep!*'

The British press anticipated yet another dress controversy: headlines appeared asking if Gussy would be banned from this Wimbledon; others asked pointedly what would happen if she were banned. Louis Greig, still peeved over the 1949 'indignities' announced, 'Wimbledon needs no panties for its popularity.' In another interview he said, 'Tinling's clothes are designed to keep everybody's eyes off the ball.'

I was approached by the press asking if I was going to dress Gussy again, but I released only the letter she sent me. Then, following demands that I give a reply, I issued a statement through the Associated Press to the effect that if Gussy wanted 'practical and attractive garments' from me, I would be happy to take care of her.

This was my first experience of the new era of communications, the first time I was able to have a dialogue with a client right across the world through the news media. Our dialogue soon raised another question, 'Surely if you design another Gussy sensation, Wimbledon will throw *you* out?'

It suddenly hit me that I had made no public mention of my break with Wimbledon six months previously. I decided to speak out and John Olliff, tennis writer for the *Daily Telegraph*, reported my differences with Louis Greig for the first time. Unbelievably, they made the lead columns on the front page. As soon as the first editions hit the streets I was besieged by all the other London newspapers. The phone rang all night without stopping, and by dawn reporters from the next day's evening newspapers were already on my doorstep.

Features and readers' letters went on for weeks. Hundreds complained about the 'dictatorial' attitude of Wimbledon attempting to impose its wishes on the players. Photographers from all over the world lurked round my design studio hoping to catch me snipping a piece of fabric that would give them a clue to my plans for the next 'Gussy sensation'. And it was not long before other designers started to get in on the act: Emilio Schuberth, one of Italy's top names, made Gussy an outfit that she wore at Beckenham, on the same court where we had met less than a year before. The week before Wimbledon Pierre Balmain, of Paris, staged a press show in London at which Gussy modelled his creation. Fortunately for me this was composed of yard upon yard of flimsy silk chiffon and was totally unwearable for tennis.

Finally Wimbledon was three days away. I had not heard one word from Gussy in four months, so I called the Dorchester and said, 'What in the hell goes on? Is Schuberth dressing you, is Balmain dressing you, or am I? What's the score?'

Gussy was distinctly embarrassed and said she would

'explain everything' if I would see her immediately. She received me in an apricot-coloured négligée, looking absolutely divine. She said she became 'caught up with those guys' and really did not know what she was doing. She excused herself, saying, 'I guess I just got carried away. You know how it goes.'

I went back to my workrooms and slaved until the early hours of the morning of 'Ladies' Day', finally coming up with a shirt-and-shorts outfit in white Swiss embroidery. At that time I had never made any shorts, but I decided this was my best insurance against Gussy's self-consciousness. Although I was assailed by doubts all through the night, my instinct kept me working.

Later that day the outfit was delivered to Wimbledon with a note, 'I thought you might not feel like a dress today, so how about this?'

All I could do then was to sit back and wait. Once again she was scheduled on the No. 1 Court where the panties had made their first Wimbledon appearance. Once again the crowd was seething with anticipation. The United Press International wire service put out a story that read, 'The lips of every woman and the eyes of every man are asking the same question, "What will she wear this time?" '

The wait was agonizing. This was the first time in my life I was at Wimbledon without any duties, which also meant without any privileges, so I had difficulty in even making my way to the free standing room, the crowd was so dense. Suddenly Gussy appeared for my moment of truth. My knees went quite limp as I saw her looking dazzling and as sexy as ever. The tight-fitting embroidered shorts seemed to enhance her already provocative long stride. The press quickly dubbed it the 'Peek-a-Boo suit' because the embroidery had holes in it and the deep suntan of her shoulders was visible through the shirt. Her appearance was a smash hit.

Within a few months of Gussy's first appearance, lace was to be seen on swimwear, ski wear, leisure wear, and every other conceivable type of garment. We had initiated a tide of fashion progress.

Destiny linked me with Gussy through the common cause of believing the word 'feminine' could be a reality in women's sports. Our association had to survive many storms and stresses before we emerged, amazed by the whole thing, perhaps a little scarred in the process.

Today, after two wildly publicized broken engagements and two broken marriages, Gussy lives in quiet solitude near the Pacific Ocean in California. She spends most of her time teaching tennis to incurably deaf children at a nearby clinic.

But together, in less than three weeks in 1949, Gussy and I changed the entire concept of how sportsgirls could look. Her name has already become a part of the folklore of tennis and in years to come her story will still be told, as a legend, wherever the game is enjoyed or discussed.

Kitty Godfree

Roy McKelvie

Mrs Biddy Godfree, formerly Miss Kitty McKane, and Jean Borotra, 88 and 85 respectively, are the oldest living champions. They both won their first singles titles in 1924 and thus celebrate their Diamond jubilees this year. But Mrs Godfree, who still lunches at the All England Club once or twice a week, and bicycles to her local shops in East Sheen, south-west London, is the only survivor of the old Wimbledon ground at Worple Road. She first played there in 1919; her last Wimbledon was 1934.

Understandably Mrs Godfree's memory of Worple Road has dimmed but she does recall playing on one of the outside courts separated from the old Southern Railway only by a hedge. 'When the Southern Express passed the noise was so great that we couldn't hear the umpire calling the score. It was an awful distraction,' she said. Indeed, she claims it was worse than the clatter of the Long Island Railroad that ran along the old US Championships stadium at Forest Hills where she reached the singles final once, won the Ladies' doubles twice, with Mrs Phyllis Covell and Ermyntrude Harvey, and the mixed once with the Australian Jack Hawkes.

'The courts at Worple Road were good, more like a croquet lawn than a tennis court, but not as good as they were at Wimbledon last summer. I wasn't a member of the All England Club in the Worple Road days – I became a member in 1923 – but I don't think it was more than a players club. No social life and fewer younger players and members than there are today.

'The old Centre Court – it really was in the centre of the stadium – held about 7,000 but on the days when Suzanne Lenglen was playing goodness knows how many people got into the ground or tried to. People trampled down the hedges to get a sight of her. They couldn't play her anywhere other than the

Centre Court,' Mrs Godfree continued. Here history repeated itself. Over 50 years later the same happened when Bjorn Borg reigned at Wimbledon.

The Centre Court was surrounded by nine other courts, four of them adjoining the railway line. There was a tea room, a bar and a pavilion, refreshment areas for the public, extra dressing rooms for the Championships though not as sumptuous as they are today. The Centre Court had covered stands on three sides. The south stand on the railway side was uncovered and the scoreboard stood above it. There were four summer houses adjacent to the four corners of the Court. The committee, members and the press were housed in the west covered stand, an arrangement similar to today where the committee and members stand is separated from the press by the royal box on the south end of the Centre Court.

According to Eric Simond, the most senior living male member (1921), the men's changing room with its Royal Doulton wash-basin, now to be seen in the Museum, was part of the one he changed in at Worple Road. 'We also had four baths – long ones, well over six feet – and there was always the smell of liniment.'

Simond also recalls the move from Worple Road to Church Road, completed in 1922. 'Some members accepted it. Some said the Club was mad; that it would never fill the place. But old Major Sloane-Stanley claimed that the new Club would be nothing like big enough. How right he was! Today the Club bears not resemblance to what it was like in 1922. Then the buildings were new and uncovered by creeper. Now they have been enlarged, built on and matured. They didn't build the No. 1 Court for a couple of years and the arrangement of the courts today is very different. They used to separate each court with a hedge. Since the last war, thanks to Duncan Macaulay, the social life has changed and there are more young members. In the old days the Club was closed during the winter. The Championships then were like a garden party. Today they are big business.'

Mrs Godfree's recollections of the players of her era are clear. 'When Wimbledon began again in 1919 after the First World War the English players had lost four and a half years of their playing life. There was virtually no play in this country during the war. The Americans were able to play and so had Suzanne Lenglen in the South of France. Even before the war she had made a name for herself though only 15. But none of us thought she would be as good as she proved to be in 1919 when, at the age of 20, she won the first of her six titles beating the holder, Mrs Lambert Chambers. That was a wonderful match and Suzanne was twice within a point of defeat. Mrs Lambert Chambers was the outstanding English player; clever, steady and thoroughly reliable from the back of the court. She hardly ever volleyed. Like Mrs Larcombe (1912 champion), Mrs Beamish, Phyllis Satterthwaite and others, all baseliners, she served underarm for most of her career though later she learned to serve overarm. The change in style came with the young post-war players, Evelyn Collyer and Joan Austin, known as 'The Babes' – they reached the doubles final in 1923. They were all-court players. Phyllis Covell and Mrs Shepherd-Barron were volleyers but Mrs Holcroft Watson remained essentially a baseliner. Suzanne could do anything and everything perfectly.'

Mrs Godfree was an all-rounder. It has been said that her best two strokes were her forehand drive and her backhand volley. She was to use these and more when she faced the new invader from California, Helen Wills, aged 19, in the 1924 final. Suzanne, by the way, had retired sick after a very hard match against Elizabeth 'Bunny' Ryan and given Mrs Godfree, then Miss McKane, a walk-over into the final.

'I had beaten Helen Wills in the Wightman Cup, but at Wimbledon she led by a set and 4–1 with points for 5–1. I remember saying to myself, "Well, you're not going to win playing the way you are. You must do something different." The only thing I could do was to change my game; hit out and attack.' She did and won 4–6, 6–4, 6–4; the first of her two singles titles.

Mrs Godfree abbreviates, indeed, understates her achievement. At the time Helen Wills was US National champion and the only player in the world who might conceivably unseat Suzanne Lenglen. In fact they did meet two years later in Cannes and Suzanne beat Helen in two close sets. But Mrs Godfree's win was the only defeat inflicted on Helen at Wimbledon which she won eight times. I can do no better than quote from a commentary of the match written by A. Wallis

People

Myers, the *Daily Telegraph* correspondent, in his book *Great Lawn Tennis.*

July 4th, American Independence Day. All the attributes of a great occasion were there. The sun was shining, the Centre Court was packed as it had never been packed this year; the Queen, and with her the Duke and Duchess of York (later King George VI and Queen Elizabeth), were in the Royal Box. At the end of an hour and a quarter's play Miss McKane had beaten Miss Helen Wills by two sets to one.

But, what an agony of suspense and fluctuation before the Championship point was scored. What a match for both ladies to dream about. What a brilliant break of all court play which carried the American champion three times within a stroke of 5–1 in the second set – a lead which, had it been secured, must inevitably have given her the British Championship as well!

What a wonderful recovery of Miss McKane who, when all seemed lost, captured six games in succession and tipped the scale in her favour! Finally what a thrilling final set, with every stroke of vital value, with Miss Wills twice needing only a point for a 4–2 lead, and with Miss McKane determined she should not get it; with each country dead level at 4—4, and with England, drawing on deeper experience, just winning in the end.

The play, except in an early phase when Miss Wills lost twelve successive points, was of a remarkably high standard. I doubt whether any Lenglen match at Wimbledon (except the first in 1919) has provided rallies so keenly contested or strokes of such resource, variety and skill. Miss Wills was as near her American best as I have ever seen her. If you ask why with her commanding lead she did not win the answer must be that Miss McKane's volleys in the last set were more incisive than her own. When the advance for the kill was finally undertaken it was Miss McKane with her longer experience of net play who stowed away the ball to a spot from which it never returned.

Miss McKane finally reached match point, 40–30, at 4–5 in the final set after a tense rally. Miss Wills attempted a low backhand drive off her body. It hit the band; Miss McKane was champion. The crowds acclaimed; the tea enclousres were choked. As she approached the umpire's chair, so I gathered afterwards, Miss Wills asked Commander Hillyard the score. She had forgotten it; she had not actually realized the match was over.

The new Lady champion, a native of London, is the first English title-holder since 1914. Miss McKane had no coach to fashion either her strokes or her tactics. She is a self-made player and an example and inspiration to all girls who, whatever their opportunity for practice, can push their way to the front by individual effort!

Thus wrote Wallis Myers many years ago and it seems to me that Miss McKane, or Mrs Godfree as she soon became, stands as a shining example to those who, in this day and age, want everything done for them. She was, of course, a natural athlete.

Mrs Godfree's career record:

Wimbledon singles champion 1924, 1926
Mixed doubles champion with L. A. Godfree 1924, 1926
World Hard Court Championships, doubles 1923
Olypic Games bronze medal 1920, 1924; doubles: gold 1920, silver 1924; mixed: silver 1920, bronze 1924.
US Championships doubles (with Mrs Phyllis Covell) 1923, (with Ermyntrude Harvey) 1927; mixed (with J. B. Hawkes) 1925
British Wightman Cup team 1923–27, 1930, 1934
First Wimbledon 1919, her last 1934, during which she won 38 singles matches and lost 11. In all she played 147 matches at Wimbledon, winning 112.

Less than three months earlier Mrs Godfree had won the all England Badminton Championships at the Horticultural Hall, Westminster. 'Badminton had taught me to smash and to volley. It showed too that you could switch and adjust from a lighter to a heavier racket. In those days our tennis season was restricted by the weather. We stopped playing from October to the end of March. In the winter months we switched to badminton or golf. Today they play all the year round, are athletically fitter and most of the modern players volley. They also have better equipment and facilities and, of course, the incentive of huge prize money to be won.'

When Mrs Godfree won that final against Helen Wills she wore a white piqué dress with pleats for fullness, short sleeves, a cardigan and a blue bandeau which she admits copying from Suzanne, and, of course, stockings. 'We all wore stockings in those days though skirts had just crept up to mid-calf or higher. It wasn't until later when the South African, Billie Tapscott, appeared on the Centre Court without stockings – 'we don't wear them in South Africa', she said – that we played in bare legs. The change in clothing came gradually.

'At those old Wimbledons,' said Mrs Godfree, 'there was never a chair on the court. When you changed ends you picked up the towel, mopped up, had a sip of water and carried on. You couldn't sit down as they do nowadays. Borotra used to rush from end to end, throwing his towel over his shoulder in his hurry. Nor were there any presentations on the court as there are now. We never saw the cups or trophies we won. No razzmatazz or anything like that. Until recently there were no replicas. I remember my husband, Leslie, having had some luck on the stock exchange, buying me a replica of the Championship trophy.'

Mrs Godfree and her husband are the only married couple ever to win the mixed title (1926). Leslie Godfree hit the first ball at the new Wimbledon in 1922 when he opened the Centre Court against Algy Kingscote, won the toss and served.

Looking back over the years Mrs Godfree said, 'I don't think the individual strokes have changed much since the days of Tilden and Suzanne Lenglen. But the speed of the ball has increased and the rackets are now much tighter strung. We didn't hit as hard as they do nowadays. Today's players are very probably physically stronger than we were. They are fitter, much more dedicated and highly competitive. They have the incentive to become millionaires.'

I wondered about Suzanne Lenglen and Helen Wills who between them won 14 singles titles; the former never beaten at Wimbledon, the latter only once, by Mrs Godfree. 'They were totally different. Suzanne was a complete player with an all-round game. Helen Wills hit harder but played almost entirely from the back of the court. Suzanne was more versatile. She had a much better doubles record. But as to who would win if they had met at their best – ah.'

Teddy Tinling the Go-Between

Julie Welch

There may be ways of making Teddy Tinling less noticeable but they would involve the use of sound-proof panels and several yards of blackout curtain. Wimbledon's Player Liaison Officer, the Director of International Liaison to the Virginia Slims World Championship, and the designer of the most famous pair of knickers in history, is a lively 73-year-old who is to the low profile what Cyril Smith is to middle-distance running.

The sort of bloke who would go outside and shoot himself rather than be seen in gymshoes at a dinner party, Tinling likes to pour his lean 6ft 7in frame into such discreet little numbers as gold quilted satin jackets, lemon shot-silk shirts and jumbo bow ties. Bald as a coot, his suntanned dome rises in a slightly unearthly point as though he's just dropped in from far-off Krypton, and his *pièce de résistance* is the beautiful diamond stud that twinkles in his left earlobe. 'It's going to pay the expenses for my funeral,' he explains. 'I've left my body to the University of Pennsylvania Medical Center. No use having a tomb – I've no kids so no one's going to put flowers on it in 50 years' time. I'd rather someone read my book and be nervous about my coming back in another life.'

Tinling, you will gather from all this, is not the man you need if you're hunting for Mr Average. On the other hand, he's a lot more fun. At an age when he's entitled to be thinking about bus passes and free specs, he goes on kitting out the likes of Billie Jean King, acting as middleman between the Wimbledon committee and the players and, last month, publishing his memoirs, *Sixty Years in Tennis*. 'I never expected to be earning my living at my age,' he says, 'but I'm very grateful to be wanted. I'm treated with great charm and respect by the establishment and others and at the end of my life I'm very happy.' He says he's had to work hard all his life to make up for not being talented, but you could fill a hall with people who'd be prepared to argue with him about that.

Ted Tinling and the game of tennis have been entwined since he was a weedy schoolboy of 13 in love with the sport's first goddess, Suzanne Lenglen. In his time he has umpired, reffed, been confidant, mediator and television commentator, played competitively against the likes of Lew Hoad and Bill Tilden, been shown the door by Wimbledon, then welcomed back again. He is sharp, witty, outrageous and charming, and what he doesn't know about the game could be written on the back of your dry-cleaning ticket.

The youngest son by several years of a well-heeled chartered accountant, Tinling hit planet earth on 23 June 1910 at Eastbourne. He had two dashingly named brothers (Collingwood and Banastre), a God-fearing Victorian for a father, a progressive free thinker for a mother and a chronic chest problem that kept him out of school and took the family to reside in Nice in an effort to put the brakes on his wheezing. 'I had hell till I was 25, when they discovered antibiotics. And I wasn't educated. I went to morning classes in Nice at a Catholic school.'

While they lived the high life on the Riviera, his mother gave him a gift subscription to become a schoolboy member of the Nice Tennis Club, Suzanne Lenglen's personal domain. Miss Lenglen was his Raquel Welch and on Thursday and Sunday afternoons, the only times schoolboys were allowed to play, Tinling hovered around like a groupie waiting for her to arrive. He even lined his bedroom walls with her picture. 'If I hadn't met Suzanne Lenglen,' he says, 'I might never have realized how beautiful tennis could be.'

But meet her he did; on a day that is obviously so seared on his mind that 59 years later he can still tell you time and date. It was 4 January 1924. Our young blood was as usual lurking amidst the potted palms gawping at La Lenglen as she waited to go out on court for a tournament, when suddenly the jolly-hockey-sticks voice of the tournament organizer boomed in his ears. 'Young man,' she said, 'have you ever umpired a match?' Eyes glued to the delectable Suzanne, the 13-year-old Tinling muttered to the effect that no, he never had. But the tournament organizer had already turned to Miss Lenglen. 'Would you mind this young man umpiring your match?' she trumpeted. '*Mais avec plaisir,*' said Miss Lenglen. And that was it – Tinling's future decided.

He spent the next two years with the Lenglen entourage, and when, at 17, he arrived in England to learn the dress-designing business, he was, he remembers, already 'a fully-fledged person' with a background of what his friend, another tennis legend Elizabeth Ryan, scathingly referred to as Continental Behaviour. 'I wore a belt instead of braces,' he explains, 'which was considered very fast.'

Take a tennis nut with a flair for style, a sense of mischief and an empathy with women, pit him against a stuffy and prurient post-war Wimbledon committee and what do you get? Well, in 1949 you got The Great Panties Scandal.

The background to it was as follows: Tinling had had a successful war; rising to Lieut.-Colonel in the Intelligence Corps – he was with Eisenhower in Algiers, then joined Montgomery's staff in Germany. He was an established figure on the tennis circuit, both as player and officiator, and every summer did duty as Wimbledon call-boy, responsible for getting players to their matches. He was also, by now, a dress designer of some accomplishment, and the butch severity of the women players' gear almost brought him to tears. What they needed to do, he decided was bring back a bit of the old feminine bezazz.

There had already been several clashes with the Wimbledon officials about his outfits, both those he designed for players and some of his own more *outré* apparel. Once the chairman of the All-England Club buttonholed him in the dressing-room. 'Your ties', he announced, 'are your worst enemy.'

Then on to the scene came Gorgeous Gussy Moran. He sewed her a pair of pretty lacy panties to wear under her tennis dress, and Wimbledon went potty. Blimpish colonels dropped their monocles, titled ladies clapped their hands over their eyes, the switchboard was jammed, newspapers fired off editorials, vicars the world over preached thunderous sermons about the wicked implications of wearing this kind of garment and a committee member bellowed to Tinling over Sunday lunch, 'You have put sin and vulgarity into tennis!'

Meanwhile, the sight of 200 press photographers lying on their backs trying to snap a picture of Gussy in The Knickers proved that as far as the rest of the world was concerned, the more s. and v. in tennis the merrier. Gussy Moran's rococo smalls made Tinling an international celebrity and the shock waves were still rippling for years afterwards.

Tinling paid a price, though. As far as the Wimbledon old boys were concerned, he was now a Grade A Bad Smell and his services were no longer wanted. Despite his increasing involvement with women's professional tennis in the United States and the unstinting enthusiasm and effort he'd given to the tournament in the past, Tinling was to spend the next three decades as the person the All England Club least wanted at their parties.

It took them 33 years to forgive him, but last year they finally did. They made him Player Liaison Officer, referee in the often stormy relationship between players and officials, and at Christmas he was made an honorary member of the club. If the Lord spares him a few more years he hopes to spend them helping to straighten out the increasing contentiousness in the sport: 'So much money, so many people getting uptight – the need for mediation if probably greater than it's ever been, and I am in a unique position to represent one person to another, stop them going berserk and start a dialogue. Having been both sides of the counter in the business, it gives a broader outlook on life.'

It was time to ask the final question – in all the time that has passed since 4 January 1924, has there ever been, in his opinion, a woman player to match his first love, Suzanne Lenglen? He is diplomatic: 'I have to represent them all. But the women in America are so anxious to equal men that they only want athleticism these days. I think that's quite wrong. I think tennis along with ice skating has a sort of grey area where aesthetics have to be considered along with athletic ability. That's why Chris Evert has been so popular – her grace, her prettiness, her sporting spirit, her feminine attractiveness. She's not primarily an athlete, though she is one. But I think she may represent an era which is passing, and now we're into the age of Martina Navratilova. The first Bionic Tennis Woman. Martina may well turn out to be the best woman player ever. She's probably playing the best tennis I've ever seen.' Better, even, than – gasp – his Suzanne Lenglen? 'Yes. And it's taken me 50 years to say that.'

Quelle Explosion!

Richard Evans

I am not sure, from all Ted Tinling has told me about her, that Suzanne Lenglen would have enjoyed being turned into an alley – either literally or figuratively. However, that is what has occurred at Stade Roland Garros, where each passing year sees another example of Philippe Chatrier's fashion.

This year the changes have been the most visually dramatic since the number one court stadium was built four years ago. A field that was used as a rugby pitch until Christmas 1983 was acquired by Chatrier's French federation and rapidly transformed into nine new courts. As the field was previously separated from the main Roland Garros tennis complex by a road called Rue Suzanne Lenglen, a slight alteration in name was necessary because it is no longer a road – certainly not a public one. Its entire length is now encompassed by the expanding Roland Garros territory and guarded at both ends by gates that might look more decorative but are just as effective as Checkpont Charlie. So 'Rue' became 'Allé'. I hope Suzanne will forgive them. Needless to say it took Monsieur Chatrier a little while to get his hands on the rugby field but as Jacques Chirac, the highly ambitious mayor of Paris, can count as well as any other politican, the statistics on tennis in France did not have to be pushed across his desk more than once. By any standards of economic, social or sporting growth, they make startling reading.

In 1984, almost a million more spectators attended the French Open than had gone ten years before. In 1974, there were 2,700 tennis clubs in France and 7,500 courts. Now there are 7,300 clubs and more than 18,000 courts. But if the number of courts has more than doubled, the way in which they are being used is even more impressive. Just six years ago the French Federation ran 1,178 tournaments of all categories. In 1983,

217

there were 8,432. And just one more statistic: ten years ago there were 7,750 men and women players ranked nationally in France. Now that figure is 130,400.

So Philippe Chatrier needed the rugby field and Jacques Chirac understood why. If Chirac ever becomes president of France, which is more than a possiblity, look for the name of Chatrier in his cabinet.

Chartier, of course, epitomizes what has happened to international tennis over the last ten years. In 1974, the professional game was still very young. The Association of Tennis Professionals was only two years old and, mainly as a result of the players' surprisingly solid stand over the Nikki Pilic affair, which resulted in the 1973 Wimbledon boycott, there was talk of creating a governing body for the men's pro game. Eventually the Pro Council was born.

Chatrier, meanwhile, had been carefully laying the foundations for a role he knew would eventually be created – that of full-time head of the International Tennis Federation. When he took over from Britain's Derek Hardwick as president of the ITF in 1977, he was well equipped to break a long-standing tradition and get himself re-elected to a second two-year term. That had never been done before, and the ITF membership needed to retire to the heady mountain atmosphere of Gstaad in the Swiss Alps to make a decision that would, in effect, acknowledge that the bespectacled Frenchman, who had been a good junior player just after the war, was now the only man with sufficient drive, knowledge, leadership qualities and, most importantly, time to take on the role of leading an old amateur organization into the modern professional world.

With David Gray, the former *Guardian* writer who died so tragically during the 1983 U.S. Open, as his general secretary, Chatrier was able to cut through much of the old red tape and turn what he likes to call his 'elephants' around. By elephants he means his colleagues from the nations who make up the ITF, dedicated but often slow-moving component parts of a far-flung worldwide organization that is inevitably difficult to mobilize.

Chatrier was able to find the time because, as a young journalist, he had founded the magazine *Tennis de France* and was now able to live off the trust fund that had been set up on his behalf. So he could work as a professional for the ITF without the stigma of actually being one. What delicious irony! That way he could talk to even the blimpiest of the old blimps who still thought of professionals as being, well, not quite gentlemen, and get them to listen to him.

It wasn't easy, not as president of the ITF or in his other influential role as president of the Pro Council, and although I have disagreed with a few moves he has made in the past I know the kind of problems he was facing in those early days. Trying to turn an amateur world professional is a far more complicated and sensitive operation than it may appear at first glance. Rewriting a rule book is one thing, but tampering with the way people have done things all their lives uncovers a snake pit of prejudice, fear and just plain bloody-mindedness that is sometimes difficult to comprehend.

While Chatrier toiled away at Stade Roland Garros, trying to whip his elephants into shape, it became my job, in 1973, to reorganize the numerous and diverse European tournaments that were forming part of a new pro calender. I had just taken over the Paris office of the ATP as European Director, and I soon discovered that my primary task involved the business of upgrading old amateur tournaments to a hopefully acceptable level of professionalism. Considerable barriers needed to be broken down. Some required patient negotiation with gentlemen; others necessitated scare tactics with little despots.

It was in Italy that I ran into one of the latter. The elderly official, all dressed up in his faded blue blazer, seemed to be some leftover relic from Mussolini's day. There were certainly plenty of Fascisti undertones in the way he started shouting at John Yuill to get back on court immediately for a doubles. Yuill, as sweet-tempered a player as you could find, was merely trying to gulp down a cup of tea, having three minutes before come off court after a long and exhausting singles on the red clay. The official looked absolutely amazed when I told him to shut up. I told him that the days when he could get away with treating players like cattle were over and that he would henceforth offer them the respect and courtesy due to any professional athlete who was conducting himself in a proper manner. He didn't like it but the next time he spoke to the player I actually heard him saying 'please'.

But, thankfully, the gentlemen were more numerous. Miguel Lerin, who, to my mind, has always epitomized the Spanish grandee, was one. Senior Lerin had been running the Godo Cup at the elegant Real Club de Barcelona for years and he had been running it his way. He was never rude to players and he always tried to act as the perfect host. But his ways were those of the amateur, and with the coming of bigger and bigger prize money, computerized rankings and entry lists that had to be striclty adhered to, changes were needed.

One day, after Jan Kodes had complained about the lack of practice balls and Steve Turner, Eddie Dibbs's great mate who acted as the classic barrack-room lawyer, had come up with another of his wonderfully inventive complaints, I took Lerin aside and tried to make him see that certain changes would have to be made. Inevitably some were going to cost him money but that was not the main problem. He had an abundance of Spanish pride and did not enjoy having some foreigner come and tell him how to run his tournament.

However, being the perfect gentleman, he was never going to lose his temper so, drawing himself up to his full height, he cut short our conversation by saying, 'You have made me quite cross, but I shall go away and have a coffee and think about what you have said to me. Then I may feel better.'

There was the faintest suspicion of a twinkle in his eye as he said it, and a short while later he did feel better and ultimately his tournament was better, too. A lovely man, Miguel Lerin.

Even Monte Carlo took a little while to come around and face the fact that the 32 pros who made up the main draw in the mid-seventies needed to be treated just a little differently from the 300 other players, ranging in age from 12 to 65, who used to pack the courts of the Monte Carlo Country Club for various tournaments every Easter. At first a blanket in the locker room was all that separated rod Laver, Tom Okker and Ilie Nastase from the multitudes. And even then they were expected to fork out ten francs as a deposit on a towel.

It was a situation that obviously couldn't last, but I must admit it was Wojtek Fibak who brought about changes at a far faster rate than I had managed. It all came to a head because players were banned from the clubhouse restaurant in those days, which was only a problem in cold weather because the terrace at the Monte Carlo Country Club is one of the most idyllic places in the world to have an alfresco meal. However, it can get very chilly on the Côte de'Azur in early April, and when Fibak was ordered out of the restaurant just a couple of hours before he was due to play a match, the young Pole was understandably incensed.

It so happened that John Vinocur, then with Associated Press and now the *New York Times* Bureau Chief in Paris, was giving himself a week's tennis reporting as a change from other more laborious duties at NATO or the European Parliament, and he sniffed a good story. Fibak was quick to provide him with it.

Suggesting that it was a scandal that professional players should be made to sit out in freezing weather to eat their lunch before – or, indeed, even after – their matches, Fibak went on to list all the things that were wrong with the Monte Carlo event. It all appeared with great prominence in the next day's *New York Herald Tribune* and the Monagesque officials, who are proud of their image and sensitive to criticism, were appalled. But to their immense credit, they immediately set about restructuring the entire tournament, setting new priorities and building, in a very short time, some of the most luxurious and comfortable players' quarters to be found anywhere in the world. Bernard Noat and his ebullient assistant Ed Lampel have seen to it that the pros are no longer left out in the cold in Monte Carlo. After a couple of years absence to let things quieten down Wojtek went back to discover just how much can be set in motion by one well-timed outburst.

The ATP was foraging in Africa in those days, too, creating new events in places like Khartoum and Algiers. Khartoum, in particular, prospered for a while because the Sudanese had studied form and were keen to do everything by the Wimbledon rule book. At least they had the grass courts to lend some credence to their ambitions. We all drank evil-smelling but good-tasting beer from the Blue Nile Breweries and Mike Estep loved the grass courts so much he won the tournament. But then my sponsor disappeared into the desert, politics reared its ugly head and all our good work was laid to waste. But they tried in Khartoum, they really did.

Another tournament of longer tradition in the region viewed life a little differently. They had one good local player and felt, with some justification, that the success of the event depended on his surviving until the later rounds. So they fixed the draw. It was quite simple, an ageing gentleman told me with great dignity. That was what they had always done and that was what they would continue to do.

'Oh, no you won't!' I exclaimed with some vehemence. 'There are ATP rules now that lay out very clearly how the draw will be made. Not only that but it will be made in public with players and press present, and if your man gets a tough first round that's what is known as the luck of the draw.'

I looked around the table and was confronted with a line of horrified faces. The committee, most of whom were from a generation well trained in bureaucratic pragmatism by the British, usually thought as one and acted as one. Now their spokesman turned on me.

'You are stupid, you English,' he spat out. 'You come here with your high-minded rules and all you do is ruin our tournament!'

There were moments during the next few hours when I envisioned being carted off in the dead of night to some Middle Eastern jail and left to rot along with my ATP rule book, written in large part by Arthur Ashe, who was black and not British at all.

But the committee's oriental nose sniffed the winds of change that were blowing across deserts and oceans and they were afraid of being ostracized from this brave new world of professionalism. So they relented and staged a public draw. And their man got his tough first round match and lost. But I still got out alive.

The Way to Win

Terry Wogan

Nowadays, when I play tennis, there's usually a doctor in attendance. He's a cheerful, stocky man with powerful Welsh thews, that make him the fastest tennis player in the world over two metres. I've never seen a retriever like him, right down to his little damp nose. I don't know whether its Welsh 'hwyl', or sheer Celtic bloodymindedness, but this man is never beaten. No ball is ungettable, every forlorn chance is chased down. Jimbo Connors, nosediving into the crowds at Flushing Meadow, has nothing on this boy A rally with this merry man of medicine is a scurrying, scrambling, heavy-breathing affair, and it's usually followed by a long thoughtful pause, because neither of us is exactly in the first flush of youth.

Our games together are characterized by fierce bursts of frenzied activity, freely interspersed by longer periods of airy badinage and manly joshing. Perhaps if old John and big Ivan could approach it in the same way, we might all have a few more laughs, or at least, respite for our frazzled nerves.

Don't run away with the idea that the Doc and I are not competitive, that senility has sapped either of our wills to win. Not likely. Why do you think he chases every ball as if it were his last? Why do you think I make him? It would be just as health-giving and a lot less exhausting to pat the ball back and forward over the net, with civil apologies every time you hit it out of your opponent's reach. No, we're trying to kill each other, the Doc and me. Six-love, six-love, that's what we're shooting for. We sometimes lose track of the score, or what side of the court we're serving to next, but make no mistake, we're both going for the whitewash. It's the Corinthian ideal, you see. Play up and play the game . . . smile apologetically when you hit a screamer down the line, past your opponent's outstretched racket, murmur 'Bad luck!' at his double faults and shout 'Good

223

shot!' when he leaves you for dead in the middle of the court. I tell you, Baron de Coubertin would be proud of the Doc and me . . .

It's the way we were dragged up I suppose. You went out to win, bending every nerve and sinew, giving everything, but never, never showing it. No show of overt jubilation was encouraged for a good shot, still less for victory. That was accepted almost apologetically, and you covered your embarrassment with three cheers for the loser. Call it hypocrisy, self-delusion, suppression of our natural spirits. Do modern tennis stars seem to you to be better-balanced, sweeter-tempered, more rounded human beings than those of yesteryear? Have all the tumult and the shouting, the obscene gestures, the arrogant postures, the flagrant abuses, produced happier players, a better game?

You'll be blaming the coloured element, of course. When the Founding Fathers of the two great continents landed on Plymouth Rock and Botany Bay, having flown, or been forced to flee, the tyranny of the Old World, they naturally rejected the old values, the cant, the hypocrisy, the two-facedness. Honesty and openness were the watchword, telling it like it was. Strive, work hard and everything and anything you want can be yours. Achievement became the goal, and over-achievement even more laudable. To win was what counted, and a loser was nowhere. Even second wasn't awfully good. If you're not a winner, thank you for taking part and good-night.

This glorification of the Great God Win was never more evident than at the Olympics this year in Los Angeles. I was there, and saw an entire nation become obsessed with *gold*. It couldn't have been more frantic in California during the Great Rush of a hundred years ago. The United States Women's Volleyball team won a silver medal, and it was as if they had failed to qualify! 'What were those four years of training about?' carped the American pundits, forgetting the hundreds, perhaps thousands, of hopeful young women who had been training equally as hard for four years, perhaps more, and hadn't even got as far as Los Angeles, not to mind win a medal. The American swimmers, in the absence of the Soviet Bloc countries, particularly East Germany, swept all others aside in the pool, and the days seemed to be filled with the 'Star-

Spangled Banner', crewcuts, teeth and that peculiar American whoop that characterizes not only their sporting triumphs, but their political conventions and TV quiz shows, as well.

However, there was one United States swimmer who was a grave disappointment. Not that he hadn't obliged with a gold medal. It was his manner, that, it was felt among the commentators, left something to be desired. *The bounder hadn't whooped.* Not only that, but he hadn't jumped around, leapt into his team-mates' arms, waved to his mother in the stand, or burst into tears as the American flag was raised. There was even some question of whether he had his hand over his heart during the playing of 'The Star-Spangled Banner'! The nation was shocked. It wasn't exactly a clenched-fist Black Power Salute, but such behaviour was flying in the face of all that was best in American life, including Disneyland and Mom's Apple Pie. The guy was obviously un-American, soft on Commies and probably didn't even chew gum . . . The poor unfortunate claimed in mitigation that although delighted to win for himself, the United States and President Reagan, he had been disappointed at not breaking a world record. It wasn't good enough. Somebody talked to him about his responsibility to The Flag, The American Dream, and his athletic scholarshiip, and the following day our hero made an abject apology to the entire American nation through television and the press for 'letting everybody down by not being enthusiastic enough at my victory' . . ,. He won another gold medal a couple of days later, and you never in your life saw such whooping, jumping, bounding, waving, laughing and crying. It did your heart good. The Prodigal had returned and repented the error of his ways . . .

Not mine, though, I kept thinking of my old tennis coach, who doubled as the rugby trainer in the winter. He would have given the American swimmers a dressing-down and probably a thick ear, for 'showing off'. Boastful self-glorification at the moment of triumph is not a pretty sight, though an increasingly common one, these days.

But here, my little ones, I'm begining to sound as old as I look. I'll just sit here a while and ponder over my pictures of that greatest of all Corinthians, C. B. Fry. Played for England at cricket and rugby, *and* everything else, 'treated triumph and disaster just the same', was a hero to every Englishman of his generation and never cursed an opponent or kissed a team-mate in his life. 'Old-fashioned buffer,' I hear you cry. Maybe, but do you think they'll ever offer the kingship of Albania to John McEnroe?

A Funny Thing Happened . . .

How Tanner Turned a Nation on

Bud Collins

You may not even miss R. Tanner, absent from Wimbledon after 11 generally productive years, but for early awakening tennis degenerates in America, and the folks responsible for televising the Big W back to the States, he will forever be enshrined as St Roscoe.

St Roscoe's call of nature – a wrong number as it turned out – was the answer to the big-dollar prayers of the NBC-TV task force just five years ago when Wimbledon made its first significant impression on the colonials of North America. Until Roscoe Tanner's gallant five-set holding action, against the champion Bjorn Borg in the 1979 final, Americans could take Wimbledon on telly or leave it alone – mostly the latter. Although the final has been beamed to the United States for more than 20 years, it was, prior to 1979, delivered in a limp taped-and-condensed form, seen five or six hours after the fact on a Saturday afternoon. By the time the telecast appeared the result was generally known. As my Uncle Studley says 'This is as thrilling as marrying a woman after you've lived with her for a couple of years.'

The delayed concept may seem as ghastly to you as it is, and possibly unbelievable that Wimbledon wouldn't be seen live. But the tournament, despite its pre-eminence, wasn't considered commercially strong enough to risk showing as it happened: that is, starting at 9 a.m. in the Eastern US, and 6 a.m. on the West Coast.

Presenting tennis at those hours on a Saturday morning seemed as reasonable as piping a Golda Meir documentary into Damascus. The viewing audience would be about the size of Twiggy's waistline. True, American TV sets are extremely well attended on Saturday mornings, but then the fans are juveniles and the fare cartoons. Could tennis possibly go up against Loony Tunes and survive? As likely as Tom devouring Jerry, was the conventional thought.

Yet the executive producer of NBC Sport at the time, a big, young, persuasive guy, named Don Ohlmeyer, boldly believed otherwise. Ohlmeyer felt that the immediacy of allowing Americans to eavesdrop on a Centre Court battle in progress, and watch every stroke, would overcome the obstacles, chiefly the American sporting public's unfamiliarity with Wimbledon and indeed life in all places at such an unsympathetic hour on a non-working day.

Nevertheless, Ohlmeyer sold it to his superiors, and a minion, Robert Basche, coined a phrase that has entered the American sporting lexicon: 'Breakfast at Wimbledon'.

But what kind of breakfast? A beigel and a cup of coffee would have been more than enough to get you through last year's dawn execution of Chris Lewis by John McEnroe. A final such as that would probably have finished off 'Breakfast at Wimbledon' before it got out of the frying pan in 1979.

What NBC desired was a match as long and satisfying as a good old English breakfast of kippers, porridge, eggs, sausage and bacon, plenty of toast and marmalade, bolstered by innumerable cups of tea – a match to linger over (garnished with innumerable revenue-yielding commercials), and one that might even intrude on lunch.

But despite the lack of enthusiasm at upper network levels the commitment was nevertheless made to an innovative Wimbledon-as-is production. However, as the climactic Saturday neared, with Borg the archangel of Centre Court looking more divinely anointed than ever, Ohlmeyer and his NBC brigade began to sweat and grope like Bjorn's victims. Naturally we wanted Bjorn on one side of the net aiming for his fourth successive title, but nobody was cheering Roscoe Tanner on to the other spot.

Early first choice was Jimmy Connors, but, strangely, he got seeded third, to be squashed by Borg in the semis. Second seed John McEnroe would have been fine, but Tim Gullikson evicted him in the fourth round. A rematch of the glorious 5-set 1977 semi, Vitas Gerulaitis's near miss against Borg, would have been well received, only Pat Dupre got rid of Vitas at the outset.

NBC had allotted six hours of time to the broadcast, and Tanner was hardly anybody's idea of a time-killing antidote to the Swede.

The only consoling thought when Tanner came through was his American origin. But he had the charisma of a cigar store Indian and visions of a quick knockout, audience withdrawal, and all that time to fill made the NBC camp tense as the tradiditional 2 p.m. starting hour approached. Tanner, in his little orphan Annie coiffure, as tightly permed as our nerves, didn't have a prayer to put the fight on Borg. But does any saint-to-be arise knowing this will be the day he earns his wings?

Apprehension was the theme as Donald Dell and I, the commentators, walked towards the broadcast booth with Ohylmeyer. Puffing on a cigarette, the boss said to Dell (who was also Tanner's agent), 'Can your guy at least win a set?'

'I wouldn't bet much on it,' Dell replied frankly. Tanner's wrongness as a finalist wasn't the only problem. Ohlmeyer had just learned that the All England Club wouldn't budge on the starting time for his grand experiment. Customarily the players marched on at 1.50 with the first ball to be struck in anger at two precisely. That was no good for NBC, scheduled to come on the air at two, with about five minutes of build-up, plus the necessary and lucrative commercials.

Ohlmeyer had assumed the AEC would be amenable to a five-minute delay, which has since been granted. Wrong, said the clubbies.

But Saint Roscoe saved the day, at both ends. Dell got to him a few minutes before the walk-on and explained NBC's predicament. 'Tie your shoes a lot just after the knock up,' was one suggestion. Roscoe improved on that. As he and Borg were making the walk from the changing room, St Roscoe stopped, saying he heard a call of nature which couldn't be put on hold. Could they deny a condemned man his last wish? He vanished to a loo where he remained, though the call was a wrong number, for the crucial five minutes.

But he wasn't finished with his patriotic stint on behalf of the homeland network. Once the match began tardily, but with the requisite precis fully shown, Roscoe began to play like a saint. When Tanner won the first set the cheering from the NBC production unit could be heard in Calais. It was going to be a match, not a slaughter so much so that the Yank damned near won in five sets.

'Breakfast at Wimbledon' was a critical and financial success, and got tastier with the McEnroe/Borg epics of 1980/81 and Connors's five-set unseating of McEnroe in 1982. By the time we at last got a clinker in Lewis–McEnroe, 'Breakfast at Wimbledon' was so well established that the men's final was moved to Sunday and even the Ladies' final gets the live treatment on Saturday.

It's a double breakfast portion now, but we wouldn't be doing it at all if Saint Roscoe hadn't held off a couple of dragons – traditional start and Bjorn Borg – five years ago.

The Not So Merry-go-round

David Irvine

Travel broadens the mind. Or so it is often claimed. It also heightens one's awareness of the insularity of many who, through choice, design or circumstance, remain in one place throughout their days, innocently tending their misconceptions of life elsewhere.

For example, there was an occasion recently when I returned home, tired and unshaven, from Philadelphia. My neighbour, the one in insurance, arrived back simultaneously from his office three miles away. 'Lucky Devil,' he said enviously. 'I bet you've spent the past week sunning yourself beside some pool.' Nudge, nudge . . . wink, wink.

Pool! In Philadelphia? In January? It snowed non-stop for 12 hours before I got out. Mountains of the stuff. It was cold enough to freeze the knocker off a door. Or worse. We aborted our first take off (not funny), I missed the London connection at JFK, and ended up in Frankfurt the next morning.

Admittedly it's not always that gruesome – occasionally one does arrive on time at the specified destination. But the point is that what those earth-bound, home-loving dreamers tend to refer to as 'the glamorous jet-set life' – you know, non-stop parties, bikini-clad lovelies, blazing sunshine and exotic poolside cocktails – is, in reality or for the most part, a very tiring and often tedious routine.

'Now don't go giving me that hard-luck story,' chided a friend when I put forward the alternative view of a tennis traveller's life. 'You see the world.' And one has to admit that's true – if you can get a window seat and there's no cloud cover restricting the view from 35,000 feet. But it's pretty repetitive. From that height nowhere even appears to be inhabited.

In a decade of globe-hopping I have been over some of the most wondrous sights on earth – but almost sitting on the wrong side of the aircraft. 'On our right' intones the captain, 'you can see the Grand Canyon, one of nature's greatest miracles.' I'm on the left. And the Fasten Your Seat Belts light is on. It was just the same when I flew by Mount Fuji as the sun was coming up!

Yet air travel must be acknowledged as the greatest single factor in changing the face of tennis. Before the war tournaments followed the sun along the same path as they do now, but at a far more leisurely pace. It took a long time to go, say, from Los Angeles to Melbourne and, because of that, big international events were few and far between.

Now a player can contest a final in Stockholm and make the first round of another tournament in Johannesburg or Memphis or Sydney two days later. And then be off to yet another continent the moment he loses.

Frankly, I envy my journalistic predecessors who took a week to cross the Atlantic in the *Queen Mary*. Not for them the hassle of the quick dash to, and the long wait at, those oh-so-familiar airports. Not for them the omnipresent effects of jet lag. Not for them the plastic food dumped in your lap when the plane encounters clear air turbulence. They journeyed in style. *That* was the good life.

For players before the jet age, the entire lifestyle of the circuit was more relaxed and casual. It was still a game for amateurs (which usually meant those at the upper end of the social and economic scale). Now it is a job – with fabulous rewards, it must be said, for those good enough to achieve the most dominant positions but still providing a good enough income at ground level for many more to maintain a reasonable standard of living.

Reluctant as I am to use it, because it is the most overworked noun in sport, the greatest difference between the old game and the new is the pressure. That is not to say that those who enjoyed the golden age of amateurism didn't feel it – but they certainly did not live with it as a daily companion. Nor was it so intense.

Today's pressure comes from the unrelenting quest for computer points, the mad-cap schedules which all players are virtually obliged to undertake, and the enormous glare of publicity to which all the exposed if they so much as touch gold. That is the difference.

Now, I hear someone say, you are not really suggesting that tennis is a real job. What, hitting a little fluffy ball around a court? Come off it! But I am. In fact the professional commitment of most modern players is considerable – almost damagingly so. Matches form only a part of their working week. They put in long hours of hard practice daily, make personal appearances, give coaching clinics and are frequently in demand for interviews. Many are also closely involved with the actual running of their sport.

If they were to remain in one place for months on end it would be easy to work out a pleasant routine. The pressures would ease and they would have more spare time. And they would get a break from hotel living. But the modern tennis circuit has no beginning and no end. Like Old Man River, it just keeps rollin' along.

The term 'season' is obsolete as far as today's game is concerned. When the European section of the tour finishes, the American leg begins. Sometimes they run simultaneously. And there's always another stop just along the line.

Travelling has become a lifestyle in itself for some and, perhaps not surprisingly, there are those who can no longer settle anywhere. Equally there are others who stand it for so long and then get out.

Flying from continent to continent; through time zones; with the clock, against the clock – all these shifts produce stress which most of us never experience. No wonder players say eight-day clocks were designed for them and airline crews and, even when fully wound, only last a week. If it's Monday it must be Brussels . . . or is it Cincinnati?

Drop Your Drawers, Fella

Mike Lupica

Here is the way every one of my eight Wimbledons began: a nurse would put a Western grip on a needle and say, 'OK, fella, drop 'em.'

I never really had a great Wimbledon. It was because of hay fever. My last official act on American soil before flying to London was showing up at a New York doctor's office, listening to that dread command from the nurse, and getting the dread cortisone shot in the you-know-what.

Then the doctor would give me enough Sudafed, gift-wrapped, to put the entire British Isles to sleep. If I ever get around to writing my Wimbledon memoirs, the title will be 'I was a Sudafed Junkie'.

And nothing helped. Hay fever sufferers, as they say in the commercials, know that nothing helps, especially in England, where the pollen count at Wimbledon time is something that compares favourably with Martina Navratilova's annual earnings. You really only have two options: (1) wheeze and sneeze for the entire fortnight, and do it wide-awake; or (2) keep popping the Sudafed. Be drowsy all the time. Say 'Greaaat' a lot when people ask you how you're feeling. And still wheeze and sneeze.

Remember when John McEnroe played the great tie-breaker in the 1980 final? How it went for 22 minutes and 34 points? I remember it vividly because I sneezed 26 times. It's in my notes, or what I can read of them. Made me such a popular boy in press row.

Hay fever always made me crankier at Wimbledon than the rain did. Wheeze and sneeze. Hack and cough. Blow the nose. Have the eyes constantly look like a Hawaiian sunset. I finally knew hay fever had won three years ago, at my last Wimbledon, when one of those nice officials in Wimbledon tie and a Wimbledon blazer tried to get me to wait for a changeover before taking my seat at Court No. 1. I wheezed, sneezed and said to the nice man, 'If you don't take your hand off my arm, I'll kill you.'

I was starting to tell the nice man I would wait for him in the parking lost when Bud Collins shoved another Sudafed down my throat.

What I'm saying is that allergies are not tennis's friend. Even if you don't play.

One of the reasons why Ken Rosewall always had a problem at Wimbledon was because he had such bad hay fever. Now maybe Rosewall was just not destined to win at The Big W, but it never helped much that as soon as he showed up at the All England Club, his allergy would close his eyes and ears, and turn his nose into Niagara Falls.

I'm told that before Brian Gottfried would take off for Europe each spring, a nurse would say 'Drop 'em' to him too.

Ivan Lendl skipped Wimbledon in 1982, explaining that he was allergic to grass. A lot of people thought Lendl might just be allergic to *tennis* on grass – or allergic to McEnroe or Jimmy Connors – when he showed up playing golf in a pro-am at Westchester (New York) Country Club not long after than. But well-known tennis trainer Bill Norris says that Lendl's hay fever is real.

'I remember one time when Lendl was playing Andres Gomez at the Italian Open,' Norris said. 'The pollen at Foro Italico is always terrible, and when you mix it with the dust from the clay courts, you've got a disaster if you have allergies. So Lendl is running for this forehand and just as he strikes the ball, he lets out the loudest sneeze I've ever heard. I mean, *loud*. Gomez reacted like he'd been shot and immediately hit the ball into the net.'

Jimmy Connors, according to Norris, always had a rough time at West Side Tennis Club in Forest Hills, when the US Open was still played on Har-Tru courts there. For some reason, the dust bothered him there more than any place else. By the time Connors got to the 1975 final against Manuel Orantes, which he lost, he had been absolutely Rosewalled by that dust, and was left dead in it.

In 1964, when the Open was still known as the National Championship at Forest Hills, and was played on grass, Carole

Graebner had such a bad reaction to the medication she was taking for hay fever that she had to play the final against Maria Bueno with her arms swathed in cotton bandages, because her skin had become so sensitive to the sun. Graebner lost.

There is also a flip side to these stories. Steve Denton is a player who can credit his allergies for his tennis career. Denton grew up in a little town in south-west Texas caled Driscoll (pop. 638). In Driscoll, there were only two sports, as the Texas saying goes: football and spring football. Denton, a big guy, couldn't play football basically because he couldn't be rolling around in the grass a whole lot. A doctor suggested tennis. Denton's mamma began driving him to Corpus Christi to play, since Driscoll had only one asphalt court, one that time had forgotten. Denton never missed football much after that.

And there are other allegies besides hay fever. Eliot Teltscher once broke out in a rash because of the polyester in the tennis clothes he was wearing at the time. Now some might say that the world might be a better place if *everyone* was allergic to polyester, but the itching made Teltscher a little testy.

See, the thing is tennis is a sport that requires such extraordinary concentration and constant movement – plus the ability to *see* the damn ball – that an allergy can just drop you in your tracks if it's serious enough. Of course, there are allergies for other athletes in other sports. When Jim Ryun went to the 1972 Olympic trials in Eugene, Oregon – known to track people as the Hay Fever Capital of the United States – he was so beset by allergies that he was afraid to leave his hotel. And Ryun didn't have to carry a racket when he ran the 1,500 metres. Or face McEnroe's serve. Or look up at the ball on his own second serve with blue eyes cryin' in the rain, as Willie Nelson says.

My favourite allergy story is the one about the old Aussie, Jack Crawford. In 1933 Crawford had won the Australian Open, the French and Wimbledon. He was on his way to what would have been the first Grand Slam, even if people might not have called it that at the time. Crawford also had asthma. The asthma was bothering him so much by the time he got to Forest Hills that he was sipping brandy on changeovers to fight it off. He made it to the final at Forest Hills and then either Fed Perry got him, or the brandy. No Crawford Slam.

Still, I feel very strongly that brandy had to be much more

civilized than Sudafed, or having a nurse say, 'Drop those drawers.'

Wimbledon might not have been easier for me, or for Rosewall, if we'd known about Crawford's, ah, medication. But we probably would have had a hell of a lot more fun.

The Most Loveable Championship

John Oakley

The sun was beating down on the Foro Italico and British stalwart Tony Pickard was battling for his life in the Italian championships in Rome. But New Zealander Ian Crookenden would not be denied and after three hours of sweat and toil had reached match point in this first round drama. Then Pickard, lunging desperately for the ball, hit his return over the baseline to lose the match. But hold on there folks, there was no call of 'Out'.

Crookenden, aghast at this daylight robbery, looked up to see the basline judge leaning over the rail that fenced off the court and talking to an ice cream vendor. 'Come on mate,' called the frustrated Crookenden. 'I've won the bloody match.' But he was wrong.

The line judge, shrugging his shoulders, waving his arms and breaking out into a torrent of Italian, explained the situation.

Roughly translated it went something like this. 'I'm very sorry but I did not see the ball. I was buying an ice cream at the time and was not watching'.

No, not journalistic licence but a perfectly true story. Such was my introduction to Rome, the Eternal City, and, in the early 1960s, home of the most hilarious, most disorganized yet most loveable tennis championship in the world.

Crookenden, still swearing under his breath in pure New Zealand, had to replay the point, won it and said: 'How about that mate?' Back came another burst of Italian: 'This time I see the shot'.

The year was 1963 and the Italians believed in doing things rather differently. Take the mixed singles.

Onto the court marched gladiator Billy Knight of Britain for yet another blood-bath on the slow red shale. At the other end on

240

marched Australian Judy Tegart.

It didn't seem quite right. Billy was a boy and Judy a girl and both glared at each other, uncertain of the next move. On came the umpire and the line judges but no other players. Well, really chaps, this just wasn't on. Even the umpire thought it a bit odd.

A hasty conference and two other players, one male and one female, were summoned to the court. Knight insisted he play his match, but Judy was equally sure that she had first claim. On to the court stalked Bill Watson, Judy's coach and mentor. 'You stay there Jude,' he yelled, 'Don't let no bloody Pom give you the heave-ho. Tell him to get lost.'

Stalemate appeared to have been reached. But no, the Italians had the perfect answer. Knight and Judy were sent muttering to the sidelines. In their place, another match featuring an Italian was greeted with rapturous applause.

Then there was the Bobby Wilson v. Marty Mulligan all-star clash. Only one problem. No umpires or line judges appeared to watch this classic. Twenty minutes later Wilson, fed up with knocking up in the midday heat, summoned a ball boy. 'Here you play,' he said, pushing his racket into the startled lad's hand. 'I've had enough.'

Ten minutes later the ball boy was outplaying a tiring Mulligan. The Australian summoned yet another ball boy. 'Here you play your friend,' he said as he flopped by Wilson's side in the shade of the backstop.

All that was in 1963. But 1964 was no better.

Angela Mortimer and Liz Starkie were playing a doubles. The sun was booming down again and the umpire, with dark glasses and big straw hat, sat motionless in the chair. So motionless they thought he was dead.

Well, not quite. He was merely asleep. Angela hit a forehand winner but no score came from the chair. All four players looked enquiringly at the umpire but he was long gone into the world of dreams. Liz, with typical Yorkshire bluntness, tugged his leg and said she would simply love it if he would wake up so they could get on with the game. The umpire, coming out of his daze, called 'Trenta pare'. Well, it was close.

Yet for human drama and personal embarrassment, worse was to follow. Big Mike Sangster, then Britain's top player, was toiling on the Centre Court against unknown American Mike

Senkowski and at the interval was down two sets to one. Then came my big mistake. I opened my mouth.

Senkowski came into the restaurant and said to a waiter. 'Tea with lemon, bud, and make it snappy. I've got to beat this guy Sangster.' The Italian looked on in wonderment at Senkowski's American drawl. 'Non comprendo,' he replied. 'Now look here bud, I want tea and lemon.' 'Non comprendo.' It could have gone on all night.

Then came the Oakley howler. 'Can I help?' I said. 'I speak a little Italian.' 'Tell this jerk to get me tea and lemon,' snapped Senkowski. 'And you', pointing at me, 'bring it down to the Centre Court. I've got to go.' Well, really lads, I'm not much good as a waiter.

Cursing under my breath I walked down the tunnel leading to the Centre Court with a tray of tea, lemon and sugar and stopped at the Court entrance. 'Here', I said to an official, 'Give this to Senkowski.'

'Not my job,' snapped the official. 'You take it yourself.' So on I popped, waiting for Sangster to turn his back. After all, I *am* a patriot.

I laid down the tray and was about to rush off when Senkowski barked: 'Pour me one out.' Britain's Australian coach, George Worthington, shouted from the stand: 'What's your game, helping the enemy?'

Reluctantly I poured out a cup and turned to go. 'Three lumps,' snapped the American. I could have shot him. So could Sangster, who lost in five sets.

Glorious Rome, where the officials once made Manuel Santana top seed when he wasn't even playing. Then they made Roy Emerson top seed and he was not there either, as I was quick to point out. 'Here you tell us who's in the tournament,' yelled an exasperated official, and I did.

Then came the moment when I thought I would be banned from Rome. Summoned to the referee's office I was shown a cutting from my paper, the *London Evening News*, in which a certain John Oakley had said the Italian championships were the world's worst when it came to organization. 'Monkeys could have done it better,' I had written.

Speaking in rather loud and clearly bad-tempered Italian the referee said the paper had been sent from London 'by a friend' and he was just a little upset.

Diplomatically I explained that I loved the tournament, the officials, the line judges, the umpires, the spectators, Italian women, shoes and ties and even the odd cats strolling around the arena. At crawling I was number one.

Suddenly the frowns turned to smiles as my outburst was translated by the referee's seductive secretary.

'Have a drink,' he said.

Loveable Rome. What a pity they now run the championships in an orderly fashion.

The Cup that Caught Fire

Barry Newcombe

The first tournament you attend as a tennis writer tends to remain in your memory much longer than most of the others. Mine was at the Hurlingham Club in West London. I was short on knowledge and background and ended up basing my first day's report on Gardner Mulloy, a man of some repute in the game, who turned out not to be playing in the tournament at all but was involved in a veterans' event.

Things did not improve. Next I was despatched to a Davis Cup match between Great Britain and Israel, played at the Chandos Club at Golder's Green, and beforehand I had enraged the good membership of that club by predicting that Israel's team, fledglings on the world circuit, would not win a set. Of course, they did more than that – they actually took a rubber from Britain on the first day. But Britain won the tie.

I am grateful for that win because Mike Sangster, Bobby Wilson, and Roger Taylor gave me an introduction to something I had heard about but never experienced: journalistic foreign travel. We were off to Copenhagen for the next round.

I was so excited on the flight over that I spilled my first airline meal all over the colleague in the next seat. In Copenhagen I found myself booked into an hotel miles of tramlines away from the team, my colleagues, and the stadium. But Britain won the tie.

That night I went on to Paris for the French Open. I had never been before and when I jumped into a cab at Orly airport I asked the driver for the Hotel Dubois – and spent the next three hours visiting the 90-odd establishments of that name before finding the correct one.

I enjoyed those French championships. I went out for a night with 'Moody' Mike Sangster, 'Resentful' Roger Taylor, and Graham 'The Runt' Stilwell, as they were styled in those days, and only just made it back to the Dubois and my early morning telephone call from London. I met John Newcombe for the first time, an experience from which we both seemed to benefit.

But the Davis Cup was beckoning again. Next stop: Budapest. On the way there seemed to have been a little friction between the team and the British press and when I arrived early, alone, I stayed in the Grand Hotel and had the strange experience of eating solo in their massive but unpatronized restaurant while the players ate at another table. There was little communication.

There was little communication at the tennis stadium, either. One telephone was the link with the world, Hungarian or otherwise, and this lone instrument, which appeared to have been used by pigeons since its installation, somehow worked as a dramatic story of British guts abroad unfolded. Roger Taylor beat Istvan Gulyas, a dark and wiry creature of untold stamina and persistence, in a final rubber which stretched over two days.

Taylor and I had agreed not to be friendly at the mid-point of that match and on the final morning I found myself summoned to the room of the team captain, Headley Baxter, a caring man at all times with his players, to cool things down. Taylor needed no cooling – he fought like a lion to defeat Gulyas and all of Hungary on that little island of tennis in the Danube.

We never went away again that year. South Africa, who played in the Davis Cup in those days, put us out in the early summer. The Davis Cup used to finish earlier then and with the tournament scene far less structured than it is now the world's greatest team competition commanded huge interest.

It has taken me to a few places since Copenhagen and Budapest, none perhaps more startling than Sofia where Bulgaria provided unlikely and predictably tame opposition for the British players of that time.

But Sofia stays in my mind for one reason – it was the city where a tennis court was set on fire. Torrential rain had flooded the clay court and to help disperse it the happy Bulgars poured petrol on the troubled waters and then lit up, a real king-size smoke.

This was fascinating stuff to the onlookers but no good at all to visiting journalists who were unable to communicate. Slowly the time ticked away to final editions, impatiently we stood and stared at the two telephones which existed in the club. We knew there were only two lines linking Bulgaria to the outside world . . . and, with minutes left to deadline, they both came alive, Sofia to Fleet Street, just like that.

It took a while to escape from Sofia because the plane, a vibrating four-engined thunderer of Russian design, had what is known as a dummy run before taking off. Bobby Wilson, who hated flying, definitely did not like that.

All this was before open tennis came into being, when the tennis circuit meant following the sun, not following the dollars, and the people involved travelled around like a moving village.

Open tennis arrived in 1968 and we all know what has happened since, with the game groaning under the weight of ever-burgeoning prize money and the structure being very clearly defined. Including the Davis Cup.

I think it was a sound idea to alter the Davis Cup so that there is an elite top 16 grouping, the so-called world group. For a time, Britain had its part in that group but now the team is playing at a lower level. That means no matches with the United States or Australia or Sweden or the other big nations of the game.

But it might mean going to Copenhagen or Budapest or Sofia once more. And we could kick a few ghosts around in those cities, that's for sure.

Not Quite Write

Reginald Brace

All sorts of things can go wrong with the work of a tennis writer before it achieves its basic object of appearing in print. Many years ago I scribbled a caption for a picture of two pretty Rhodesian girls who were playing the English circuit for the first time. The picture and the caption were duly published in the *Yorkshire Post* with the hilarious addition of the words 'who have fancied mounts at Thirsk tonight'. Thirsk is a well-known Yorkshire racecourse. Somehow, part of the caption for a photograph of two jockeys riding there had crept under that of the unsuspecting and highly respectable tennis players. The mistake was spotted after a couple of editions, and I doubt that the girls ever saw it. But I still have the cutting; a yellowing reminder of the gremlins that so often bedevil tennis journalism.

Every tennis writer has at least one anecdote about some incident which made him want to call game, set and match to his career. John Oakley, then of the *London Evening News*, was covering a Davis Cup tie between Britain and Yugoslavia in Manchester and thought he was doing splendidly as he put over three fresh opening paragraphs to a running story about a marathon set between Mike Sangster and Nikki Pilic. Each of the piping hot introductions had the latest score, and was designed to replace its predecessor. Unfortunately, the *News* ran them all in sequence. 'Tell me', wrote a reader to the editor, 'was John Oakley drunk in Manchester?'

It was about the same time – we all go throught these periods – when Oakley, filing from Paris, was amazed to find that the French hard court championships had suddenly become the 'French grass court championships' in his paper. 'But surely,' said the sub-editor responsible, 'isn't all tennis played on grass?'

The *London Standard's* Barry Newcombe managed to

247

produce a tight-lipped grin at his paper's treatment of the 1967 Wimbledon men's final. The by-line 'By John Newcombe' indicated that not only had the Australian beaten Wilhelm Bungert but that he had found time to describe his triumph for the *Standard* as well.

Roy McKelvie's favourite bloomer is a connoisseur's choice. One year Beppi Merlo, the slack-stringed Italian virtuoso who never hit the ball hard in his life, beat Neale Fraser in the Italian championships. 'Merlo crushes Fraser,' trumpeted the *Daily Mail* next day. 'Just an example of what can happen when tennis copy lands on the subs' table', sighs McKelvie.

Sub-editors often come up with headlines like that, although occasionally they make sense in a lunatic way. A *Times* headline which said a celebrated woman player 'carries all before her' could have been interpreted as an admiring reference to her physique. But the tennis vocabulary is full of potential pitfalls. It only takes a slight spelling error to convert simple terms like 'drop shot' and 'passing shot' into phrases of extreme vulgarity. 'Forehand' can so easily become 'fourhand' while it is amazing how often 'surface' appears as 'service'.

Lance Tingay, of the *Daily Telegraph*, was perturbed to find that he was apparently guilty of describing Tilden as one of the great all-time sinners of the game. He had, of course, written 'winners', but how was the reader to know?

However, it is on the telephone that the majority of errors are spawned. The typists who tap out the deathless prose of far-flung tennis journalists often seem to be deaf, stupid and handicapped by a pair of boxing gloves.

Tingay, phoning from Stockholm to London, referred to the 'peripatetic Scandinavian championships'. This went down as the 'very pathetic Scandinavian championships' although, to be fair, the typist queried the phrase before Lance hung up. Judy Alvarez was referred to as 'the Jewish number five' when she was really the US number five. Gardnar Mulloy became 'the Army lawyer' instead of the Miami lawyer. Raul Ramirez is still called 'Paul' from time to time in print.

And so it goes on. Most tennis writers have experienced that awful feeling of doom, doubt and apprehension after a crackling call in which the typist has asked for the spelling of such words as 'the' and 'that'. The journalist's clammy hand replaces the receiver in its cradle. He screams for a drink. Later, through an alcoholic fuzz, he indulges in a manic reverie about what has actually gone down on paper at the other end of the line.

Sometimes the process of gaining contact with a newspaper office is agonizing. Laurie Pignon of the *Daily Mail* recalls a Davis Cup tie in Spain in which the British press corps was almost silenced by a breakdown in telecommunications. Miraculously, an office was found where wiring facilities still existed. The lone operator was liberally tipped by journalists determined to do anything to ensure that their stories went over first. Anxious to please everyone, he sent out everything at high speed but with scant concern for the proper destination of the copy. Fleet Street was even more chaotic than usual that night.

Calling direct from the United States can have unscheduled moments of mirth. Pignon, after asking to speak to a copy taker, was put through to the *Daily Mail* canteen. The operator thought he had said 'coffee maker'. Ronald Atkin once found himself filing to the foundry at the *Observer*. Yes, the nerves can take a pounding. Telephoning from the Masters at Houston, I found myself bellowing 'Hello' at an idiot on the line who could only use same word in reply. 'Sir,' said the girl operator, 'would you mind shutting up? You are talking to your own echo.'

It was on the same trip to Houston that I was trapped in a lift on the way to the telex. My copy was clutched in a damp palm; the deadline was minutes away. I tilted my head back and let loose a good old-fashioned Anglo-Saxon expletive, which made at least one Texas rose go pink around the petals. It was not claustrophobia which caused the howl. Merely the thought that those tennis demons were ganging up on me again.

Some days, it seems that fate is out to crush you. It certainly felt like that the day after the Masters ended in Boston in 1973. I will skip over irrelevancies like broken shoebuckles, mutinous suitcases, and the sheer agony of coaxing a story out of a thoroughly uncooperative typewriter. But on the way to the Western Union office, I opened the cab window, to be rewarded by a deluge of water as we sloshed through a dip in the road. And my cup of misfortune was not yet filled.

No, said the lady behund the Western Union counter, they could not telex my story to Leeds. Cable, yes. Telex no. 'When will the cable arrive?' I asked. 'Tomorrow', she replied, brightly.

A Funny Thing Happened...

Frustration mounting, I directed the cab to the home of Bud Collins, where I was having lunch.

'Bud', I said when I eventually arrived – the driver lost his way and had to radio to base for instructions – 'lead me to the phone.' 'Only too glad,' said Bud, 'But it went out of order an hour ago.' So we roused a lovely kimonoed lady who lived next door. Sure I could use her phone, she said.

Hand and voice trembling, I picked up the receiver, reached the overseas operator and put in my call. 'I'm sorry, sir,' said the operator, 'but there's a delay of 20 minutes. I'll call you back.' Well, I finally got through and my piece appeared in the paper. Just. But it had been one of those not infrequent days when tennis reporting is invested with all the joy of the Chinese water torture.

One Night in Bucharest – or Budapest

Laurie Pignon

Mr Dwight Filley Davis donated his giant Cup in the cause of international friendship and world peace in 1900. He was later to become the US Secretary of War, a role for which he would have been ideally suited in 1972 – the year that the Challenge Round was abolished and the United States survived hostilities and beat Rumania 3–2.

Several players have been mentioned in despatches for showing bravery beyond the call of tennis duty on that occasion, but should anyone ever wish to start a lawn tennis chamber of horrors I suggest that the cheating that went on during those three days would be a prize exhibit.

In contrast the entry of the tennis writers into Rumania was pure Whitehall farce with Ilie Nastase upstaging Brian Rix in every scene. From past and sometimes painful experiences we have learned that even with the right visa, and no dollars to sell on the black market, entry in East European countries can be a long-winded business; but not this time.

Nastase was at the airport to meet his French fiancée and we were on the same flight. When he saw us he gave one of those clownish grins which angered some linesmen, stole a cap from an armed immigration officier, collected our passports, told officials we were his friends, and ordered them to hurry with our baggage. Such is the magic of a national hero in this part of the world, but I can't see it working at Heathrow or Kennedy. Considering the bad press Nastase had received from us over the years it was a generous gesture.

Accommodation, even when confirmed, was not so easily settled. David Gray, in his *Guardian* reporting days, and I had to share a tiny, oddly shaped room which had a dungeon of a window from which we could see no 'little tent of blue which prisoners call the sky'. Apart from dodging Gray's wet socks which he had a passion for washing, and working on a table with two typewriters which only had space for one and a half, we had no problems. Unless of course you count Gray's snoring.

There was, however, one member of our party who did suffer some embarrassment; he was a young, rather serious New Yorker whose identity wild horses, or even the threat of expulsion from the All England Club, could not force me to divulge.

He was 'ordered' by the Rumanian interpreter who understood English well enough until it came to protesting about anything, to share a room with the very attractive daughter of an English sports photographer.

I am not suggesting that the rest of us would have jumped at the chance, but at least we would have been gentlemen enough not to make such a public fuss. Not that it did him any good. We were left to understand that a compromise was agreed upon: she undressed in the dark, and he got up before she was awake.

Such curious things do happen in some parts of the world, as on the night that Gray and I met the Rumanian Minister of Sport and finished up by sharing a bottle of wine with a lady whose dress was remarkable, if only for its brevity. I could say that we were driven to it at gun point but that would be rather overstating the case.

We were in fact peacefully making our way back to our hotel after an excellent dinner – Gray was a great picker of restaurants – when we passed a police or army headquarters where nocturnal visitors were definitely not welcome. Two angry-sounding little men appeared as if by magic out of the shadows and with sub-machine guns at their hips prodded us to the other side of the road where outside a night club we all but collided with a man wearing – of all things – a Tottenham Hotspur FC tie. He was the Minister of Sport, and wished to talk only about the golden era of Danny Blanchflower, Jimmy Greaves and Dave MacKay who were making soccer history during his residence at the Embassy in London; he insisted we went inside.

There are times in all our lives when our embarrassment is such that we wish that the ground beneath our feet would open up to give us some escape from an awful gaffe. Such a man was

Mr Dwight Filley Davis's son, and the ground he was standing on was the red clay centre court of Progresul Sports Club.

The United States had escaped from threatened kidnapping and won his father's Cup and he was making a 'thank-you' speech. He thanked the good people of Budapest for their kindness. He told them what a beautiful city Budapest was, and what wonderful memories of Budapest he would be taking back to the United States. He was, of course, in Bucharest, but the red, yellow and blue-flag waving crowd cheered him just the same.

Budge's Racket

Dennis Cunnington

It may come as a major surprise, or even a serious shock, to the great Donald Budge to learn that a racket he discarded *circa* 1950 is still being wielded with some zest.

I can assure him of that because only the other week I was caught an almighty whack around the ankle with it after the user had executed the finest double-handed forehand cum backhand you could ever wish to see. The fact that my right ankle was in such close proximity to the shot was entirely my own fault. I was doing a spot of coaching at the time and my pupil was, and still is, the loveliest, most gorgeous blue-eyed blonde imaginable – and she is only six!

But I am telling the story back to front. It really begins some 35 years ago when Donald Budge and my old school friend Big 'Oggie had an eyeball to eyeball confrontation over the relative weight and design of a tennis racket.

Now if ever Donald Budge made a mistake in life, it was to get into an argument with Big 'Oggie, a fellow he had seen neither before nor since. Many people had engaged in discussions, debates or plain heated arguments with this fine fellow, and to the best of my knowledge, they always ended second best. That also included a motley collection of German soldiers on the Anzio beachead, but that is another story.

Big 'Oggie – his real name was Maurice Oglethorpe, but he was never addressed as such – always shone at school when it came to physics and relative things such as that. He always knew what he was talking about, which was another good reason for the Great American Tennis Player to avoid such a meeting with my friend, especially in the draughty corridors of Nottingham Ice Stadium one bleak November night.

We had all gathered there to witness one of these four-man professional one-night stands which were so popular in the years just after the war. They always caused a bit of a flutter whichever town they visited, and this occasion was no exception. Apart from Budge, the other gladiators on that foggy night were Jack Kramer, Fred Perry – our Fred was still going strong then – and Dinny Pails, who, despite his Australian accent, some claimed was as Nottingham as Robin Hood himself.

Results did not matter much then, but I know we all had a good night's entertainment, and in the little corner of the ice rink that did duty as a press room there was much talk afterwards of the merits of the players.

All was going well until Big 'Oggie heaved his body into view to see it I was ready for going home. I was, but he wasn't, it seemed, for he had just spied Budge chatting to some spectators, and he wanted a few words with the great man himself on, as I explained earlier, this business of weight and design.

Budge tried patiently to explain, but as far as my friend was concerned he was not very convincing. As I said, people tended to lose their way when they talked with Big 'Oggie. A straightforward conversation always became an argument, and he always won, no matter how long it took to turn the tide his way.

This one, I recall, was no exception, but even as the cross fire was taking place I had a feeling all was not as it should be. It wasn't, not by a long chalk, for we had been locked in by a caretaker anxious to cut through the city fog and reach the sanctuary of his home as quickly as possible.

Tennis players in those days, even Wimbledon champions, were not so desperate as they are now to rush to a courtesy car to take them back to hotels and other such palaces. So Don did not mind lingering one little bit, but being locked in Nottingham ice rink as midnight approached was a situation not to be taken lightly.

It was Big 'Oggie who got us out of that mess, too, by locating a nightwatchman in the bowels of the earth who was doing his best to ensure that the mass of pipes which surrounded him would still be manufacturing ice after the wooden floor of the court had been lifted and taken away.

Thankfully, a side door was at last opened and the Great American Tennis Player disappeared into the pea-souper. And there was Big 'Oggie, all six feet four inches of him – and some said twice as wide – standing there still clutching the racket which had been the centre of such earnest discussion.

'He gave it to me, he said I could keep it,' he said, almost weeping with joy.

Well, I can vouch for the fact that that racket has been handled as lovingly as any object could be. Big 'Oggie used it effectively as he became quite a passable club player. Then a change came over him. He became a Methodist Minister and devoted all his time to caring for his flock. But this magical racket stayed in existence, used by all members of his family in turn.

Sadly, Big 'Oggie was called to Higher Things a few years ago, and is no longer with us. But Don Budge's racket is, safe for years to come in the hands of my friend's six-year-old grandchild Samantha. I can vouch for that, for the bruise is only just fading!

A Tennis Star is Born – and Dies in Sudden Mystery

Frank Rostron

Whatever happened to Baby Jane? Bette Davis and Joan Crawford answered the questions in their eerie movie. But whatever happened to that meteoric Yugoslavian Davis cup star Anton Zagnes?

No record books detail his exploits, and even that social register 'Who's Who' of the sport, the BP/Commercial Union Annual Almanac of this or any other year fails to include him in its biographies of past or present 'greats'.

Yet 'Zaggie' is a by-word, a legend almost, among veteran European sports correspondents who know of his distant relationship with Count Dracula because of his mysterious origins and equally obscure disappearance into either the Carpathians or the Tatra Mountains.

Well, whatever did happen to Zagnes whose emergence on the international scene was as sudden and obscure as his mysterious death? This is one subject on which even critical colleagues cannot challenge my authority. For I now have a confession to make. I was his illegitimate father and was responsible for his sudden appearance literally on the eve of a Davis Cup match in Belgrade between Great Britain and Yugoslavia and his obscure disappearance and subsequent burial in indecent haste.

In a long, industrious and mainly respectable career devoted to revelations of truth, unravelling of fact and the pursuit of scoops, I have scorned fiction in the pages of newspapers. But the fatherhood of Zagnes was thrust upon me, like greatness, through an accident I have for long, and vainly, been trying to conceal.

It happened this way. Shortly after the Second World War, when air services and communications generally with mid-Europe were crude and erratic, I arrived with the British team, and two or three other correspondents from London including the *Daily Telegraph's* Lance Tingay, to report a Davis Cup tie against Yugoslavia in bomb-scarred Belgrade. None of us knew the composition of the rebuilt Yugoslav team, though having personally helped their pre-war star Kukuljovic to emigrate to South Africa (where he prospered) like his team mate Puncek, leaving only Josef Palcada of their once formidable team, we knew they would be mainly newcomers.

Britain's non-playing captain, the late Herman David, and his players headed by Tony Mottram (father of Buster) and Geoff Paish did not know the team either. Phone calls from the then primitive Hotel Moskva and even a quick taxi trip to the deserted stadium proved abortive. My deadline was nearing alarmingly with no sign of my booked telephone call to London.

But fate rescued me, or so I thought. In my linguistic crisis, my foreign correspondent colleague Eric Bourn, a Balkan specialist recently transferred from Vienna to Belgrade, appeared like a rescuing angel and quickly transported me to the comfortable sanity of his flat. While he and his lovely wife generously poured Scotch into my travel-weary frame, we started to translate the local sports pages. But no official team had been named. There was only speculation. At last he contacted an official who named a team. But by one of those cruel tricks the hated and unpredictable continental telephone plays suddenly the phone rang. It was my call to London booked a couple of hours earlier from the Hotel with instructions when I left to divert it to Bourn's flat. Horrors! I did not want a call for at least another half hour nearer my deadline and prepared to tell the telephone exchange.

But Eric, wise to the whimsies of mid-European telephones, warned: 'The speed of this call is a miracle. Take it or you may have to wait all night.'

So, on a crackling phone inaudible at both ends I had to ad lib a hasty preview of the tie, with my pal Bourn, a complete non-sports fan, pushing scribbled names, ages and general data in front of me. Next day we shuddered to see that a player from Zagreb had become one Zagnes, occupation: university student.

So the unwanted Zagnes was hastily dropped when the official draw was made in the City Hall over genial glasses of Slivovic, their plum brandy, with no explanation of his embarrassing appearance and rapid disappearance. Fortunately, Zagnes is no longer referred to in polite European society. But ribald colleagues keep reviving him in a plain attempt to embarrass his father. There have been periodic stories about a man, who so far from being a university student, is now said to have been the desperado leader of a raiding guerilla unit operating in the Carpathians and Tatras. One malicious colleague has spread the story of Zaggie's marriage to a Ruritanian beauty. Another is suggesting he actually is now at a university being groomed to become Secretary-General of the ITF. His embarrassed father merely begs that he should be allowed to rest in peace.

Oh for the ancient days of straightforward foreign cabling before the correspondent's life was ruined by the telephone. In those days, pre-teleprinter, one could file the day's cables and have done. If they were delayed and missed the edition, there was nothing one could do about it. Queries and requests for follow-ups would arrive too late for immediate attention and allow the correspondent to dine and party in peace.

Now the telephone, outside the United States anyway, permits no peace and through inaudibility and sound distortion multiplies errors of spelling, grammer and general context. Yet the results can be hilarious as well as maddening. I once had to telephone a story from Hamburg about Max Schmeling the one-time world heavyweight champion and Baron Gottfried von Cramm, former Wimbledon finalist and one of Barbara Hutton's several husbands, to the defunct *London Star*, whose sports editor was named Gunning. After dictating the opening paragraphs to a mystified receiver I found I was talking to A. J. Cummings, one of the world's foremost political commentators, who worked for the sister paper, the *News Chronicle*, also now defunct, in the same building. But an even simpler mishap caused Peter Wilson, sports columnist of the *Daily Mirror*, to dictate his French championships tennis report from Stade Roland Garros in Paris, only to discover after a heated altercation with the receiver that he had dictated his copy to the *News of the World*, who were awaiting the athletic report from their track and field expert Doug Wilson, one of Britain's leading milers.

Such comic mix-ups must be legion. But imagine delivering a

scoop to your rivals, which happened to me during the last war when my message in its passage through the censors got re-addressed from the *Daily Express* to our then closest rivals the *Daily Mail.* They published it. And that reminds me. I've never been paid.

But my favorite tennis mix-up story, which has nothing to do with transmission problems except of food and drink, is worthy of a Danny Kaye movie. Picture the scene: visiting British writer Rostron spic and span in tuxedo all set for the US Tennis Writers' dinner dance, that year at the New York Hilton. Jack Kramer and friends, going by car the brief distance from the Hotel Roosevelt to the Hilton, offer a lift gratefully accepted because it is raining. Politely they drop the visiting scribe at the front entrance while going off to garage the car. Rostron, directed up the escalator amid a Grand Central Station style crowd, enters a banqueting room, is received ceremoniously by the host and hostess, wonders why there are no familiar tennis faces but soothes embarrassment with offered martinis. Wonders why there is general surprise and renewed hospitality offers when it is discovered he is from London. Checks with head waiter who says, 'Tennis party? No that's the next floor. This is the Amalgamated Goldsmiths Guild.' Rostron sneaks out, slinks upstairs. More gladhanding greeting from smart hosts, generous offerings of martinis and rival bids from friendly hosts to join their table when it is discovered he is a visiting limey. This time suspiciously, though beginning not to care, checks about the tennis dinner. 'Tennis? No. This is the Rotary Reunion, but you are welcome.' One more narrow escape from martinis by false pretences on the next floor where cautionary enquiries are made before entry. Further up the stratosphere I made it at last with faces identified as Billy Talbert's, Gene Scott's and Will Grimsley's signifying 'home at last'. Now at least one Londoner, the inventor of Zagnes, knows he need never starve or die of thirst in New York.

Wimbledon Profit Fails to Ease the Loss Account

Rex Bellamy

The Wimbledon championships produced a record surplus of £4,252,193 an increase of 55 per cent on last year's £2,751,154. 'Buzzer' Hadingham, the dapper and breezy chairman of the management committee said yesterday: 'We were pretty lucky because we had marvellous weather and record crowds.' The surplus goes to the Lawn Tennis Association for the greater good of British tennis.

Hadingham made the customary polite protest about the fact that the LTA would lose about £1,310,00 of the surplus in corporation tax. Jim Cochrane, the avuncular president of the LTA council, said much of the balance would be devoted to development and schools ('development' is a popular multi-purpose word with the LTA) and added that an expensive director of coaching would be appointed within a few weeks.

The LTA seem to appoint chiefs more readily than they recruit Indians. But they can now put more money into regional development schemes and, later, hope to add county tennis centres to the existing network of regional centres. And there will be extra funds, instantly, for loans to clubs.

As usual, this Wimbledon press conference was ritualistic and relentlessly genteel. Sunshine streamed through the windows across the inevitably green furnishing and the inevitably suited and tied assembly. All-England Club ties were evident even among the press corps. Are there drama critics, one wondered, who belong to Equity? True, a serenely Polish journalist was tieless, the BBC neckwear was hidden under a crew-neck sweater, and the *Guardian* served a double-fault with a reddish tartan shirt gashed by what looked like pendant mustard. The rest of us played the game by wearing the expected uniform – which makes everyone feel secure because conformity of clothing encourages conformity of thinking. At Wimbledon, people who wear their independence are regarded as eccentric and potentially difficult.

The top table was embellished by cards identifying Mr Christopher Gorringe, Mr Jim Cochrane, Mr R.E. Hadingham (nobody knows what the initials represent), Mr John Curry, and Mr Tony Hughes. The repetitive 'Mr' seemed a broad hint to those of us lumbered with the chore of drawing up the birthday honours list.

Coffee was served to wake everyone up and, an hour later, sherry was provided as a sedative for those mentally disturbed by the mass of figures that formed the main course. The press were given copies of the accounts and an explanatory statement. The latter was read out by Gorringe, innocently implying that although he was literate, he was none too sure that the literati of Fleet Street were similarly accomplished.

We read, and heard, that the heaviest item of expenditure was the £2,071,705 devoted to improving the premises. Broadcasting and television fees made up £5,986,043 (a jump of £1,989,393) of Wimbledon's total income, £9,934,158. In the United States championships, the preferences of television bosses have a ludicrous effect on the scheduling. But Wimbledon, Hadingham insisted yesterday, will not dance to the TV tune. Presumably, he hopes they will play it again anyway.

When we had been laid low by the financial report, the Wimbledon chairman tossed us provocative crumbs in response to supplementary questions.

'The worst thing that could happen to tennis', he said, 'would be a standardized surface throughout the world.' Agreed. But you and I could reasonably debate his belief that a player who hits a lucky winner off the net cord should say 'Sorry!' Does he advocate public insincerity as a sop to the unlucky?

It was a cosy and comforting occasion, for all that. Once again, Wimbledon has done us proud. Yet one's final thought for the day was a teasing paradox. Britain can obviously make money out of tennis players. If only we could make tennis players out of money.

The Press Gang

Laurie Pignon

It might surprise some readers of the daily and Sunday newspapers to know that writers of lawn tennis not only like the game, but some actually play it.

It is commendable that they should take such a lively interest in their livelihood, but it is sad to report that there appear to be unhealthy trends towards professionalism among the typewriter tappers which are causing concern.

So far I have not met a pressman (or woman) with his own manager or agent, but some have from time to time been spotted having secret coaching sessions, which is entirely contrary to the Corinthian concepts of our unwritten code.

David Irvine of *The Guardian*, for example, has been seen having practice matches with his son in the parks of Cheadle Hulme. This has, not unnaturally, resulted in a noticeable improvement in his rather unorthodox method of play in which he has mastered the world's first lobbed return of service. In fact, he lobs everything.

Barry Newcombe of the *Sunday Express*, a long-time admirer of the moon-ball system, is showing the same dedicated determination, but his inclination towards impetuosity when a rally lasts more than three strokes is holding him back. He has not learned to relax like Irvine, who often practises his ability to keep loose (as the Americans say) by falling asleep during dinner.

Ronald Atkin of the *Observer* has without doubt a professional approach towards fitness. In spite of attempting to keep his training schedule secret by working out when he knows that his colleagues are still in bed or telephoning their early morning copy, he has been mistaken for an escaping mugger while running five miles or more around the uneven, unswept streets of Manhattan, or any other city where the circuit takes him. He is also a great believer in vitamins usually from the valleys of the Rhône, the Loire or the Rhine which results in commendable concentration when following the flight of the ball.

There are certain delusions of grandeur about Nigel Clarke's (*Daily Mirror*) all-court game, but he too deviates from the Olympic principle that taking part is more important than winning; in fact he suffers from the Jimmy Connors syndrome that he would rather fall down dead than lose. There was ample evidence of this when we were partners in San Francisco in a match which for some reason the Americans took seriously.

Clarke, in spite of pulling a ligament in his arm and in considerable pain, insisted on continuing. This bravery not only put him out of the game for several months but forced him to drink the celebration champagne left-handed.

For some curious, claustrophobic reason Rex Bellamy of *The Times* prefers the confines of a squash court to the wider horizons of tennis, and fortunately restricts his professional tendencies to that peculiar game.

Not so John Parsons. One might expect the lawn tennis correspondent of the *Daily Telegraph* to be a simon pure amateur and to know when he is beaten, but not a bit of it. He even underwent spare-part surgery so that he might return to active service, and any day now he is expected to make a triumphant entry to the hackers circuit. Even more unsportingly I understand he is to bring the nurses from his transplant unit in Oxford as his personal cheer leaders. Lance Tingay would never have pulled such a trick.

No one, not even the Association of Tennis Professionals, has thought of such a wheeze as Gerald Williams of the BBC. To improve his forehand he married a Wightman Cup player. Sadly it did not last but at least Williams has a back swing beautiful to behold, and his former wife has become an expert tennis broadcaster. It is called give and take.

Getting too good at lawn tennis is a mistake all professionals have made. Reg Brace (*Yorkshire Post*) is almost such a man; he only has to play a couple of loose strokes and he is miserable for the next ten points. The idea of actually smiling if a drop shot plonks into the bottom of the net or a lob splashes into a swimming pool appals him. He is tennis's Geoff Boycott who takes over the baseline as if it is the wicket crease, and thinks that it is not cricket if you give him anything short.

John Barrett, so conscious of his television 'cool' image and aware of his professional past, which is really nothing to be ashamed about, only plays under duress, but he does have half a dozen good excuses: he is either working for the BBC, the *Financial Times*, Slazengers, Channel 9 in Australia or his annual *World of Tennis*.

Gone are the halcyon days when with borrowed rackets, a box of well-used practice balls and a stolen court somewhere between the rhododendrons and the groundsman's rhubarb the press used to stage their playing pleasures.

Now we 'compete' at such lordly venues at Stade Roland Garros, Flushing Meadow, and Foro Italico. The Italians foot fault as if training for the long jump, the Germans bring a fistful of rackets, the Americans arrive an hour early so that they can get in some crafty practice, while the French arrive late and win. Sponsors give prizes and as these get more valuable so the laughter gets less.